Structure in Milton's Poetry

Structure
in Milton's Poetry

From the Foundation to the Pinnacles

Ralph Waterbury Condee

The Pennsylvania State University Press

University Park and London

Copyright © 1974 by The Pennsylvania State University
All rights reserved
Printed in the United States of America
Designed by Glenn Ruby

Library of Congress Cataloging in Publication Data
Condee, Ralph Waterbury, 1916-
   Structure in Milton's poetry.
   Bibliography: p. 193
   1. Milton, John, 1608-1674—Criticism and inter-
pretation. I. Title.
PR3588.C6 1974   821'.4   73-12934
ISBN 0-271-01133-5

For Bym

Contents

Acknowledgments

Parts of this book appeared in earlier versions as articles in *The Journal of General Education, Philological Quarterly, Studies in the Renaissance, Studies in Philology,* and *The Yale Review.* I am grateful to the editors of these journals for permission to reprint parts of those articles here.

I am indebted to The Pennsylvania State University for the research leaves and grants which enabled me to write this book, and to Glasgow University for its hospitality in affording me the haven in which much of it was written. I am especially grateful to Professor Henry Sams of Penn State, whose faith that I would finish this book seems never to have wavered, and to Professors John Bryce and Peter Butter of Glasgow University, who welcomed me as a Senior Research Fellow in 1969-70. Carl Jackson of the Pattee Library, The Pennsylvania State University, and Robert Ogilvie McKenna of the Library of Glasgow University and their staffs were unfailingly helpful. My thanks to Professor and Mrs. Sydney Checkland of Glasgow University for their continuing support and help is greater than I can express. To Harris Fletcher, Thomas Whitfield Baldwin, Marcus Selden Goldman, and Bruce Weirick of the University of Illinois, whose guidance led me this way, I am deeply grateful.

My debt to my wife, who not only endured the writing of this volume but also understood it, removed the most glaring of the infelicities, and helped to recast my tortured prose, is of a nature so long and deep that no mere sentence here can do it justice.

I

Milton's Poetical Architecture

Whoever purposes, as it is expressed in Milton, "to build the lofty rhyme," must acquaint himself with this law of poetical architecture, and take care that his edifice be solid as well as beautiful; that nothing stand single or independent, so that it may be taken away without injuring the rest, but that from the foundation to the pinnacles, one part rest upon another.

Samuel Johnson, *The Rambler*[1]

Milton's skill in constructing poems which are "solid as well as beautiful" was one which he developed through false starts, experience, and the creation of poems whose structure was sometimes weak and awkward, sometimes deft and strong. The pages that follow will analyze some of his poems—early and late, well and badly organized—in order to see how his ability to construct a solid poetic edifice developed. An examination of the structural weaknesses of some poems and of the techniques Milton used to overcome or avoid these weaknesses will help to explain the increasingly complex poetic structures which he created as he matured.

This study, therefore, concerns the development of several aspects of Milton's poetic structure as he moves from early works such as the poem on the death of the Fair Infant to the two great epics. The most important of these aspects is his increasing mastery of the ability to make a poem move from one set of ideas (or state of mind) at the beginning of the poem to another at the conclusion; that is, his ability to make use of a functional rather than an inert structure. This functional structure is progressive or dynamic, and carries the poem from initial perturbation to final insight.

Milton attempts this technique with little success in the early poems, yet in *Samson Agonistes* and the two great epics it is a gross understatement merely to say that he masters it. Rather, in the later poems the dynamic structure is not only a pattern in which Milton sets forth the ideas he describes; it is also an instrument by which the significance of the poem's events fulfill the kind of larger meanings which only structure can impart. For example, in *Paradise Lost* the actual events of Adam's temptation, fall, and partial restoration set forth a Miltonic concept of heroism. Related to the narrative of these events is the fact that epic poetry has been the traditional form for setting forth an ideal of heroism. Milton does not simply build the Adam-story, with its concept of heroism, into the epic pattern with its inevitable heroic implications; he creates a poem in which the new Christian ethical ideal of heroism, the heroism of patience and heroic martyrdom, emerges within and by means of the structure of the poem. Consequently, the new ideal in the poem supersedes, both structurally and ethically, the old pagan heroism of physical courage. The result is that *Paradise Lost* inextricably fuses its structure with the events described and makes this structure move dynamically toward a resolution which exists in both the organization and the narrative.

But this achievement of uniting a progressing or dynamically moving structure with the actual events was not one that Milton arrived at easily. Therefore we shall examine this concept of dynamic structure as it occurs feebly and awkwardly in many of the early poems, then observe his development of it to the point where it is one of the richest and most complex achievements of the later poems.

In order to observe clearly the intricate operation of this dynamic progression, working as it does with both the structure and the actual events of the poem, we shall need to look at other aspects of Milton's use of poetic structure. First and most obvious is the relation of the parts to the whole and to other parts. Secondly, we shall examine Milton's increasing ability to unite two important elements of his poetry: (1) the extra-poetic situation—that is, the actual events (the death of the Infant or the birth of Christ)—and (2) the poetic situation—the writing of a poem of a particular kind, using particular literary devices. Finally, we shall study the increasing skill with which Milton uses the literary tradition, especially the Greco-Roman tradition, to bring about structural unity.

An analysis of the early poems will show that structural gaps result from a lack of clearly organized progressions. The later poems not only solve these problems of structural progression, they also draw much of their strength from the specific poetic techniques Milton creates as solutions.

Four points on the ordering of the following chapters need to be explained. It seems best to begin a detailed examination of these structural aspects of Milton's development with a study of *Paradise Lost*, rather than with Milton's first poems. In *Paradise Lost* we can see most clearly his ability to create a poem in which the structure progresses by firmly built steps from initial perturbation to ultimate resolution so that one part rests upon another from the foundation to the pinnacles. By beginning at a major point of Milton's achievement, we can understand more clearly how he arrived there. Having seen the fulfillment of the specific facets of Milton's poetry with which we are concerned, we shall be in a better position to recognize the first signs of these facets in the early poems, where they are often half-realized, botched, or altogether avoided.

For clarity's sake, I have placed "Lycidas" beside "Elegia Tertia," although these poems are separated by eleven years and by such important poems as the Nativity Ode, the Companion Pieces ("L'Allegro" and "Il Penseroso") and *Comus*. My reason for this departure from chronological order is that the extra-poetic situations in "Elegia Tertia" and "Lycidas" are quite similar; while the poetic patterns of the two poems have several interesting resemblances, "Elegia Tertia" falters in integrating its poetic patterns with its extra-poetic situation. This failure helps to point out why, where, and how "Lycidas" makes a successful fusion of its poetic structure with its extra-poetic events of grief, the injustices of death, and the ultimate beatific vision.

Furthermore, this study places *Samson Agonistes* immediately after the discussion of "Mansus" and "Epitaphium Damonis," and therefore before *Paradise Lost* and *Paradise Regained*, thus perhaps departing yet again from chronology. But the question of the date of *Samson Agonistes* is still not firmly answered, and an evaluation of all the external evidence is not relevant to this study. Because it must come *somewhere* in the sequence of Milton's poems and because of certain important differences between it and *Paradise Lost*, the discussion of

Samson Agonistes is in a position which intentionally implies that it is earlier than the two epics.

Last of all must come *Paradise Regained*. It has never been a popular poem; Bartlett's *Familiar Quotations* gives it half a page to *Paradise Lost*'s eight pages. But it seems to me to stand clearly as the logical *terminus ad quem* of Milton's development. It is not so much a sequel to *Paradise Lost* as it is the logical consequence of many of the important implications of the earlier poem. *Paradise Regained* takes the "epicness" of *Paradise Lost* and carries this epicness to its logical conclusion. The poetic patterns and extra-poetic situation have reached their ultimate fusion: just as, for Milton, Christ surpasses any other conceivable epic hero, so the structure of *Paradise Regained* carries the epic tradition beyond itself to a point appropriate only to this hero of this poem. Whatever may have been the popular appeal of *Paradise Regained*, from the standpoint of the scope and direction of Milton's poetic career, it is his triumph of poetical architecture.

II

The Dynamic Structure
of *Paradise Lost*

Dream not of thir fight, As of a Duel

Paradise Lost ends quietly, with Adam and Eve departing in tears, but not in despair:

> Som natural tears they drop'd, but wip'd them soon;
> The World was all before them, where to choose
> Thir place of rest, and Providence thir guide:
> They hand in hand with wandring steps and slow,
> Through *Eden* took thir solitarie way.
>   (XII. 645-49)[1]

But this is not merely the end of a tale that has now been told. It represents a resolution and a stasis following conflicts embodied not only in the narrative but in the abstract ideas, the images, the feelings, the sounds, the metrics—in almost every conceivable aspect of the poem. This closing scene is quiet, but it is at the same time a culminating triumph-and-defeat, a vision-and-exile which is highly charged with a momentum that derives from the dynamic structure of the whole poem. By "dynamic structure" I mean that quality of a literary work which gives it its character of thrust, movement, or progression from one set of ideas or patterns of feelings at the beginning of the poem to a related but different position at the end of the poem.

Thus at the beginning, the poem speaks of the need for justifying "the wayes of God to men"; this line is followed by scenes in Hell, of Satan's hatred, of a universe of unrest. Some ten thousand lines later the poem arrives at a point where Michael reveals to Adam that a loving God will dissolve

> *Satan* with his perverted World, then raise
> From the conflagrant mass, purg'd and refin'd,
> New Heav'ns, new Earth, Ages of endless date
> Founded in righteousness and peace and love
> To bring forth fruits Joy and eternal Bliss.
>
> (XII. 546-51)

Adam, who has lived in innocence, then in sin and rebellion, and then in contrition, has at last progressed so far as to say,

> Henceforth I learne, that to obey is best,
> And love with fear the onely God, to walk
> As in his presence, ever to observe
> His providence, and on him sole depend,
> Mercifull over all his works, with good
> Still overcoming evil, and by small
> Accomplishing great things, by things deemd weak
> Subverting worldly strong, and worldly wise
> By simply meek; that suffering for Truths sake
> Is fortitude to highest victorie.
>
> (XII. 561-70)

There have been, of course, innumerable studies of the structure of *Paradise Lost*,[2] and this is only natural since the complexity of the structure, or "structures," as Summers would prefer the term,[3] demands a multiplicity of approaches. Here we shall be concerned especially with the dynamic or progressive aspect of the structure. As Arthur E. Barker says, in discussing Milton's revision of *Paradise Lost* from ten to twelve books, "*Paradise Lost* was always meant to be a poem whose beginning is disobedience, whose middle is woe, and whose ultimate end is restoration. It may be that the intention was clouded in 1667, or that Milton's view of restoration was obscured. The 1674 revision is at any rate an effort to clarify the poem's ways."[4] Barker argues that *Paradise Lost* is "to be read as a metaphor of spiritual evolution. Its structural pattern is neither rigidly fixed nor shifted; it is shifting."[5] But the structural pattern is more than shifting; it is progressing strongly toward ends which are implicit in the total pattern of the poem.

We can see this dynamic or progressive structure most clearly in Milton's treatment of the figures of Adam and Satan. The relation of these two figures to the structure of *Paradise Lost* is a complex one and it gave rise, especially during the nineteenth and early twentieth centuries, to the celebrated Satanist controversy. As we all know, it was fashionable for a time to maintain that Satan was really the hero of *Paradise Lost*. And, as we also know, this position has fallen badly into disrepute. But it will be fruitful to stop and reexamine this controversy briefly because embedded in some of the crucial critical positions are perceptions of an important aspect of the poem. It is not strange that this should be so if we remember that some of those who held various Satanist positions were poets of the caliber of Dryden, Blake, and Shelley. By examining their approaches to the poem we can cast light on Milton's technique of creating a dynamic structure by using—not following, but using—literary tradition.

I propose that Satan is not *the* hero of *Paradise Lost*, but that he is in a very significant way *one* of the heroes; that when we examine in precisely what way he is a hero, we shall move closer to comprehending the poem's use of the epic tradition in developing a dynamic momentum. In simple terms, Satan fades and Adam emerges as a hero during the course of the poem. Underlying this fading and emergence are concepts of heroism which Milton presents, juxtaposes, and brings to fruition, as he moves through the story of Adam's creation, fall, redemption, and exile.

The earliest existing record to suggest that Satan is the hero is John Dryden's preface to his translation of the *Aeneid:*

> The file of heroic poets is very short.... Spenser had a better plea for his *Fairy Queen,* had his action been finished, or had been one; and Milton, if the Devil had not been his hero, instead of Adam; if the giant had not foiled the knight, and driven him out of his stronghold, to wander through the world with his lady errant.[6]

William Blake, in a famous passage in his *Marriage of Heaven and Hell*, suggested the idea that Satan was the hero; then Shelley explored the position in more detail in *The Defence of Poetry:*

> Nothing can exceed the energy and magnificence of the character of Satan as expressed in *Paradise Lost*. It is a mistake to suppose that he could ever have been intended for the popular personification of evil.... Milton's Devil as a moral

being is as far superior to his God as one who perseveres in some purpose which he has conceived to be excellent in spite of adversity and torture is to one who in the cold security of undoubted triumph inflicts the most horrible revenge upon his enemy.[7]

Innumerable nineteenth-century critics followed in Shelley's footsteps, the ennobling of Satan reaching perhaps its most impassioned statement in Lascelles Abercrombie:

> But in *Paradise Lost,* Satan *is* the idea: the character of Satan is the presiding thing; he is the essence and force and scope of the originating motive; and in his character, in the immense consistency of his superbly personal energy, resides the significance of the whole poem; for he is the focus of it all, and out of him and his destiny radiates that mutual relevance of things, which is what we call significance.[8]

These three statements clarify an important point which pervaded and confused the Satanist controversy. Dryden's argument is structural; it is based on the premise that in an epic poem the hero wins, as opposed to tragedy, in which the hero loses.[9] Dryden's statement implies that it is Satan who wins; therefore if the poem is an epic, the poem's structure assigns the role of hero to Satan.

Parenthetically, one should note the rejoinder of several critics, including Samuel Johnson, that Dryden misread the poem: at the end, Satan was degraded and, Johnson points out, "Adam was restored to his Maker's favor." For our purposes at the moment, however, this is beside the point.

Although Dryden misread Adam's position at the end of *Paradise Lost,* he surely saw Satan as a villainous person—the "giant" who drives out the "knight." And here his position differs radically from that of Shelley, who maintains that Satan is morally superior to God and, one presumes, to Adam as well. Note the shift which has taken place: Shelley, who also misread the poem, is talking about the ethical hero, while Dryden is talking about the structural, or functional hero—that is, the figure whose relation to the other parts of the poem is one which the epic tradition assigns to the hero. Therefore, as Odysseus is to the action of the *Odyssey,* as Aeneas is to the action of the *Aeneid,* so Satan is to the action of *Paradise Lost.* The fact that both Dryden and Shelley are quite mistaken complicates the argument, but their positions ultimately enlighten the poem. Like Dr. Johnson's objections to *Samson Agonistes,* their arguments are both invalid and invaluable.

Abercrombie's premise (also mistaken) is closely related to Shelley's but differs enough to make it worth looking at. He does not defend Satan's ethics, but he sees the Arch-Fiend as the central figure or the "focal hero" of the poem—just as Shakespeare's Richard III, who is contemptible by almost any conceivable ethical standards, is unquestionably the central character of the play.

It is helpful to introduce this idea of the "focal hero" for two reasons: (1) to differentiate the patently false argument that Satan is the ethical hero from the subtler argument which admits his evil but still claims for him a central role on the ground that his very evil, like Richard's, is what fascinates us and therefore becomes the vortex of the whole work; (2) to suggest that the term "hero" indicates not merely one or two, but several different concepts. For example it is also used simply to mean a "warrior of great prowess or renown." This was an important meaning of the term 'ηρος in Homer as he applied it to the dead warriors in the fourth line of the *Iliad;* he also so characterized a minor chieftain named Peiroos as 'ηρος in the second book (line 844) of the *Iliad.*[10] In the same manner Vergil spoke in the *Aeneid* of Ilus, Assaracus, and Dardanus as

> pulcherrima proles,
> magnanimi heroes, nati melioribus annis.
> (VI. 648-49)

Family most fair, high-souled heroes born in happier years.[11]

And this is what Milton meant by the term in *Samson Agonistes* when he had Harapha address Samson:

> Thou durst not thus disparage glorious arms
> Which greatest Heroes have in battel worn.
> (1130-31)

If we were to apply this terminology to *Paradise Lost,* we might describe not only Satan, but Christ, Gabriel, and Beelzebub as heroic.[12] Because of such ambiguities, the term "hero" cannot be precise; thus we must recognize a multiplicity of types of heroes such as the ethical hero, the structural hero, the focal hero, or the heroic warrior.

Dr. Johnson brushed aside as "indecent" Dryden's comment that Satan triumphs and thus is, like Aeneas, an epic hero. Indeed, Satan is not the victor and Adam is not "foiled," but departs in a state of enlightenment which defies reduction to a single phrase. Milton is a very subtle and complex poet and never more complex than in the ways he interweaves his structure with the generic tradition in which he is working. Dryden has hold of an important aspect of the poem: in many respects Satan *is* the most Aeneas-like figure in *Paradise Lost*. Take his first speech in the poem:

> If thou beest he; But O how fall'n! how chang'd
> From him, who in the happy Realms of Light
> Cloth'd with transcendent brightness didst out-shine
> Myriads though bright.
>
> (I. 84-87)

Countless editors have pointed out the resemblance of this speech by the Arch-Enemy to one by Aeneas, who is addressing the ghost of Hector:

> Ei mihi, qualis erat! quantum mutatus ab illo
> Hectore, qui redit exuvias indutus Achilli
> vel Danaum Phrygios iaculatus puppibus ignis!
> squalentem barbam et concretos sanguine crinis
> volneraque illa gerens, quae circum plurima muros
> accipit patrios.
>
> (II. 274-79)

"Ah me! what aspect was his! how changed from that Hector who returns after donning the spoils of Achilles or hurling on Danaan ships the Phrygian fires! with ragged beard, with hair matted with blood, and bearing those many wounds he gat around his native walls."

We must not miss the accompanying fact that the ensuing dialogue in *Paradise Lost* is between the Arch-Fiend and his "bold Compeer," Beelzebub, and that in the comparable passage in the *Aeneid* it is between Aeneas and his comrade-in-arms, the noble Hector.

Satan and Beelzebub discuss the catastrophe which has befallen them, and then Satan calls the other fallen angels from the fiery lake:

> Princes, Potentates,
> Warriers, the Flowr of Heav'n, once yours, now lost,
> If such astonishment as this can sieze
> Eternal spirits; or have ye chos'n this place
> After the toyl of Battel to repose
> Your wearied vertue, for the ease you find
> To slumber here, as in the Vales of Heav'n?
> Or in this abject posture have ye sworn
> To adore the Conquerour? who now beholds
> Cherube and Seraph rowling in the Flood
> With scatter'd Arms and Ensigns, till anon
> His swift pursuers from Heav'n Gates discern
> Th'advantage, and descending tread us down
> Thus drooping, or with linked Thunderbolts
> Transfix us to the bottom of this Gulfe.
> Awake, arise, or be for ever fall'n.

(I. 315-30)

Not only does "all the hollow Deep / Of Hell" resound with Satan's rousing summons to his scattered forces; but the epic tradition back to Homer echoes through the speech. This is how Odysseus cheered his men as they approached the dangers of Scylla:

> My friends, we are not unacquainted with trouble. This is no greater danger than when the Cyclops imprisoned us in his cave by brute force; we escaped from that place, thanks to my courage and my ingenious plan, and I think we shall live to remember this no less. Now then, attend to my instructions. Keep your seats and row away like men, and then we may hope that Zeus will save and deliver us out of this danger. Now for you, steersman, pay careful heed, for you hold our helm in your hands. Keep her well away from the smoke and surge, and hug the cliffs; whatever you do, don't let her run off in that direction, or we shall all be drowned.[13]

(XII. 208-21)

And surely that encyclopedic reader for whom Milton wrote, who presumably had total recall of all literature from Homer and Hesiod to Reginald Scott and Sir Robert Fludd, would instantly remember the first book of the *Aeneid,* where Aeneas rallies his warriors, disheartened after their buffeting at sea, just as the devils are demoralized after their defeat and expulsion from Heaven. And it is Aeneas who addresses these lines to his men:

> O socii, (neque enim ignari sumus ante malorum),
> o passi graviora, dabit deus his quoque finem.
> vos et Scyllaeum rabiem penitusque sonantis
> accestis scopulos, vos et Cyclopia saxa
> experti revocate animos maestumque timorem
> mittite; forsan et haec olim meminisse iuvabit.
> per varios casus, per tot discrimina rerum
> tendimus in Latium, sedes ubi fata quietas
> ostendunt; illic fas regna resurgere Troiae.
> durate, et vosmet rebus servate secundis.
>
> (I. 198-207)

"O comrades—for ere this we have not been ignorant of evils—O ye who have borne a heavier lot, to this, too, God will grant an end! Ye drew near to Scylla's fury and her deep-echoing crags; ye have known, too, the rocks of the Cyclopes; recall your courage and put away sad fear. Perchance even this distress it will some day be a joy to recall. Through divers mishaps, through so many perilous chances, we fare toward Latium, where the fates point out a home of rest. There 'tis granted to Troy's realm to rise again; endure, and keep yourselves for days of happiness."

After Milton's devils have extricated themselves from the lake and have been catalogued in the traditional style, Satan addresses them:

> He now prepar'd
> To speak; whereat thir doubl'd Ranks they bend
> From wing to wing, and half enclose him round
> With all his Peers: attention held them mute.
> Thrice he assayd, and thrice in spight of scorn,

Tears such as Angels weep, burst forth: at last
Words interwove with sighs found out thir way.
O Myriads of immortal Spirits ...

(I. 615-22)

In a situation quite different, Aeneas similarly addresses his father
Anchises in the sixth book. But by these verbal parallels Milton
clearly implies a comparison of Satan with Aeneas:

Sic memorans largo fletu simul ora rigabat.
ter conatus ibi collo dare bracchio circum,
ter frustra comprensa manus effugit imago,
par levibus ventis volucrique simillima somno.

(VI. 699-702)

So he spoke, his face wet with flooding tears. Thrice there he
strove to throw his arms around his neck; thrice the form,
vainly clasped, fled from his hands, even as light winds, and
most like a winged dream.

When Satan begins his perilous journey to Earth he encounters the
threatening figure of Sin, who tries to stop him. Satan responds coura-
geously:

Incenst with indignation *Satan* stood
Unterrifi'd, and like a Comet burn'd,
That fires the length of *Ophiucus* huge
In th' Artick Sky, and from his horrid hair
Shakes Pestilence and Warr.

(II. 707-11)

And the epic warrior that Satan most resembles is not the antagonist
Turnus nor the villainous Mezentius, but, again, the heroic Aeneas:

Ardet apex capiti, cristisque a vertice flamma
funditur, et vastos umbo vomit aureus ignis:
non secus ac liquida si quando nocte cometae
sanguinei lugubre rubent, aut Sirius ardor
ille, sitim morbosque ferens mortalibus aegris,
nascitur et laevo contristat lumine caelum.

(X. 270-75)

On the hero's head blazes the helmet-peak, flame streams from the crest aloft, and the shield's golden boss spouts floods of fire—even as when in the clear night comets glow blood-red in baneful wise; or even as fiery Sirius, that bearer of drought and pestilence to feeble mortals, rises and saddens the sky with baleful light.

We must see that the relation of *Paradise Lost* to the *Aeneid* is more important than mere literary borrowing or than the dependence of one epic poet on another. Epic poets, indeed all poets, tend to borrow from their predecessors and to bend their borrowings to fit the poetic situation at hand. Vergil took from Homer and molded his material to fit his poem: the drunkenness of the Trojans at the fall of Troy (in Homer) is transferred by Vergil to the Rutulians killed by Euryalus and Nisus *(Aeneid* IX. 189-236). But Milton's treatment of Vergil in *Paradise Lost* is bolder than Vergil's treatment of Homer. Milton's borrowings are more organically integrated into his poem; they are part not merely of what Milton says but of how he says it.[14]

Milton is using Vergil, using the relation between Aeneas and Satan, as an instrument to integrate the extra-poetic patterns involving God, man, and the justification of the human condition with the poetic patterns of his epic. The events in the Garden of Eden are extra-poetic in that, in Milton's view, they actually occurred, regardless of whether anyone wrote a poem about them or not. In the same sense, the death of Edward King was extra-poetic, in that it was a historical event, independent of poems such as "Lycidas," which were written about it. In *Paradise Lost* Milton integrates the extra-poetic patterns of events in the Garden with the poetic patterns of the epic tradition—in particular, those of the *Aeneid,* which serves as a functional background against which to establish the patterns and progressions of *Paradise Lost.*

One of the most important functions of the *Aeneid* in *Paradise Lost* is to establish this background against which Satan appears as an epic hero of the traditional sort. Like Aeneas in the midst of the flames of Troy, Satan fights for his homeland; he loses; he is forced into exile. Like Aeneas, he rallies his forces and with great courage he leads them through hardships and adventures. After his victory over Adam in the Garden, after founding his new realm on Earth, Satan specifically points to his epic achievements as he addresses his followers:

> Now possess,
> As Lords, a spacious World, to our native Heaven
> Little inferiour, by my adventure hard
> With peril great atchiev'd. Long were to tell
> What I have don, what sufferd, with what paine
> Voyag'd th'unreal, vast, unbounded deep
> Of horrible confusion.
>
> (X. 466-72)

Aeneas and Odysseus might well have spoken with these accents, and with far smaller achievements to point to.

It would not be true, however, to say that only Satan, of all the figures in *Paradise Lost,* resembles Aeneas. The parallel between Adam's vision of the future, explicated by Michael in Books XI and XII of *Paradise Lost,* and that of Aeneas, explicated by Anchises in Book VI of the *Aeneid,* is very close, and the parallelism is important to *Paradise Lost:* as Aeneas sees the trials, the sorrows, and the ultimate triumphant destiny of a Rome guided by the Immanent Mind, so Adam sees the sins and sufferings of mankind, and the ultimate raising up of

> New Heav'ns, new Earth, Ages of endless date
> Founded in righteousness and peace and love
> To bring forth fruits Joy and eternal Bliss.
>
> (XII. 549-51)[15]

The ultimate destiny of mankind, which Adam witnesses, surpasses the glory of Rome that Aeneas foresees, just as the victory of Satan in the Garden is of greater magnitude than that of Aeneas over the wrath of Juno.

The poem departs from any pat comparisons in another way as well: not only is Adam occasionally equated with Aeneas, but the poem's general tendency of relating Satan with the old epic virtue of martial courage is not a simple, unvarying formula. In the Heavenly battle in Book VI of *Paradise Lost,* the frequent military echoes of the *Iliad* and the *Aeneid* seem in fact to follow no particular design. To create a neat pattern, Milton could have used the martial echoes from Homer and Vergil only in relation to the devils, but he did not: for example at one point (VI. 832), he likens Christ to Hector *(Iliad* XII. 462). Still it is safe to say that Milton's tendency, especially in the early books of *Paradise Lost* and occasionally at later points in

15

the poem, is to relate Satan the warrior-adventurer with Aeneas the warrior-adventurer by having Satan imitate the phrases, speeches, and actions of Aeneas.

In contrast to Satan, whose role is in some ways that of a super-Aeneas, Adam embodies a virtue of another sort, the tale of which is

> Not less but more Heroic then the wrauth
> Of stern *Achilles* on his Foe pursu'd
> Thrice Fugitive about *Troy* Wall; or rage
> Of *Turnus* for *Lavinia* disespous'd,
> Or *Neptun's* ire or *Juno's,* that so long
> Perplex'd the *Greek* and *Cytherea's* Son.
> (IX. 14-19)

It is true that Satan has fought battles and endured wounds. But as *Paradise Lost* moves to its conclusion it specifically rejects this kind of heroism:

> Warrs, hitherto the onely Argument
> Heroic deem'd, chief maistrie to dissect
> With long and tedious havoc fabl'd Knights
> In Battels feign'd; the better fortitude
> Of Patience and Heroic Martyrdom
> Unsung; or to describe Races and Games,
> Or tilting Furniture, emblazon'd Shields,
> Impreses quaint, Caparisons and Steeds;
> Bases and tinsel Trappings, gorgious Knights
> At Joust and Torneament; then marshal'd Feast
> Serv'd up in Hall with Sewers, and Seneshals;
> The skill of Artifice or Office mean,
> Not that which justly gives Heroic name
> To Person or to Poem. Mee of these
> Nor skilld nor studious, higher Argument
> Remaines.
> (IX. 28-43)

In the eleventh and twelfth books Michael helps to re-educate Adam after his sin, and at one point Adam loses track of this "higher Argument." When he hears from Michael of the Incarnation and of Christ's coming triumph over Satan, Adam looks forward to a tale full of the grand old epic blood and thunder:

> Say where and when
> Thir fight, what stroke shall bruise the Victors heel.

But Michael quickly brings him back from ideas of any martial struggle:

> Dream not of thir fight,
> As of a Duel, or the local wounds
> Of head or heel.
>
> (XII. 384-88)

These lines reverberate not only with overtones of Genesis, which foretells that the serpent will bruise the heel of Adam's seed, but also with the legends of Achilles, who will meet death in epic combat through a heel-wound from the arrow of Paris. Michael's rebuke to Adam in these lines, scorning the battles of the flesh for the trials of the spirit, reinforces the momentum of the poem. Now in Book XII the poem thrusts itself upward to a height where it can look down on the traditional epic battles of Achilles, Hector, and Aeneas as merely "local wounds of head or heel." This new vision of true heroism is built on a loftier ethical base:

> not therefore joynes the Son
> Manhood to God-head, with more strength to foil
> Thy enemie ...
> . . . .
> But by fulfilling that which thou didst want,
> Obedience to the Law of God ...
> . . . .
> So onely can high Justice rest appaid.
> The Law of God exact he shall fulfill
> Both by obedience and by love, though love
> Alone fulfill the Law.
>
> (XII. 388-90, 396-97, 401-4)

And Adam goes on to set forth his newly acquired understanding of true virtue in a passage which clearly reflects Milton's rejection of tinsel trappings, martial glory, and physical combat:

Henceforth I learne, that to obey is best,
And love with fear the onely God, to walk
As in his presence, ever to observe
His providence, and on him sole depend,
Mercifull over all his works, with good
Still overcoming evil, and by small
Accomplishing great things, by things deemd weak
Subverting worldly strong, and worldly wise
By simply meek; that suffering for Truths sake
Is fortitude to highest victorie,
And to the faithful Death the Gate of Life;
Taught this by his example whom I now
Acknowledge my Redeemer ever blest.

(XII. 561-73)

This speech creates structural resonances throughout the whole of *Paradise Lost*. For example, it is a purified, rectified counterpart of Mammon's perverted pacifism[16] in Book II:

Our greatness will appeer
Then most conspicuous, when great things of small,
Useful of hurtful, prosperous of adverse
We can create, and in what place so e're
Thrive under evil, and work ease out of pain
Through labour and indurance.

(II. 257-62)

And this placing of Adam and his perils beside the conventions of the traditional epic hero creates a functional force which drives the poem by poetic means to its extra-poetic resolutions, its "justification." It is this emergence of the figure of Adam, as the poem progresses, out of the complex pattern of relations among Adam, Satan, and the traditional hero of epic poetry which imparts some of the dynamism we are discussing to the structure of the poem.

Milton's Adam never demonstrates these virtues in action; the poem closes before this can happen. But Michael, whose wisdom we can hardly doubt, is satisfied that Adam has achieved an internal state of true heroism, with the hope of greater victories to come:

To whom thus also th'Angel last repli'd:

> This having learnt, thou hast attained the summe
> Of wisdom....
>
> . . . .
>
>   ... onely add
> Deeds to thy knowledge answerable, add Faith,
> Add vertue, Patience, Temperance, add Love,
> By name to come call'd Charitie, the soul
> Of all the rest: then wilt thou not be loath
> To leave this Paradise, but shalt possess
> A Paradise within thee, happier farr.
>
>   (XII. 574-76, 581-87)

To elevate Satan to the role of sole hero of the poem is to misread the poem badly; but to dismiss him from any heroic role is to turn a deaf ear to those vast Homeric and Vergilian echoes which Milton causes to reverberate through so many of Satan's best speeches and grandest deeds. And the clash of those martial Homeric-Vergilian echoes in Satan's adventures with the saintly spiritual "summe of wisdom" of the mature Adam is one of the structural forces which drives the poem forward from its violent, distorted, malevolent beginning to its peaceful, harmonious resolution.

To oversimplify in another direction—perhaps it is impossible to talk about great poetry without oversimplifying in some fashion—Satan stalks through the poem not only as the Father of all Evil, but also as the embodiment of an outmoded system of epic values. The poem explicitly and implicitly claims a high place for Satan in this old system of values; his physical courage, his unconquerable will to triumph, his willingness to make the daring epic voyage into an unknown world to found a newer, better realm—all these traits mark him as an epic hero. As a heroic figure he dwarfs Aeneas in the same manner that his new realm of the whole Earth dwarfs Aeneas's Rome. But to stop here, of course, is to trace only one theme in the vast dynamic structure that Milton has created.

The unity of *Paradise Lost,* throughout its vast expanse of ten thousand lines, is established by many elements; but the unity which the poem achieves is not a static fusion of a single plot with a single theme. It is the dynamic progression in which the initial evil of Satan moves forward to find its resolution in the concluding vision of Adam, who is superior to Satan ethically, and more central to the poem structurally. At the conclusion of the poem, Adam prepares for a type of heroism beyond that of Achilles, Odysseus, or Aeneas. He fights no military battles as he journeys forth on the greatest of all epic voyages; his goal is not to gain Rome or all the kingdoms of Earth, but rather to win a kingdom "happier farr"—the "Paradise within." These traditional epic heroes—Achilles, Odysseus, Aeneas, and Satan—establish the base from which *Paradise Lost* thrusts itself upward to the true heroism which Adam ultimately learns.

The result of the functional dissonance between Milton's kind of epic hero and the hero of the epic tradition is that the unique epicness of *Paradise Lost* is not merely an inert Greco-Roman box which contains a Biblical tale. It is part of the dynamic metaphor which both carries the poem forward from its initial positions in Book I to its ultimate resolutions in Book XII, and which helps to integrate the poetic pattern of the poem as a whole with the extra-poetic patterns implied in Milton's intent to "justify the wayes of God to men."

III

The Early Latin Poems
and "Lycidas"

Fundat et ipsa modos querebunda Elegeia tristes

Milton's first three Latin elegies differ greatly from *Paradise Lost* in almost every respect—in their subjects, in their overt purposes, and even in their language, which is Latin, not English. Yet in them, as in *Paradise Lost,* Milton also faced problems of structural unity and attempted solutions to these problems. Further, the first three Latin elegies, like *Paradise Lost,* create poetic situations which call for a dynamic structure: in the elegies the poet must find a way to get from initial conflict to ultimate resolution.

"Elegia Prima" is ostensibly a letter, written probably in the spring of 1626,[1] to Milton's friend Charles Diodati. At the same time it is an elaborate nosethumb at Milton's alma mater, Cambridge University, which had just rusticated (suspended) him. The other two early Latin elegies were written on the occasion of the death of someone Milton admired and lead almost inevitably to a comparison with "Lycidas."

Thus "Lycidas," although written eleven years later and in English rather than in Latin, is an excellent *terminus ad quem* for these early Latin poems. It succeeds at what they attempt but fail to do. Since much of what Milton does in the mature poems such as "Lycidas" and *Paradise Lost* is managed with such skill that we do not see how the poems could have been otherwise, an examination of these immature Latin forerunners will show that the earlier poems are similar to the later masterpieces in some ways, but are in other ways clumsy and disorganized. A study of the earlier poems will clarify some of the adroitness and structural skill of the mature poems.

"Elegia Prima" is written in part as an explanatory letter to Milton's friend Charles Diodati, who was then a student at Oxford, but who was, at the moment, in Chester. As the result of a quarrel Milton seems to have had with his tutor in the Lenten term of his second year at Cambridge (1626), he apparently was sent home.[2]

Like almost all of Milton's early poems, "Elegia Prima" is deeply influenced by Ovid,[3] and this is perhaps even more to be expected in this poem since, as James Holly Hanford points out, Milton saw "the analogy between his own exile and the fate of Ovid ... [and] made a kind of imaginative identification of himself with his Roman predecessor."[4] This observation is true, but the relation that Milton establishes between himself and Ovid is, for the seventeen-year-old poet, a complex and clever one. He uses Ovid not as a simple model, but as a weapon for taking a retributive whack at Cambridge. Milton does not make a direct comparison between himself and Ovid, but a cross-comparison: Milton's exile to London is as happy as Ovid's residence in Rome; Milton's residence at Cambridge was as miserable as Ovid's exile to Tomis.

The Ovidian parallels in "Elegia Prima" are almost numberless,[5] and some of them, as so often in Milton's early poems, are mere frosting. For example, line 9 of Milton's poem, "Me tenet urbs refluâ quam Thamesis alluit undâ" recalls Ovid's "Et quas Oceani refluum mare lavit harenas" *(Metamorphoses* VII. 267); Milton's "Irrita nec nobis tempora veris eunt" (48) repeats Ovid's "et primi veris erunt" *(Fasti* II. 150). Another parallel that is important but too well known to dwell on is the fact that Milton's exile-poem takes the form of a letter, as did Ovid's forty-six *Epistulae ex Ponto,* written from Tomis to his various friends in Rome. Many of the poems in the *Tristia,* written in exile from Tomis, are also letters. In addition, Milton uses Ovid's verse form, the elegiac distich. But merely noting these parallels misses the point of Milton's gibes at Cambridge. It leaves the poem as little more than a personal record of his exile and his random experiences in London, with some similarity to the Companion Pieces, but with neither their vividness nor their organization. The elegy seems to ramble from Milton's rustication to the plays he had read, then to the women he had seen, and finally returns with reluctance to its theme of exile.

What actually gives the poem much of its organization is a device quite similar to that which, over forty years later, was to help so powerfully in organizing the ten thousand lines of *Paradise Lost*. There Milton establishes the proper relation of Adam and Satan to the true Christian epic virtues by means of the relation of Aeneas and Achilles to the pagan, martial virtues. So, in a small, undergraduate way, the organization of the ninety-two lines of "Elegia Prima" depends on this cross-comparison of Milton's rustication to Ovid's exile. When Milton says (21-24) he wishes Ovid had had as pleasant an exile as his because then Ovid could have outdone Homer and Vergil, he echoes (and wants us to remember) the first book of Ovid's *Tristia*, where Ovid complains that not even Homer could write poetry under the conditions at Tomis.[6] Milton implies that Ovid would have surpassed even Homer under the pleasant conditions in London:

> Si sit hoc exilium patrios adiisse penates,
> Et vacuum curis otia grata sequi,
> Non ego vel profugi nomen, sortemve recuso,
> Laetus & exilii conditione fruor.
>
> (17-20)

But if this be exile, to have returned to the paternal home and to be carefree to enjoy a delightful leisure, then I have no objection to the name or to the lot of a fugitive and I am glad to take advantage of my banishment.[7]

A major reason for Ovid's hatred of Tomis was that he could not write poetry in such a place.[8] Milton uses this as a barb for the university that sent him home; instead of fostering poetry, Cambridge is as hostile to it as Tomis, Milton implies (13-16); but unlike Ovid, Milton is writing about the place *from* which he has been exiled.

The three central sections of Milton's poem (25-36, 37-46, 47-84) now appear not as digressions but as developments of the theme of Cambridge-equals-Tomis, London-equals-Rome. These lines record the joys to which Milton was rusticated and from which Ovid was exiled. Milton writes of London:

> Tempora nam licet hîc placidis dare libera Musis,
> Et totum rapiunt me mea vita libri.
>
> (25-26)

Here my hours are free to be dedicated to the quiet Muses;
and my books, which are my life, quite carry me away.

Milton's exile in London supplies what residence at a university
should, but does not; conversely Ovid's complaint in exile is

Non hic librorum. per quos inviter alarque,
copia: pro libris arcus et arma sonant.
(Tristia III. xiv. 37-38)

Not here have I an abundance of books to stimulate and nourish
me: in their stead is the rattle of bows and arms.[9]

In a pitiful elegy on the belated coming of spring to Tomis, Ovid
remembers the Roman games and he can almost hear the applause of
the crowded theatres.[10] Milton in exile has "Sinuosi pompa
theatri" on every hand, and he revels in them for twenty lines,
delighted by the "catus senior," the "prodigus haeres," and
"furiosa Tragoedia" herself.

The section in Milton's elegy concerned with the pretty girls of
London (47-84) is laden with Ovidian parallels—echoes of the
delights which Ovid remembered from Rome and which Milton finds
in exile from Cambridge. For example Milton's lines, "Saepius hic
blandas spirantia sydera flammas / Virgineos videas praeteriisse
choros" (51-52) ("Here, like stars that breathe out soft flames,
you may see groups of maidens go dancing past") recall Ovid's
"Quot caelum stellas, tot habet tua Roma puellas" ("As many as
are the stars of heaven, so many maidens doth thine own Rome con-
tain")[11] from the *Ars Amatoria* (I. 59), the book which was probably responsible in part for getting Ovid exiled to Tomis. The story of
Venus and Adonis, to which Milton refers in line 62, Ovid told in the
Metamorphoses (X. 503-738). More important, Milton's "Tarpëia
Musa" (69) is of course Ovid himself, who once enjoyed in Rome
what Milton is enjoying in exile.

While the shady lanes near London make exile pleasant (49-50),
the very landscape of Cambridge is bare, shadeless, and repulsive to
Milton (13)—echoes of Ovid's complaint against the barren Pontic
landscape, with no apples bending the branches, no grapes, nor even
vines, but only a treeless plain whose typical vegetation is worm-
wood.[12] Even the marshy banks of the Cam, which Milton will

remember eleven years later in "Lycidas," here give him occasion for sneers (11,89) reflecting Ovid's feelings about the swamps of Tomis.[13]

This is not to say that the poem is only a paraphrase of Ovid's feelings about Tomis, but rather to point out that Milton gives pungency to his exile-poem by means of a submerged metaphor involving the well-known dreariness of Tomis. For Milton in this poem[14] there is nothing good about Cambridge, *from* which he has been exiled, and nothing bad about London, just as for Ovid there was nothing good about Tomis, *to* which he had been exiled, and nothing bad (in the *Tristia* and the *Epistulae ex Ponto)* about Rome.

Again and again, in his early poems, Milton makes the mistake of needlessly plastering his lines with remembered passages from books he has read. But his use of Ovid in "Elegia Prima" is a functional metaphor of some skill and bite; it is one of the seeds of the structural ideas which flowered in *Paradise Lost.* This structural concept in "Elegia Prima" differs from its counterpart in *Paradise Lost* in that it primarily depends on a static, albeit inverted, relation to Ovid's exile poems. Where the organization of *Paradise Lost* embodies the emergence of a new heroic ideal out of an outmoded heroic form, "Elegia Prima" makes use of a reversal of the relations of exile, residence, civilization, and barbarism.

But "Elegia Prima" also develops, in a small way, its own internal dynamic pattern in a manner that faintly foreshadows the structure of *Paradise Lost.* Once the poem has condemned, in its opening lines, the crudities, indignities, and ugliness of Cambridge, it moves into a contrasting passage, containing good poetic logic, on Milton's serious studies during his London exile—"totum rapiunt me mea vita libri" (26). Unfortunately the passages on Roman comedy and Greek tragedy which follow (27-46) are not Milton at his most vivid; the kindest judgment is that they helped prepare him for some of the best parts of "Il Penseroso," such as:

> Som time let Gorgeous Tragedy
> In Scepter'd Pall com sweeping by,
> Presenting *Thebs,* or *Pelops* line,
> Or the tale of *Troy* divine.
> Or what (though rare) of later age,
> Ennobled hath the Buskind stage.
> But, O sad Virgin, that thy power

Might raise *Musaeus* from his bower,
Or bid the soul of *Orpheus* sing
Such notes as warbled to the string,
Drew Iron tears down *Pluto's* cheek,
And made Hell grant what Love did seek.
(97-108)

While the Latin precursors of these lines are duller poetry, they are not out of place, and they act as an effective bridge to the resounding culmination of "Elegia Prima." Milton notes that he has been out watching the girls of London:

Ah quoties dignae stupui miracula formae
Quae possit senium vel reparare Jovis.
(53-54)

Ah, how many times have I been struck dumb by the miraculous grace of a form which might make decrepit Jove young again!

With increasing, self-kindling enthusiasm, he raises his poem to a climax which manages to be both amorous and chauvinistic:

Cedite laudatae toties Heroides olim,
Et quaecunque vagum cepit amica Jovem.
Cedite Achaemeniae turritâ fronte puellae,
Et quot Susa colunt, Memnoniamque Ninon.
(63-66)

Give way, ye Heroïdes, so much praised in olden times, and every mistress who made inconstant Jove her captive. Give way, you Achaemenian damsels with the turrets on your brows, and you, whose home is Susa or Memnonian Nineveh.

We may smile at the seventeen-year-old scholar who finds the London girls even more exciting than the study of Ovid or Euripides, but the passage does serve the function of carrying the poem forward, giving it impetus and structural integrity.

Gloria Virginibus debetur prima Britannis,
Extera sat tibi sit foemina posse sequi.
(71-72)

The prime honor is due to the virgins of Britain; be content, foreign women, to follow after.

There is an over-solemnity to the culmination of the poem in these passionate and patriotic lines which carry an unconscious touch of comedy, but the vitality and enthusiasm of the young scholar-girl watcher pull the poem together:

> Tuque urbs Dardaniis Londinum structa colonis
> Turrigerum latè conspicienda caput,
> Tu nimium felix intra tua moenia claudis
> Quicquid formosi pendulus orbis habet.
>
> (73-76)

And you, London, the city built by Trojan colonists and now widely conspicuous with towered head, yours is the excessive happiness of bounding within your walls whatever beauty the pendant world possesses.

This progression from the drabness of university studies to the beauties of the girls of London by means of Ovid, Homer, Plautus, Euripides, et al., is obviously naive and adolescent poetry; but it is surely the work of a young craftsman who has a feeling for integrating his extra-poetic experience of rustication into a poetic pattern which has a strong and fairly well unified impetus toward its climax.[15] "Elegia Prima" is obviously an immature poem, but running all through it are embryonic techniques which Milton will gradually, over the years, perfect and bring to bear on the masterpieces of his maturity.

Later in 1626 Milton wrote the first of the many epicedia which recur in his works. "In Obitum Procancellarii Medici" was composed on the occasion of the death of Dr. John Gostlin, Regius Professor of Medicine and Vice-Chancellor of Cambridge University, on 21 October 1626. This would probably place the writing of the poem within six months after "Elegia Prima." The poem for Dr. Gostlin is the first of the four Latin epicedia[16] which Milton wrote that year, and the first of a sequence of epicedia which reached its culmination in "Lycidas" and "Epitaphium Damonis."

The poem for Gostlin has had its defenders, though not many.[17] It parades a great deal of classical learning, but little of the learning serves any poetic purpose, and in this respect the poem is a step backwards from "Elegia Prima." The mythological figures mentioned in the Gostlin poem (Hercules, Hector, Sarpedon, and so on) are linked to Dr. Gostlin chiefly by the fact that they, like him, are all dead. Even the order of their appearance seems haphazard. The poem struggles for some unity and integral imagery with the introduction of Machaon (23), a surgeon with the Greek army before Troy. Machaon is said to have been the son of Aesculapius, and Aesculapius himself appears (25-28). The deceased Gostlin was, of course, a physician. The poem has a momentary flash of life at lines 37-40 as it contrasts Gostlin's career in rescuing men from death with Persephone's meeting men after death:

> At fila rupit Persephone tua
> Irata, cum te viderit artibus
> Succoque pollenti tot atris
> Faucibus eripuisse mortis.
> (37-40)

But Persephone broke the thread of your life, angered because she saw you snatching so many victims from the black jaws of death by your arts and powerful potions.

But it concludes in drab conventionality:

> Colende praeses, membra precor tua
> Molli quiescant cespite, & ex tuo
> Crescant rosae, calthaeque busto,
> Purpureoque hyacinthus ore.
> Sit mite de te judicium Aeaci,
> Subrideatque Aetnaea Proserpina,
> Interque felices perennis
> Elysio spatiere campo.
> (41-48)

Reverend Chancellor, may your limbs find rest in the soft turf, I pray, and from your grave may roses and marigolds and the purple-lipped hyacinth spring. May the judgement of Aeacus upon you be gentle, and may Sicilian Proserpina smile! May you walk forever among the blessed in Elysium!

The weakness of this conclusion does not merely lie in its conventionality; in *Paradise Lost,* the functional manipulations of the conventions (for example, the conventional journey to found a new kingdom) are a source of the poem's strength. But in the Gostlin poem the ending has no structural relation to the rest of the poem except in its routine fulfilling of the epicedic conventions. The poem never actively uses the conventions as poetic techniques; it is merely obedient and therefore flat. Milton's path onward from the poem for Gostlin leads eventually to the poems for King and Diodati, and ultimately to *Paradise Lost* and *Paradise Regained* but the path has a long way to go.

"Elegia Secunda," for the University Beadle, written at about the same time as "In Obitum Procancellarii Medici," is a brief trifle with little poetic value, but it has one good image in it—that of Death as "magna sepulchrorum regina," which Leigh Hunt thought was worthy of Dante or of Milton in his "maturest imagery."[18] And the closing lines have a certain grand resonance to them:

> Vestibus hunc igitur pullis Academia luge,
>   Et madeant lachrymis nigra feretra tuis.
> Fundat & ipsa modos querebunda Elegéia tristes,
>   Personet & totis naenia moesta scholis.

> (21-24)

Therefore grieve for this man, O Academe, in robes of black, and make his dark hearse wet with your tears. Let wailing Elegy herself pour out her sad dirge and fill all the schools with its sound.

"Elegia Tertia," commemorating the death of Bishop Lancelot Andrewes on 25 September 1626, is a far better poem and more interesting as a step in Milton's development. More than any other early poem it foreshadows the two great epicedia of Milton's maturity, "Lycidas" and "Epitaphium Damonis." It uses some of the same devices as the two mature poems, and it faces the same conflict: the justification of God's ways to men at the time of the death of a man of virtue. For our purposes, the poem is chiefly valuable because it tries and partially fails at what "Lycidas" and

"Epitaphium Damonis" magnificently achieve. It states the extra-poetic problem, the death of Bishop Andrewes, and then moves on to its extra-poetic resolution, the vision of Andrewes in Heaven. But unlike "Lycidas" and "Epitaphium Damonis," the progression is always extra-poetic; that is, the transfiguration of Andrewes is stated as a fact in the concluding section of the poem, but it is never integrated into the structure of the poem. In "Lycidas" and "Epitaphium Damonis" the progression and the resolution are not only stated in the poem, they *are* the poem itself; in each of these, such structural elements as imagery, language, and the relation of parts to the whole, are inseparably unified with the "subject," which consists of such elements as grief, loneliness, and the ultimate vision of God's mercy. In "Elegia Tertia," this union never takes place; the structure of the poem gives only the feeblest foundation for the statement that a resolution has taken place.

"Elegia Tertia" divides itself into three sections: I: 1-14, the poet's grief; II: 15-36, his complaint to "Mors fera" for carrying off the beloved Bishop; III: 37-68, the poet's vision of the Bishop in Heaven. The opening fourteen-line section repays close examination and comparison with the opening of "Lycidas":

> Moestus eram, & tacitus nullo comitante sedebam,
> Haerebantque animo tristia plura meo,
> Protinus en subiit funestae cladis Imago
> Facit in Angliaco quam Libitina solo;
> Dum procerum ingressa est splendentes marmore turres
> Dira sepulchrali mors metuenda face;
> Pulsavitque auro gravidos & jaspide muros,
> Nec metuit satrapum sternere falce greges.
> Tunc memini clarique ducis, fratrisque verendi
> Intempestivis ossa cremata rogis.
> Et memini Heroum quos vidit ad aethera raptos,
> Flevit & amissos Belgia tota duces.
> At te praecipuè luxi dignissime praesul,
> Wintoniaeque olim gloria magna tuae.
>
> (1-14)

I was grief-stricken and without any companion I was sitting in silence. Many sorrows were besetting my spirit, when, lo, suddenly there arose a vision of the baneful destruction which

Libitina wrought upon English soil when dire death—terrible with his sepulchral torch—entered the bright, marble palaces of the patricians, attacked the walls that are weighted with jasper and gold, and presumed to mow down hosts of princes with his scythe. Then I remembered that glorious duke and his brother, whose bones were burned on untimely pyres; and I remembered the Heroes whom Belgia saw rapt into the skies—the lost leaders whom the whole nation mourned. But my greatest grief was for you, most worthy Bishop, and in time past the noble ornament of your Winchester.

Like "Lycidas," the elegy begins in grief, but it is at first a diffuse and unnamed grief—"tristia plura." Even as the picture comes into focus it is irrelevant to an epicedion for Bishop Andrewes: "Fecit in Angliaco quam Libitina solo" (4). Then enter the distracting figures of "clarisque ducis, fratrisque verendi," who seem to have been Count Ernest of Mansfield and Duke Christian of Brunswick-Wolfenbüttel, both of whom had recently died.[19] But they are as irrelevant to this poem as Hercules and Sarpedon were to the poem on Dr. Gostlin; they are here only because they happen to have died in 1626. Count Ernest and Duke Christian are like actors who have wandered onto the wrong stage; their presence here has only to be compared with the massive entry in "Lycidas" of St. Peter, "the Pilot of the Galilean lake," to see the integrating power which‧ Milton developed in the eleven years between the two poems. St. Peter is not only an impressive figure; he serves a necessary structural function in the great progression that carries "Lycidas" to its appropriate resolution.

"Elegia Tertia" manages to turn to Andrewes only after Count Ernest and Duke Christian have left:

> At te praecipuè luxi dignissime praesul,
> Wintoniaeque olim gloria magna tuae.
>
> (13-14)

But my greatest grief was for you, most worthy Bishop, and in time past the noble ornament of your Winchester.

Milton's "praecipuè" looks self-conscious: Bishop Andrewes's entry into his own epicedion has been long overdue. Grief stricken,

Milton proceeds to his own lamentation (15-30) and then to the beatific vision. In itself, the section describing the vision displays real competence, but it brings Milton face-to-face with a difficult problem of poetic organization: how is he to manage this structural progression from grief to joy? The central section of "Elegia Tertia" does this first by the poet's lament to Death, but from there on the progression is crudely managed: day ends, the poet grows sleepy, and he dreams. Luckily, the dream is of Andrewes in the company of the saints:

> Illic puniceâ radiabant omnia luce,
> Ut matutino cum juga sole rubent.
> Ac veluti cum pandit opes Thaumantia proles,
> Vestitu nituit multicolore solum.
> Non dea tam variis ornavit floribus hortos
> Alcinoi, Zephyro Chloris amata levi.
> Flumina vernantes lambunt argentea campos,
> Ditior Hesperio flavet arena Tago.
> Serpit odoriferas per opes levis aura Favoni,
> Aura sub innumeris humida nata rosis.
>
> (39-48)

There all things were radiant with rosy light, like mountain-crests flushing in the morning sunshine. The earth was brilliant in a garb of many colors, as it is when the child of Thaumas scatters her wealth abroad. Chloris, the goddess beloved by delicate Zephyr, did not deck the gardens of Alcinous with such various flowers. Silver rivers washed the green fields and their sands gleamed with greater wealth than Hesperian Tagus. Through the perfumed opulence stole the light breath of Favonius—the dewy breath that is born beneath myriad roses.

And then, with the poet's awakening, the poem closes.[20]

This concluding beatific vision in "Elegia Tertia" is an interesting foreshadowing of the heavenly visions of three of the mature poems—"Lycidas" (165-85), "Mansus" (94-100), and "Epitaphium Damonis" (198-219). Since the beatific vision as a poetic device plays such an important part in these four poems (not to mention variations on the idea in *Paradise Lost),* and since Milton writes with such a deep awareness of his literary tradition, it will help to observe the ancestry of these passages. The beatific vision has of course been a usual, although not necessary, section of the epicedion for centuries. Perhaps the most famous of these is in Vergil's fifth eclogue, which is a dialogue between Menalcas and Mopsus on the death of Daphnis—probably Julius Caesar.[21] Mopsus bewails the death of Daphnis in lines which Milton will recall in some of the early sections of both "Lycidas" and "Epitaphium Damonis":

> "Exstinctum Nymphae crudeli funere Daphnim
> flebant (vos coryli testes et flumine Nymphis),
> cum complexa sui corporis miserabile nati
> atque deos atque astra vocat crudelis mater.
> non ulli pastos illis egere diebus
> frigida, Daphni, boves ad flumina; nulla neque amnem
> libavit quadrupes nec graminis attigit herbam.
> Daphni, tuum Poenos etiam ingemuisse leones
> interitum montesque feri silvaeque loquuntur."
>
> (20-28)

"For Daphnis, cut of by a cruel death, the Nymphs wept—ye hazels and rivers bear witness to the Nymphs—when, clasping her son's piteous corpse, his mother cried out on the cruelty of both gods and stars. On those days, Daphnis, none drove the pastured kine to the cool streams; no four-footed beast tasted the brook or touched a blade of grass. Daphnis, the wild mountains and woods tell us that even African lions moaned over thy death."[22]

Menalcas answers that he will raise Daphnis to the stars:

> "Daphnimque tuum tollemus ad astra;
> Daphnis ad astra feremus: amavit nos quoque Daphnis."
>
> (51-52)

"Daphnis I will exalt to the stars; me, too, Daphnis loved."

And then Menalcas sets forth his vision of the deified Daphnis:

> "Candidus insuetum miratur limen Olympi
> sub pedibusque videt nubes et sidera Daphnis.

ergo alacris silvas et cetera rura voluptas
Panaque pastoresque tenet Dryadesque puellas.
nec lupus insidias pecori nec retia cervis
ulla dolum meditantur; amat bonus otia Daphnis.
ipsi laetitia voces ad sidera iactant
intonsi montes; ipsae iam carmine rupes,
ipsa sonant arbusta: 'deus, deus ille, Menalca!' "

(56-64)

"Daphnis, in radiant beauty, marvels at Heaven's unfamiliar threshold, and beneath his feet beholds the clouds and the stars. Therefore frolic glee seizes the woods and all the countryside, and Pan, and the shepherds, and the Dryad maids. The wolf plans no ambush for the flock, and nets no snare for the stag; kindly Daphnis loves peace. The very mountains, with woods unshorn, joyously fling their voices starward; the very rocks, the very groves ring out the song: 'A god is he, a god, Menalcas!' "

Statius, in his "Epicedion in Patrem Suum," has a similar vision of his father in Heaven.[23]

Christian epicedia[24] naturally tended toward Heavenly visions, and the poems on the death in 1612 of Prince Henry, son of King James I, are filled with them. Giles Fletcher's "Upon the Most Lamented Departure of ... Prince Henrie" concludes with a vision of the Prince at the throne of God.[25] But these beatific visions are not inevitable parts of epicedia; Castiglione's "Alcon," which deeply influenced both "Lycidas" and "Epitaphium Damonis" in so many ways,[26] has only a hint of any immortality for the dead shepherd, and the poem ends in gloom, Alcon's death still unjustified:

Alconem postquam rapuerunt impia fata,
Collacrymant duri montes, & consitus atrâ est
Nocte dies; sunt candida nigra, & dulcia amara.

Now that unpitying fate has stolen Alcon,
The harsh mountains weep; day is overlaid
With darkness: fair is foul and sweetness bitter.[27]

Neither Milton's epicedion for Gostlin nor the one for the Beadle has any hint of a beatific vision.

But Milton's poem for Bishop Andrewes not only affirms the Bishop's immortality, it also envisages his entry into Heaven in a passage which is almost a rehearsal for the conclusions of "Lycidas," "Mansus," and "Epitaphium Damonis." The Angels greet the Bishop with

> Nate, veni & patrii felix cape gaudia regni,
> Semper ab hinc duro, nate, labore vaca.
>
> (63-64)

"Come, my son, and joyously enter into the delights of your father's kingdom; and rest here from your labors forever."

Milton's difficulties with "Elegia Tertia" do not arise from the concluding vision itself (except for its unfortunate last line); they are rooted in the structure of the poem as a whole. As Dr. Johnson warned, "From the foundation to the pinnacles, one part [must] rest upon another." The concluding vision (39-68) rests on a middle (31-38) which is banal and random. While it is logical that night comes, and that sleep follows nightfall, visions of Bishop Andrewes in Heaven are hardly the logical outcome of this sequence, and the poem has done nothing to necessitate this structural progression. Likewise the beginning of the poem, as we have seen, is flawed with inert irrelevancies. In short, the extra-poetic exaltation from the death to the transfiguration of a good man receives little or no support from the poetic structure, which fails to reflect this dynamic Christian apotheosis.

A comparison of the opening lines of "Lycidas" with those of "Elegia Tertia" is perhaps unfair, but it will be valuable in clarifying the direction of Milton's development:

> Yet once more, O ye Laurels, and once more
> Ye Myrtles brown, with Ivy never sear,
> I com to pluck your Berries harsh and crude,
> And with forc'd fingers rude,
> Shatter your leaves before the mellowing year.
> Bitter constraint, and sad occasion dear,
> Compells me to disturb your season due:

> For *Lycidas* is dead, dead ere his prime,
> Young *Lycidas,* and hath not left his peer:
> Who would not sing for *Lycidas?* he knew
> Himself to sing, and build the lofty rhyme.
> He must not flote upon his watry bear
> Unwept, and welter to the parching wind,
> Without the meed of som melodious tear.
>
> (1-14)

The similarities of the beginning of "Lycidas" to that of the third Latin elegy go deeper than the coincidence that both sections are fourteen lines long. The occasions, the feelings, and the persona, for obvious reasons, resemble those in "Elegia Tertia." Further on in "Lycidas," Milton will ask "What boots it with uncessant care ...," paralleling the "tristi sic ore querebar" in "Elegia Tertia," and both poems conclude in peace.

The initial sections of each poem are fourteen lines long. In "Lycidas," the opening lines comprise the first of the eleven sections into which the poem is divided. The basis for this traditional division in epicedia (which Milton also observed in "On the Death of a Fair Infant") is the association of the number eleven with mourning and specifically with the termination of mourning. Alastair Fowler points out that "Tombs were honoured in February, according to Ovid, so long as the shades wandered; but this stopped on the day of the Feralia, when 11 days of the month remained—'as many days of the month as there are feet in my verses' " (*Fasti* ii. 561-70).[28] Henry King's "The Exequy" is also divided into eleven sections.

The opening of "Lycidas" indicates the extent of Milton's development in his ability to integrate the extra-poetic pattern—grief in the presence of death—with the aesthetic problem of creating the poem and giving it a structural impetus which uses its poetic resolution to achieve its extra-poetic resolution. The poem develops two related but separate conflicts—the poet's grief at the death of Lycidas, and his reluctance to begin writing the epicedion. Explicitly, the first fourteen lines adhere closely to the dual conflict; implicitly, "Lycidas" is building up a context which foreshadows its vision of immortality and the simultaneous resolution of the dual conflict: the laurel, the myrtle, and the ivy are evergreens sacred to the fertility gods.[29] Adonis, Ovid tells us *(Metamorphoses* X. 512), was born out of a myrtle tree; Apollo's pursuit of the laurel (Andrew Marvell to the contrary notwithstanding) is a fertility myth; and the ivy was sacred to Dionysius. At the same time "Lycidas" raises other questions of death and immortality—"He must not flote upon his watry bear/ Unwept." As editors for centuries have pointed out, "Who would not sing for *Lycidas?"* echoes a reference to the poet-shepherd Gallus to whom Vergil gave immortality. "Neget quis carmina Gallo?" Vergil asks in the third line of the tenth eclogue. Milton clearly implies that a similar poem will give a kind of immortality to Lycidas. This deep and essential interaction with his Greek and Roman predecessors, as opposed to superficial mimicry, is typical of Milton's mature poems—although we have of course already seen the technique at work in "Elegia Prima."

Even the rhyme scheme of the opening lines of "Lycidas" looks forward to the closing lines and imparts both unity and progression to the poem.[30] This dynamic unity, like that which thirty years later will give *Paradise Lost* its driving force, is managed not by mere repetition of lines from the opening, but by a carefully managed progression. "Lycidas" begins with a corrupted, distorted sonnet. The very first of the fourteen lines is unrhymed, asserting immediately the distortion of the form. Lines 2-5 use the *a b b a* pattern assigned to lines 1-4 in a normal Petrarchan sonnet, with the expected pattern delayed by one line. Lines 6-9 of "Lycidas" resemble lines 5-8 of a Petrarchan sonnet, but the rhyme scheme is again delayed. Constraint, compulsion, and disturbance are not merely extra-poetic ideas which are the subject of this misshapen sonnet; they are also part of the poetic structure which will carry the poem forward. What "ought" to be the second quatrain, *a b b a,* comes a line too late and then as a blemished *a c d a.* And line 13, like line 1, remains adamantly unrhymed. Even the normal pentameter pattern of the sonnet breaks, with a truncated trimeter at line 4. All these functional dissonances of the poem's disturbed opening will be carefully resolved in the closing lines. And the resolutions will be an integration of the extra-poetic problem of death with the literary problem of a unified poem which reflects in its structural progressions the spiritual progress of the persona/poet from grief and reluctance to the tranquil awareness of a just universe.

But like "Elegia Tertia," "Lycidas" must manage its transition from grief to the beatific vision. In "Lycidas" the structural problem is solved not by a handy dream which pops in front of the dreamer but by a spiritual pilgrimage: a succession of encounters with the figures Phoebus, Neptune, Aeolus, Camus, and St. Peter, who ultimately give meaning to the ecstatic vision, logic to the resolution, and structure to the poem. The poet has journeyed from bitterness through nostalgia, anger, and other realms of the spirit. After the failure of his self-deception and "false surmise," the poet surrenders to the image of physical death:

> Ay me! Whilst thee the shores, and sounding Seas
> Wash far away, where ere thy bones are hurl'd,
> Whether beyond the stormy *Hebrides*
> Where thou perhaps under the whelming tide
> Visit'st the bottom of the monstrous world.
>
> (154-58)

The failure of his own "frail thoughts" to find a solution wrings from him an almost involuntary prayer:

> Look homeward Angel now, and melt with ruth.
> And, O ye *Dolphins,* waft the hapless youth.
>
> (163-64)

And now it is in the tenth paragraph that the justification of God's ways reveals itself—"*Lycidas* your sorrow is not dead." In the Pythagorean system the decad symbolizes the return to unity.[31] The universe, rightly understood, is not fractured but unified and manifests God's mercy and justice; Lycidas dwells "in the blest Kingdoms meek of joy and love." It is significant that this paragraph is the first in the poem to have no unbroken (trimeter) lines, and that none of the ten unrhymed lines of the poem occurs in this paragraph. The structural progression of "Lycidas" advances not only by means of the emergence of tranquillity out of perturbation, but also by means of the development of a regular prosodic pattern, a pattern in harmony with itself.

Then follows the second resolution—the resolution to the second conflict of the opening section. Just as the extra-poetic grief for Lycidas in lines 1-14 is balanced by the beatific vision of lines 165-85, so the reluctance and uneasiness evidenced in the distorted structure of the first fourteen lines resolve themselves into the immaculate *ottava rima* with which the poem closes:

> Thus sang the uncouth Swain to th'Okes and rills,
>   While the still morn went out with Sandals gray,
> He touch'd the tender stops of various Quills,
> With eager thought warbling his *Dorick* lay:
> And now the Sun had stretch'd out all the hills,
> And now was dropt into the Western Bay;
> At last he rose, and twitch'd his Mantle blew:
> To morrow to fresh Woods, and Pastures new.
>
> (186-93)

The day has ended; Lycidas's earthly life has ended. But the harmonious conclusion, with its unbroken pentameters and its impeccable *ottava rima,* both states and suggests rebirth and eternal life—not only the death and the resurrection of Lycidas, but also the completion of the poet's task along with his dedication to a creative future. "The 8-line total of the *commiato,*" Fowler says, "suits both sides of the ambiguity, since it may symbolize either the octave of harmony or the eternal life beyond mortality's 7's."[32]

The whole passage parallels the conclusion of Vergil's tenth eclogue, which sings the sorrow of Gallus (who has been merely jilted, not killed). Having spoken for his friend, the poet steps back into his own role and concludes:

> Haec sat erit, divae, vestrum cecinisse poetam,
> dum sedet et gracili fiscellam texit hibisco,
> Pierides; vos haec facietis maxima Gallo,
> Gallo, cuius amor tantum mihi crescit in horae,
> quantum vere novo viridis se subicit alnus
> surgamus: solet esse gravis cantantibus umbra,
> iuniperi gravis umbra, nocent et frugibus umbrae.
> ite domum saturae, venit Hesperus, ite capellae.
>
> (70-77)

These strains, Muses divine, it will be enough for your poet to have sung, while he sits idle and twines a basket of slender hibiscus. These ye shall make of highest worth in Gallus' eyes—Gallus, for whom my love grows hour by hour as fast as in the dawn of spring shoots up the green alder. Let us rise; the shade oft brings peril to singers. The juniper's shade brings peril; hurtful to the corn, too, is the shade. Get ye home, my full-fed goats—the Evening-star comes—get ye home.

Here Milton's recollection of Vergil's lines becomes a poetic instrument. Stepping back from his poem and using a similar cadence, he sums up and re-emphasizes the pastoral tradition which has been functioning throughout "Lycidas." Needless to say, this pastoralism has been pervasive in the poem and has been so thoroughly and competently discussed that there is no need for repetition here.[33] The justification of God's ways which "Lycidas" ultimately envisages, as its intricate structure drives the poem onward to its conclusion, lies not only in the beatific vision but in the dignity and worth of mankind as man has recorded himself in the pastoral tradition.

But one must not imagine that the essential difference between "Elegia Tertia" and "Lycidas" lies in some change in Milton's attitude toward the death of virtuous men. In simple terms, the difference lies in the fact that he was a better poet in 1637 than he had been in 1626, and there are unmistakable signs of this difference. In "Elegia Tertia," Milton uses the epicedion as a mode of statement; his grief is, presumably, sincere, and the poem is a gesture to give expression to that grief. But in "Lycidas," as in *Paradise Lost,* the poem is not merely a statement of grief and consolation; the poem itself is the means by which the conflict is resolved. In "Elegia Tertia" the poet has a vision of the Bishop in Heaven because of the chronological sequence of night-sleep-dreams-vision, and because such a vision of the deceased is a usual occurrence in a poem of this sort.

In "Lycidas" the case is quite different. The vision has its origin not only in the fact that Lycidas is dead, but in the nature of the poem itself—its images of fertility and resurrection, its developing patterns of feeling, its prosody, the peculiar nature of the two initial conflicts which fuse into one resolution, the character of the persona and his spiritual pilgrimage—and so on. The poetic pattern, or structure, of the poem has fused with the extra-poetic pattern and served the function of resolving both conflicts by means of the existence of the poem.

Between 1626 and 1637 Milton developed into a mature poet. "Elegia Prima," with its clever but superfical use of Ovid, was a brisk step in the right direction. It did more than echo Ovid; it used Ovid to help unify the poem. "Elegia Tertia," probably written a few months later, was only a hesitant step on the way to "Lycidas." It did state for the poet the resolution for an extra-poetic problem (Andrewes's death), but it never succeeded in trans-forming that resolution into a unified aesthetic structure. "Elegia Tertia" set forth the need to justify God's ways, and it stated that the ways were justified. But "Lycidas" did not merely state the struggle, it *was* the struggle; and it justified God's ways by its own powerful impetus to come into being and so discover this justification.

Thus "Elegia Tertia" was a small stride and "Lycidas" a major stride toward *Paradise Lost*. By 1637 Milton had united the extra-poetic problem (the death of Edward King) with the poetic problem—the building of an integrated epicedion, the structure of which was an embodiment of its own resolution. Without this poem, Milton would not have been ready for *Paradise Lost*—for the con-structing of its majestic parallels to the *Aeneid,* beginning with the similarities of the "pius" but martial Aeneas to the martial, malev-olent Satan, and ending with the development of the human, faltering, maturing Adam, "with wandring steps and slow," setting forth on the longest, most wearying, greatest epic voyage of them all.

IV

The Fair Infant, "Elegia Quinta," and the Nativity Ode

But wisest Fate sayes no, This must not yet be so

Between "Elegia Tertia" and "Lycidas" are six poems (seven, if one counts "L'Allegro" and "Il Penseroso" separately) that best exemplify the stages by which Milton arrived at the mastery of structure which we find in "Lycidas." These are "On the Death of a Fair Infant," "Elegia Quinta," the Nativity Ode, the Companion Pieces, "Ad Patrem," and *Comus*. They represent different stages of Milton's development and therefore deserve three chapters. The poem on the Fair Infant belongs in many ways with the awkward early poems, yet mixed with its vacillations and false starts are signs of Milton's emerging skill. Also, like "Elegia Tertia" and *Paradise Lost*, it attempts to face and resolve the problems of man's relation to God. "Elegia Quinta" and the Nativity Ode, in spite of their contrasting subjects, are closely related structurally, and together represent a significant intermediate point in Milton's poetic development. Rather than attempting a structural progression like that of "Elegia Tertia," which in many ways fails, or that of "Lycidas," which succeeds, the fifth elegy and the Nativity Ode are poems of static structure skillfully integrated in terms of the relation of the parts to the whole, but neither raising nor solving problems such as those concerning the relation of man to God.

The first of these intermediate poems, "On the Death of a Fair Infant Dying of the Cough," is a valuable poem for what it does well and an interesting poem for what it does badly. Anne Phillips, the Fair Infant and Milton's niece, was buried on 22 January 1628, just after her third birthday. Presumably he wrote the poem a little more than a year after the three Latin epicedia to Gostlin, the Beadle, and Andrewes. At the time of composition it was by far his best epicedion as well as his first in English.

The first four stanzas are superb. Milton integrates them by means of a little myth of his own making which functions in miniature as does the pastoralism which ten years later will infuse "Lycidas." Milton's myth justifies God's ways by putting the child's death into the context of "history" that, although fictive, is true in that it reminds us that the young and beautiful have died before. If the death of young Hyacinth is not a justification for the death of Anne Phillips, it is at least a flattering parallel, carrying with it not only symbolic immortality but the prospects of immortality in the legends of mankind.

The soundness of the structure in the remainder of the poem is a matter of disagreement. Like "Elegia Tertia," and so many other epicedia, "On the Death of a Fair Infant" begins in grief and concludes in Christian joy. Again there is the structural problem of the means of transition from the one state to the other. Hugh Maclean finds a "relatively successful progression of stanzas I through IX," and sees the poem structurally as a considerable advance beyond "Elegia Tertia."[1] Structurally, Maclean argues, the poem falls into four divisions: two groups of three stanzas each, a third of four stanzas, and a single concluding stanza which recalls and corrects impressions created in stanza I. Within the broad movement from grief to the final note of consolation and hope, "Milton elaborates a subtle and developing pattern." Maclean's analysis is close, sensitive, and reasonable; his praise is largely justified, considering Milton's youth at the time of composition. But a great deal goes wrong with the poem, and much of the trouble stems from the same problems that arise in the earlier epicedia.

To clarify the difficulties, let me suggest a slightly different division into sections from that which Maclean proposes. I should prefer to group stanza IV with the first three—rather than putting IV with the next three—thus:

I

O fairest flower no sooner blown but blasted,
Soft silken Primrose fading timelesslie,

Summers chief honour if thou hadst out-lasted
Bleak winters force that made thy blossome drie;
For he being amorous on that lovely die
     That did thy cheek envermeil, thought to kiss
But kill'd alas, and then bewayl'd his fatal bliss.

II

For since grim Aquilo his charioter
By boisterous rape th'Athenian damsel got,
He thought it toucht his Deitie full neer,
If likewise he some fair one wedded not,
Thereby to wipe away th'infamous blot,
     Of long-uncoupled bed, and childless eld,
Which 'mongst the wanton gods a foul reproach was held.

III

So mounting up in ycie-pearled carr,
Through middle empire of the freezing aire
He wandered long, till thee he spy'd from farr,
There ended was his quest, there ceast his care.
Down he descended from his Snow-soft chaire,
     But all unwares with his cold-kind embrace
Unhous'd thy Virgin Soul from her fair biding place.

IV

Yet art thou not inglorious in thy fate;
For so *Apollo,* with unweeting hand
Whilome did slay his dearly-loved mate
Young *Hyacinth* born on *Eurotas'* strand
Young *Hyacinth* the pride of *Spartan* land;
     But then transform'd him to a purple flower
Alack that so to change thee winter had no power.

There is justification for Maclean's concluding the first section with
stanza III, but it seems to me that the comparison in the fourth stanza of
Hyacinth, beloved but inadvertently killed in his youth by Apollo, with
the Fair Infant, beloved but (in Milton's little myth) blunderingly
killed by Winter, knits itself skillfully into the pattern of the first three
stanzas.

Then, in what seems to me the beginning of a new section, Milton steps back from his own myth:

V

Yet can I not perswade me thou art dead
Or that thy coarse corrupts in earths dark wombe,
Or that thy beauties lie in wormie bed,
Hid from the world in a low delved tombe;
Could Heav'n for pittie thee so strictly doom?
Oh no! for something in thy face did shine
Above mortalitie that shew'd thou wast divine.

Now the awkward, amorous killers of Greco-Roman legend have disappeared from the poem, and we have a stanza which would be competent enough in itself if the previous four stanzas had not been there. In the closing couplet the poet not only seems to forget that Winter, too, saw "something in thy face," but he ignores the first four stanzas, which told us that the Infant has joined the mythological world of Apollo and Hyacinth. One must not, of course, read a poem as if it were a legal contract, trying to trip up the poet with the fine print; but the mature Milton would have had a more integrated concept of where his poem had been and where it was going. The phrases "something in thy face did shine" (34) and "thou wast divine" (35) in the fifth stanza have implicit but unexplored connections with the little myth of the first four stanzas. In "Lycidas" such connections are explicitly developed. The image of the drowned Lycidas in line 11 is linked closely with the concluding image (172-73) of him transfigured and "mounted high, / Through the dear might of him that walk'd the waves," and the recurring water imagery gives the poem not only unity but impetus. So in "Mansus" the "felix concordia" (7), which seems almost a chance phrase early in the poem, is a unifying motif of companionship and mutual support which culminates with the poet "aethereo ... laetus Olympo" in the last line of the poem. *Samson Agonistes, Paradise Lost,* and *Paradise Regained,* of course, offer even more striking examples of this kind of unification.

In the sixth stanza of "On the Death of a Fair Infant," the phrase "where e're thou hoverest" (38) ought to recall the Infant's encounter with Winter only twenty-two lines before,

"Through middle empire of the freezing aire" (16); but the poem does nothing with the connection. And in the momentary uncertainty of the line "Or in the Elisian fields (if such there were)" (40) Milton seems to forget that we have already given credence to "grim Aquilo" (8), "the wanton gods" (14), and Winter's "ycie-pearled carr" (15). Surely by now belief in the Elysian fields is not likely to give us pause, and Milton in his maturity would have had a much more integrated concept of where his poem had been and where it was going.

Similarly at line 42, stanza VI, the question, "And why from us so quickly thou didst take thy flight" ignores the poetically superb answer that the poem has given us in lines 1-21. Now that this question has been unnecessarily raised, the poet showers us with proposed answers which take the form of a spattering of further questions, largely unrelated either to the opening of the poem or to each other: "Wert thou some Starr? ... or ... Some goddess fled / Amongst us here below? ... Or wert thou that just Maid? ... or ... that sweet smiling Youth! ... Or that crown'd Matron sage white-robed truth?" It is appropriate, of course, to say as many complimentary things as possible about the dead under these circumstances. But the contrast between the unorganized lists in this as well as other early poems and the careful patterns of the mature poems—between the haphazard images of the latter stanzas of the poem on the Fair Infant, and the contrasting but related pagan deities of "Lycidas"—shows that in 1628 Milton's apprenticeship was far from over.

The rest of the poem on Anne Phillips is little better, although by now further analysis would seem only bad-tempered. The question (64-65) "But oh why didst thou not stay here below / To bless ... " ignores the fact that the poem has already asked and answered that question in several ways. The last answer that the poem gives us, "But thou canst best perform that office where thou art" (70), Maclean calls "abrupt and almost glum." The final stanza seems tacked on merely to end the whole business.

Despite its deficiencies, the poem has many virtues.[2] The first four stanzas are masterful, and the imagery of the poem is often bright and, taken in isolated phrases or stanzas, coherent. The rhythmic control is usually sure and graceful. For example, "Wert thou some Starr which from the ruin'd roofe / Of shak'd Olympus by mischance didst fall?" (43-44) is a fine pair of lines; when taken by themselves they are vivid, fluent, and dramatic. The fault is not inherent in the lines themselves but in their structural relation with the whole poem.

The technical requirements of the stanzaic form are considerable (let any critic who doubts this try his hand at it); yet Milton's graceful fluency makes the stanza look easy. His grasp of the problem of fitting the poem into a series of eleven stanzas (as in "Lycidas," the number probably is associated with death and mourning), neatly and intricately rhymed, has about it the easy air of an accomplished practitioner. However, the Nativity Ode shows us how much further a poet, regardless of age and experience, can go in integrating his ideas, his images, his aural effects into a complex, repeated stanzaic form.

Suddenly, in the spring of 1629, Milton took a major stride ahead: "Elegia Quinta, Anno Aetatis 20, In Adventum Veris" is the first poem of Milton's career which needs no apologies for the poet's youth. The promise of poetic skill in the first four stanzas of the poem on the Fair Infant is fulfilled the next year in "Elegia Quinta." It begins with the poet's awareness of the spring—which arouses the nightingale in the forest and the poet in the city to sing in mutual praise of the season:

> Urbe ego, tu sylvâ simul incipiamus utrique,
>   Et simul adventum veris uterque canat.
>
> (27-28)

> I in the city and you in the forest, let us both begin together and let us both together sing the advent of spring.

This song is essentially a celebration of fertility—Aurora leaves the impotent bed of Tithonus for the embraces of Cephalus; Tellus throws off her hated old age and longs for the warmth of Phoebus:

> Exuit invisam Tellus rediviva senectam,
>   Et cupit amplexus Phoebe subire tuos;
> Et cupit, & digna est, quid enim formosius illâ,
>   Pandit ut omniferos luxuriosa sinus,
> Atque Arabum spirat messes, & ab ore venusto
>   Mitia cum Paphiis fundit amoma rosis.
>
> (55-60)

The reviving earth throws off her hated old age and craves thy embraces, O Phoebus. She craves them and she is worthy of them; for what is lovelier than she as she voluptuously bares her fertile breast and breathes the perfume of Arabian harvests and pours sweet spices and the scent of Paphian roses from her lovely lips?

She is jealous of Tethys, the sea-goddess to whom Phoebus has returned each night and urges him to "lay your glories in my lap":

> Sic Tellus lasciva suos suspirat amores;
> Matris in exemplum caetera turba ruunt.
>
> (95-96)

Thus the wanton earth breathes out her passion, and her thronging children follow hard after her example.

Cupid and Hymen run at large and all humans are filled with their spirit. The poem closes with the prayer that spring may last forever or at least that its joyful passage will be as slow as possible.

The poem differs significantly from the others which we have examined so far. It begins with no conflict, it seeks no resolution, it urges no course of action—not even the conventional "carpe diem." It quite consciously rejoices in what it is. It is significant that the questions which do arise early in the poem are rhetorical questions:

> Fallor? an & nobis redeunt in carmina vires,
> Ingeniumque mihi munere veris adest?
> Munere veris adest, iterumque vigescit ab illo
> (Quis putet) atque aliquod jam sibi poscit opus.
>
> (5-8)

Am I deluded? Or are my powers of song returning? And is my inspiration with me again by grace of the spring? By the spring's grace it is with me and—who would guess such a thing?—it is already clamoring for some employment.

Unlike those of "Elegia Tertia" or "Lycidas," which genuinely pose a problem and genuinely find a solution, these questions are expressions of a state of mind, a sense of joyful wonder which pervades the whole poem. The questions are not doubts or quests for the justification of things, but a happy surprise at apprehending the renewed freshness of the world. This awareness stands at the beginning, middle, and end of the poem, rather than being a concluding resolution. The feeling of joyful insight, resembling the concluding visions of "Elegia Tertia" and "Lycidas," suffuses even the beginning of "Elegia Quinta":

> Delius ipse venit, video Penëide lauro
> Implicitos crines, Delius ipse venit.
> (13-14)

Apollo himself is approaching—I see the locks that are braided with Daphne's laurels—Apollo himself comes.

His supernatural vision appears not only at the end of the poem but even in the early lines—

> Intuiturque animus toto quid agatur Olympo,
> Nec fugiunt oculos Tartara caeca meos.
> (19-20)

My spirit surveys all that is done on Olympus and the unseen infernal world is not impervious to my eyes.

"Elegia Quinta" is not only inherently an excellent poem; it also marks a major step ahead in Milton's ability to control the structure of a poem. The poem keeps the literary tradition under control, making the Greco-Roman deities serve the poem rather than, as in "Elegia Secunda" for example, crowding the stage as usurping irrelevancies.

One reason that "Elegia Quinta" succeeds so well is that its organization is static rather than progressive. By celebrating the world as it is, the poem avoids the problem of managing a transition from a beginning which differs importantly from its conclusion. The serious structural faults of some of the early poems, such as "Elegia Tertia," are not solved here; they are avoided. In this sense "Elegia Quinta" is not so much a step on the way to poems like "Lycidas" as it is a temporary digression. It represents a solution to some of Milton's poetic problems, but it is an evasion of others—in particular the structural problem of creating a poem that moves from its initial conflicts to a conclusion which integrates its poetic and extra-poetic resolutions. This is not to belittle "Elegia Quinta" as a poem; one must not see Milton's career as a self-conscious Poet's Progress to the Celestial City of Unified Structure. "Elegia Quinta" is an excellent poem in achieving what it attempts, but the nature of Milton's development is more clearly delineated if we are also aware that the poem is not attempting the kind of progression we find in "Lycidas."

"Elegia Quinta" is important for two other reasons: (1) the more open, joyful, and sexual character of the poem, which points to no moral at all, needs stressing as part of the recurring task of laying the ghost of the tight-lipped "puritanical" Milton who never existed; (2) that Milton wrote this most delightful and successful of his early poems in Latin rather than in English ought not to surprise us if we remember that the youthful Milton was primarily a Latin poet. Prior to his twenty-first birthday he had written nineteen Latin poems totaling over a thousand lines and only three poems in English totaling barely two hundred lines.

Assuming that "Elegia Quinta" was written in the spring, the ode "On the Morning of Christ's Nativity" came six months later. Milton dates the poem for us by referring to it in "Elegia Sexta," where he says he is writing the Latin elegy at the Christmas season and that he is also writing a poem on the birth of Christ.

Although the subject of the Nativity Ode contrasts markedly with that of "Elegia Quinta," the resemblances of the two poems are important. Like the fifth elegy, the Ode faces no extra-poetic problems at the beginning and hence at the conclusion it solves none. Its only "problem," if we look at the poem this way, is to "afford a Present to the Infant God" (16), "to welcome him to this his new abode" (18). And the poem concludes not when the poetic structure has supplied the dynamics whereby the extra-poetic problem is resolved, as do "Lycidas" and *Paradise Lost,* but rather when the "Present to the Infant God" is completed and presented—"Time is our tedious Song should here have ending" (239). As A.S.P. Woodhouse puts it, "[The Ode] is in the nature of a simple affirmation, with no problem stated or implied, and no emotional tension to be resolved." The purpose of the Ode is "simply to order and confirm his thought on the subject."[3] Similarly, Rosemond Tuve says that the poem "exists to celebrate a mystery rather than to describe and comment upon an event."[4]

Perhaps the static quality of the poem is clearer if we examine a passing remark by Merritt Hughes. His phrase, "the theme of this *Ode* [is] the triumph of the infant Christ over the gods of paganism,"[5] is mistaken in a very enlightening way: there is no triumph in the poem in the sense that, for example, Christ in Book VI of *Paradise Lost* triumphs over Satan, or Satan (in Book IX) triumphs over Eve. In the Ode, the fact of Christ's birth, His very presence on earth, refutes the pagan gods, who steal off with no confrontation, no struggle, and, therefore, no triumph in any developmental sense.

XXIV

Nor is *Osiris* seen
In *Memphian* Grove, or Green,
 Trampling the unshowr'd Grass with lowings loud;
Nor can he be at rest
Within his sacred chest,
 Naught but profoundest Hell can be his shroud,
In vain with Timbrel'd Anthems dark
The sable-stoled Sorcerers bear his worshipt Ark.

XXV

He feels from *Juda's* Land
The dredded Infants hand,
 The rayes of *Bethlehem* blind his dusky eyn;
Nor all the Gods beside,
Longer dare abide,
 Not *Typhon* huge ending in snaky twine:
Our Babe to shew his Godhead true,
Can in his swadling bands controul the damned crew.

Osiris does not struggle and go down to defeat; he merely "feels" the hand of Christ and slinks away, foredoomed. While "Our Babe" resembles the infant Hercules in his cradle, He never (in the poem) uses or needs to use His strength against the "damned crew." Thus the theme of the poem centers not on a conflict between Christ and the pagan gods but on the poet's celebration, by means of his "humble ode," of the mystery of the Incarnation.

This is not to say that the poem lacks a beginning, middle, and end; we as readers clearly progress in our realization of the Blessed Infant's power. But for Him, in Milton's poem and in Christian theology, that power exists outside the sequence of time and is therefore static. However, this quality is not an attempt by Milton to avoid poetic difficulties. When Woodhouse calls the poem a "simple affirmation," he does not mean that Milton is writing a simple poem. Rather, for reasons we cannot know, Milton has temporarily turned away from poems like "Elegia Tertia," which attempt a developmental or progressive structure, to write a poem like the Nativity Ode, which is meticulously and essentially static.

Sufficient reason for the static structural patterns in the Ode can be found in the nature of the material—the poem centers on the single focal point of the Nativity. The Incarnation is an event not only inside but also outside the sequence of time. As Lowry Nelson points out, timelessness permeates the Nativity Ode, placing it first of all in two simultaneous time-planes, and ultimately in a "momentaneous present" whereby Christ's birth in Bethlehem and Milton's writing of the poem 1,629 years later at Cambridge, are simultaneous. "The birth of Christ," Nelson points out, "and every Christmas are essentially the same."[6]

Nelson argues that "the Christian ideas of the circularity of time and the simultaneity of all moments under the aspect of eternity underline the innermost structure of the poem," and he points to the repeated but patterned shifts in the time-position of the poem.[7] Thus as the poem opens we are in Cambridge on the Christmas of 1629:

I

This is the Month, and this the happy morn
Wherein the Son of Heav'ns eternal King,
Of wedded Maid, and Virgin Mother born,
Our great Redemption from above did bring;
For so the holy Sages once did sing,
    That he our deadly forfeit should release,
And with his Father work us a perpetual peace.

By the fourth stanza of the introduction we are in a second time-plane—that of the historical event in Bethlehem, and Milton speaks in what Nelson calls the "hortatory future":

IV

See how from far upon the Eastern rode
The Star-led Wisards haste with odours sweet,
O run, prevent them with thy humble ode,
And lay it lowly at his blessed feet;
Have thou the honour first, thy Lord to greet,
    And joyn thy voice unto the Angel Quire,
From out his secret Altar toucht with hallow'd fire.

From here on the poem moves back and forth between Milton's time and that of the events in Jerusalem, sometimes contradicting its verb tenses within the same stanza:

It was the Winter wilde,
While the Heav'n-born-childe,
All meanly wrapt in the rude manger lies.
        (29-31)

The two time-planes ultimately merge as the poem ends. The focus narrows from the cosmic view of the angels to the flight of the devils and then to the Christ-child Himself, as the poem enters this "momentaneous present" which is both Cambridge 1629 and Bethlehem centuries before:

XXVII

But see the Virgin blest,
Hath laid her Babe to rest.
   Time is our tedious Song should here have ending:
Heav'ns youngest teemed Star,
Hath fixt her polisht Car,
   Her sleeping Lord with Handmaid Lamp attending:
And all about the Courtly Stable,
Bright-harnest Angels sit in order serviceable.

This concluding stanza, with its echo of the earlier "Hast thou no verse, no hymn, or solemn strein, / To welcome him to this his new abode?" (17-18), serves also as a frame within which to place the Hymn, the "Present to the Infant God," and as such it reinforces the static quality of the poem. The persona of the poem does not change or develop—as does the "uncouth Swain" in the 193 lines of "Lycidas"—but concludes the poem because he has completed the task he set for himself at the beginning.

Brooks and Hardy point out that the stanzaic structure itself in the Ode, "with its intricate, interlaced rhyme scheme and with its long final line, sets up resistance to any rapid narrative drive."[8] In other words, the stanzaic structures (the introduction and the hymn are of course different) contribute—as do the shifts in the time-planes—to make the Ode the peculiarly successful static poem that it is. Problems of a progressive structure do not arise because the poem skillfully manages its own kind of stable, celebratory organization. This is not to say that nothing happens or that there is nothing that might be called "movement" in the poem. The interplay of the two planes of time, as Nelson points out, are carefully patterned, and move to a logical resolution.

Within the stanzaic structure itself, the poet manages an artful dynamism—for example:

XV

Yea Truth, and Justice then
Will down return to men,
   Orb'd in a Rain-bow; and like glories wearing
Mercy will sit between,
Thron'd in Celestial sheen,
   With radiant feet the tissued clouds down stearing,
And Heav'n as at some Festivall,
Will open wide the Gates of her high Palace Hall.

XVI

But wisest Fate sayes no,
This must not yet be so,
   The Babe lies yet in smiling Infancy,
That on the bitter cross
Must redeem our loss;
   So both himself and us to glorifie:
Yet first to those ychain'd in sleep,
The wakeful trump of doom must thunder through the deep.

The hexameter line with which the fifteenth stanza closes—"Will open wide the Gates of her high Palace Hall"—is a marvelous crescendo not merely because of its sonority but because the line emerges with grand poetic logic out of the quieter early lines of the stanza. And then the poem quickly hushes us with its next two trimeters:

> But wisest Fate sayes no,
> This must not yet be so.

The prosody and the theology simultaneously remind us that man's salvation is a victory arising not from the Incarnation but from the Crucifixion. The fusion of the extra-poetic with the poetic here is superb, and the abrupt contraction from the hexameters to the trimeters is structurally brilliant. Yet the structural devices of the poem make no attempt to impart any progressive organization to the poem.

Unlike the haphazard structure of so many parts of "Elegia Secunda" and "Elegia Tertia," written less than four years before, the Nativity Ode is knit into carefully integrated sections. As Arthur Barker points out, "The first eight stanzas ... describe the setting of the Nativity, the next nine the angelic choir, the next nine the flight of the Heathen gods, the ... last stanza presents the scene in the stable."[9] These parts are inextricable: "The three movements each present a single modification of the simple contrast preserved throughout the poem, between images suggesting light and harmony, and images of gloom and discord." These movements are united "not by the repetition of a structural pattern, but by the variation of a basic pattern of imagery."[10]

One should note that "Elegia Quinta" and the Nativity Ode are Milton's first long poems which achieve the kind of structural unity which is so characteristic of the mature poems. Michelangelo is reported to have said that one should be able to roll a good statue downhill without having the arms and legs break off. And "Elegia Quinta" and the Nativity Ode are the first of Milton's poems which could be metaphorically rolled down a hill and remain intact.

But it is significant that these two poems never face or solve some of the structural problems which caused trouble in the earlier poems. No crucial clash of bitterness and faith, of grief and joy, provides dialectic or dynamic structures that progress toward some ultimate justification. The two poems are essentially celebratory and their structures are therefore static. Unlike "Lycidas," which would not be written for almost eight years, there are no extra-poetic problems here with which the two poems must come to terms. This is not to say that "Elegia Quinta" and the Ode are poorer poems for this, nor is it to say that Milton intentionally avoided these problems. There is no reason to think that he considered these matters relevant to the structures of the two poems. But only after producing these poems did Milton return to the problem of progressive structure and gradually solve it.

V

The Companion Pieces
and "Ad Patrem"

Ergo ego jam doctae pars quamlibet ima catervae
Victrices hederas inter, laurosque sedebo.

The Companion Pieces and "Ad Patrem" may well have been written at about the same time, shortly after the fifth elegy and the Ode; the dates have been disputed in arguments which are not relevant here. But since there seems to be general agreement that the Companion Pieces precede "Ad Patrem," I have chosen to discuss them first, although structurally "Ad Patrem" is a weaker poem. Moreover, to argue the sequence of a poet's works from the assumption of continuous, unbroken growth is obviously fallacious; the organizational difficulties of "Ad Patrem" are an inadequate basis either for dating it or for placing it in the sequence of Milton's works.

Like the Nativity Ode, the Companion Pieces have had their few and short lines explored, discussed, attacked, defended, and chewed to bits so often that at this late date one is tempted merely to print copies of the poems together with a bibliography of the best critical essays, leaving the rest to the diligence and intelligence of the reader. Somewhat in that spirit I shall leave many aspects of "L'Allegro" and "Il Penseroso" undiscussed and even unmentioned.

But we shall need to examine here the role that the two poems played in helping Milton develop the particular kinds of structure which were forerunners to the structural intricacies of "Lycidas," *Paradise Lost,* and other poems of his maturity.

The Companion Pieces, written perhaps two years after "Elegia Quinta" and the Nativity Ode, face the same structural problems of unity and impetus, but in an oblique way.[1] Each in itself is static in the sense that, once the contrasting moods in the initial lines have been exorcized, each poem becomes an embodiment of its own unique and unchanging idea. Each is an inward exploration, a probing. This is perhaps clearest if we remember that both "Lycidas" and *Paradise Lost* use a pattern which progresses from one set of attitudes at the beginning to another at the end. Moreover, in these poems the extra-poetic problems of man's place in the universe find part of their answer in the existence of the poem, the nature of the poem, and the structure of the poem. The poetic and extra-poetic problems and solutions are unified by means of the structural impetus.

The Companion Pieces proceed not to the resolution of a problem outside the poem, such as the justification of God's ways to men, but rather to a deeper insight into a situation which was essentially present at the beginning of the poem. If we consider "L'Allegro" as a journey and ourselves as Milton's companions, the poem embodies a journey in which the poet is not our fellow-struggler, as is the uncouth swain in "Lycidas," but rather our knowledgeable guide. In the Companion Pieces, we and Milton do not suffer together through the intricate but integrated patterns of a spiritual pilgrimage to the point of, at last, facing fresh woods and pastures new. Milton is our fellow-traveler but not our fellow-travailer; he has been there before and he wants us to share the pleasures he has had. In this sense "L'Allegro" and "Il Penseroso" resemble the static, celebratory structures of "Elegia Quinta" and the Nativity Ode, rather than the dialectic, dynamic structures of "Lycidas" or *Paradise Lost*.

One of Milton's methods of imparting unity to each of the poems is the use of chronology. In each poem we move through the hours of day and night—from dawn to midnight in "L'Allegro," from dusk through night into the next day in "Il Penseroso." This structural technique serves the two poems well—the appropriateness of what we see, hear, and enjoy is not dependent merely on chance or the whim of our guide. The structure has about it what one might call the illusion of the necessary. In "L'Allegro" we hear the lark and cock before we see the plowman because that is Nature's inexorable way, and in "Il Penseroso" the arrival of night carries us on through the poem without our stopping to think that the poem might be organized otherwise. There is no necessary connection between the emotional states embodied in the two poems and the circuit of the sun, which is, as A.S.P. Woodhouse points out, "in the nature of a device."[2] While the device is useful to hold each poem together and to relate each poem to the other (with just enough differences in the treatment of the chronology to avoid obviousness), all we need to do is to turn again to "Lycidas" or *Paradise Lost* to see how little the chronological progression has enriched the insight of the Companion Pieces. Whereas "Lycidas" and *Paradise Lost* move ahead through progressions inherent in their situations and ideas, the Companion Pieces depend heavily on a kind of "post hoc ergo propter hoc."

If we consider the Companion Pieces not as two individual poems but as one poem whose parts are related, the organization of the whole appears as an important step in Milton's developing control of structure. Each of the poems gains immeasurably from the existence of the other: the peculiar quality of the emotion embodied in "L'Allegro" (and I shall not join the hapless throng of those who have tried to give a name to this emotion) achieves part of its embodiment from the existence of "Il Penseroso," and the relation of "Il Penseroso" to "L'Allegro" is of course similar. For example, the description of the dawn in "L'Allegro" is so good as to be self-justifying:

> To hear the Lark begin his flight,
> And singing startle the dull night,
> From his watch-towre in the skies,
> Till the dappled dawn doth rise;
> Then to com in spight of sorrow,
> And at my window bid good morrow,
> Through the Sweet-Briar, or the Vine,
> Or the twisted Eglantine.
> While the Cock with lively din,
> Scatters the rear of darknes thin,
> And to the stack, or the Barn dore,
> Stoutly struts his Dames before.
>
> (41-52)

But the passage is deepened and enriched by the presence in "Il Penseroso" of the description of evening, occupying a comparable position early in the poem:

Sweet Bird that shunn'st the noise of folly,
Most musical, most Melancholy!
Thee Chauntress oft the Woods among,
I woo to hear thy Even-Song;
And missing thee, I walk unseen
On the dry smooth-shaven Green,
To behold the wandring Moon,
Riding neer her highest noon,
Like one that had bin led astray
Through the Heav'ns wide pathles way;
And oft, as if her head she bow'd,
Stooping through a fleecy cloud.

(61-72)

Similarly, the rural life and the "soft Lydian airs" in "L'Allegro" balance by resemblance and contrast the literary allusions, the "pealing Organ," and the "anthems clear" in "Il Penseroso."

However, the relation between the two poems is more complex than that of mere parallels and contrasts. "L'Allegro" is a necessary predecessor to "Il Penseroso." "Their relation," Louis Martz points out, "is ... that of Younger Brother to Elder Brother."[3] The treatment of music in the two poems, for example, clearly leads from "L'Allegro" to "Il Penseroso." As Nan Carpenter points out, "L'Allegro" is, among other things, a "eulogy of secular song," while *"Il Penseroso* finds its highest point in the beauties of ecclesiastical music." Milton "singles out the two most elaborate forms of religious music of his age—the Great Service and the anthem—as the high point (161-66) of *Il Penseroso.*"[4] David Miller carries the idea of the progression from "L'Allegro" to "Il Penseroso" a step beyond that of the musical patterns:

> The two poems are made up of parallels that are at the same time contrasts; the activities of Il Penseroso complement those of L'Allegro, but at each point they are nearer to the contemplation of God. There is something of the Neoplatonic ladder that organizes Spenser's four hymns. The progress of the poems culminates in the contemplation described in the final section of *Il Penseroso,* a description that has no parallel

in *L'Allegro*.... The delights of *L'Allegro* are real and valued, but like the glories of Greece they cannot stand against the ecstasy of Christian contemplation. Partial truth is inferior to complete truth. It is Il Penseroso who represents the proper Christian pattern.[5]

These readings by Martz, Carpenter, and Miller illuminate not only the Companion Pieces but the direction of Milton's development. The Companion Pieces are structurally stronger than "Elegia Tertia" in that they achieve a union of the extra-poetic emotions of the two poems with their verbal entities. They also represent a development beyond "Elegia Tertia" in the direction of the kind of dynamic structure which Milton achieves in *Paradise Lost*. "Elegia Tertia" attempts, but fails, at an integral progression of feelings and ideas; the Companion Pieces succeed at another type of structure—one which is not so much progressive as it is a relation and opposition of lower with higher. This is, however, a structure which has not reached the subtle organization of ideas and feelings which characterize *Paradise Lost*.

In some ways the structural interrelations of the Companion Pieces also resemble the technique Milton used five years earlier in "Elegia Prima." Just as the first elegy not only invited but even required Ovid's exile poems *Tristia* and *Epistulae ex Ponto* as points of reference, so "L'Allegro" and "Il Penseroso," successful as each may be in isolation, need each other for their full realization. But Milton has developed beyond "Elegia Prima," not only by creating his own points of reference for each poem in the other but also by organizing them sequentially so that the structure depends on the movement from the first Companion Piece to the second.

This technique is similar in some ways to the function of the epics of Homer and Vergil in *Paradise Lost*. Milton uses these epics as instruments for enrichment and subtlety, while in the Companion Pieces he uses the relation of each Companion Piece to the other as a point of reference. If we had only one Companion Piece without the other, we should be conscious of no structural deficiency; isolated from its companion, both "L'Allegro" and "Il Penseroso" have the celebratory quality of "Elegia Quinta" and the Nativity Ode. But given both the Companion Pieces, we find that "Il Penseroso" is the logical culmination of "L'Allegro." Viewed in this fashion, the two poems are another step toward "Lycidas," "Epitaphium Damonis," and *Paradise Lost*.

At some time after the completion of the Companion Pieces Milton wrote "Ad Patrem." All we can say with certainty concerning its date is that it must have been written no later than 1645 because it was published then. Unfortunately, the evidence for any specific date for this structurally interesting poem seems inconclusive. Bush and Woodhouse argue for 1631-32, shortly after the completion of the Companion Pieces, while Shawcross proposes 1638 and Fletcher suggests 1645.[6]

The discussion of the poem in this study is placed between that of the Companion Pieces and *Comus*—that is, about 1632—for two reasons: first, the arguments of Bush and Woodhouse for this early date seem to have great, although not ultimate, validity; second, the structural weaknesses of "Ad Patrem" point to an earlier rather than a later date. This is, of course, a weak argument, since it assumes an inevitable chronological progression of skill on Milton's part; it is unwarranted to assume that Milton could have written no poorly organized poems after writing as superbly organized a poem as "Lycidas." Nor are the strengths or weaknesses of "Ad Patrem" of such a nature as to be necessary predecessors or consequences of the other poems Milton wrote in the 1630s. Therefore a date of 1632 is not demonstrably wrong.

The only known circumstance surrounding the composition of "Ad Patrem" must be deduced from the poem itself: Milton's father seems to have objected either to his career as a poet or to his devoting so much attention to writing poetry. Many of the attempts to date the poem are based on assumptions concerning what poem or what events in the younger Milton's life caused his father to object—the conclusion of his undergraduate career at Cambridge? The performance of *Comus* at Ludlow Castle? The publication of *Comus*? We do not know and the poem never tells us. It simply says that his father objects to his poetry, that his poetry is indeed trivial and juvenile, and that he is greatly indebted to his father for gifts he can never repay, such as his knowledge of languages and philosophy. But poetry itself is a noble art, akin to music at which his father's skill is very great; and the poem closes with the conventional promise to make his father immortal by means of the poems he will write.

Milton builds his poem out of two opposing elements—deprecation of the actual poetry he has written so far ("tenues sonos"—"trivial songs") and praise of the ideal image of poetry, which is loved by the gods and has the power to bind the underworld. Kings have honored poets, and poets have preserved in song the deeds of heroes. By setting up this opposition between the real (his own poetry) and the ideal (the poetic tradition), Milton has created a structure which now needs completion or resolution in some sort of reconciliation—a scene or vision of future glory which will change his father's opinion, ensure his father's fame, and fulfill the potentialities of his own "tenues sonos." "Ad Patrem" establishes itself therefore as similar in organization to the kind of progressive or dynamic structure seen in the earlier "Elegia Tertia" and in the later "Lycidas" and *Paradise Lost.*

But "Ad Patrem" never achieves the kind of developmental structure that it aims at because it never manages to fuse its poetic position with the extra-poetic situation, and three quite different faults cause Milton's difficulties. The first of these is inherent in the crucial passage where he predicts his ultimate crowning with laurel and ivy:

> Ergo ego jam doctae pars quamlibet ima catervae
> Victrices hederas inter, laurosque sedebo,
> Jamque nec obscurus populo miscebor inerti,
> Vitabuntque oculos vestigia nostra profanos.
> Este procul vigiles curae, procul este querelae,
> Invidiaeque acies transverso tortilis hirquo,
> Saeva nec anguiferos extende Calumnia rictus;
> In me triste nihil faedissima turba potestis,
> Nec vestri sum juris ego; securaque tutus
> Pectora, vipereo gradiar sublimis ab ictu.

$$(101\text{-}10)$$

Therefore, however humble my present place in the company of learned men, I shall sit with the ivy and laurel of a victor. I shall no longer mingle unknown with the dull rabble and my walk shall be far from the sight of profane eyes. Begone, sleepless cares and complaints, and the twisted glance of envy with goatish leer. Malevolent Calumny, open not your dragon gorge. You have no power to harm me, O detestable band;

and I am not under your jurisdiction. I shall walk with heart secure, lifted high above your viper stroke.

The extra-poetic situation is the kind of vision of triumph which is appropriate to the direction the poem is taking—rather like a literary version of the beatific, religious vision which concludes "Lycidas" and "Epitaphium Damonis." But Milton gives poetic embodiment to the situation with language which vitiates the triumph it describes. He lifts us up to his vision of glory while looking over his shoulder: he speaks of himself as "nec obscurus," as no longer mingling with the "populo inerti," and the repeated negations deflate his climax rather than exalt it. Milton appears in the scene not so much as triumphing in what he strives for but rather as renouncing what he wants to seclude himself from. The vision of Lycidas in Heaven, in the next-to-last paragraph of that poem, as he "flames in the forehead of the morning sky," carries the poem to the vigorous climax that its structure demands; the corresponding section in "Ad Patrem" allows the poem to deflate in a series of negatives.

A second fault, one which also prevents the climactic lines concerning Milton's being wreathed with laurel and ivy from being an effective climax, is the haphazard arrangement of some of the previous parts of the poem. "Ad Patrem" begins (1-16) with the hope that his muse will rise with bold wings; this opening section points to the two central conflicts of the poem—his clash with his father and the difference between the potential and the actual worth of his poetry.

But the poem immediately leaps (17-40) to a pronouncement of the divine nature of poetry and its power over the gods, and then to an Olympian/Heavenly vision of an eternity in which men, crowned with gold, will sing sweet songs echoing to the vault of the stars. The poem's rapturous praise of "immortale melos, & inenarrabile carmen" (37) rises to a peak which takes on the manner of a solution to the poem's conflicts. But this passage is not a resolution; Milton still has three-quarters of his poem left to be developed. And indeed the rest of the poem tends to wander anticlimactically to lower emotional pitches and less exalted matters.

On leaving the Heavenly Realms the poem moves to the banquets of ancient kings (41-55), where bards sang of heroic subjects. This of course is relevant to Milton's justification of poetry, but one wonders why it follows—at a lower level in almost all senses—the lofty passage preceding it. Again, the section on his father's permitting him to escape careers in business and law (67-76), and the following passage (77-92) on his father's encouragement of his linguistic and philosophical studies, are logical parts of the poem. But it is difficult to see any structural reasons for their position in the poem.

The next section (93-110) is the passage which occupies a climactic position in the poem without actually being climactic. The section begins by dismissing the folly of seeking for gold (93-94), then awkwardly reverts to the subject of his father's generosity:

> Quae potuit majora pater tribuisse, vel ipse
> Jupiter, excepto, donâsset ut omnia, coelo?
> Non potiora dedit, quamvis & tuta fuissent,
> Publica qui juveni commisit lumina nato
> Atque Hyperionios currus, & fraena diei,
> Et circum undantem radiatâ luce tiaram.
>
> (95-100)

What greater gift could come from a father, or from Jove himself if he had given everything, with the single exception of heaven? He who gave to his young son the common light, the chariot of Hyperion and the reins of day and the aureole radiating a flood of glory (even assuming that those gifts were harmless) bestowed no grander gifts.

The reference to Phaëthon, destroyed by his father Hyperion's gift, takes the poem in quite the wrong direction, as Milton's "quamvis & tuta fuissent," ("even assuming those gifts were harmless"), indicates. Then the poem lurches suddenly from Hyperion and Phaëthon to a statement of its resolution:

> Ergo ego jam doctae pars quamlibet ima catervae
> Victrices hederas inter, laurosque sedebo.
>
> (101-2)

Therefore, however humble my present place in the company of learned men, I shall sit with the ivy and laurel of a victor.

One wonders where Milton's "ergo" came from. While the

laurels and ivy are reasonable resolutions of the early references to "tenues sonos" and "exiguum opus," the intervening parts have not led us in this direction. Therein lies the structural weakness of the poem. "Lycidas" and *Paradise Lost* proceed by means of inexorable poetic logic from their foundations to their pinnacles; "Ad Patrem" simply wanders from its discussion of alternative careers to Hyperion and his son, to Milton's father's generosity, and then, baldy, "ergo." Milton had not yet become a great poet.

A third difficulty in "Ad Patrem" lies in the lines which conclude the poem:

> Et vos, O nostri, juvenilia carmina, lusus,
> Si modo perpetuos sperare audebitis annos,
> Et domini superesse rogo, lucemque tueri,
> Nec spisso rapient oblivia nigra sub Orco,
> Forsitan has laudes, decantatumque parentis
> Nomen, ad exemplum, sero servabitis aevo.
>
> (115-20)

> And you, my juvenile verses and amusements, if only you dare hope for immortality and a life and a glimpse of the light beyond your master's funeral pyre, and if dark oblivion does not sweep you down into the throngs of Hades, perhaps you will preserve this eulogy and the name of the father whom my song honors as an example to remote ages.

Rather than carrying "Ad Patrem" forward, as do the last eight lines of "Lycidas" to "fresh woods and pastures new," this conclusion lets it fall back into the conflicts from which it began: "nostri, juvenilia carmina, lusus" (115)—"my juvenile verses and amusements"—simply reiterates "tenues sonos" (4) and "exiguum opus" (7). And what ought to be a resolution to the poem merely reaffirms the difference between Milton's own poetry and the ideal poetry discussed so fervently in the middle of the poem (17-40). Milton's hope that his verses will immortalize his father is a feeble one, both logically and poetically.

In other ways, however, "Ad Patrem" represents an advance in poetic technique for Milton. Written in dactylic hexameters rather than in the elegiac distichs of most of his early poems, it begins to develop rhythmic patterns which give Milton more freedom and syntactical flexibility. The elegiac distichs tended to constrict him into short sentences to fit the couplets; the flowing hexameters of "Ad Patrem" permit the development of a kind of verse-paragraph not found in the elegies. This more fluid verse form will be an invaluable instrument for Milton in "Mansus" and "Epitaphium Damonis."

The greatest strength of "Ad Patrem" lies in the personae Milton projects for his father and himself. The aesthetic problem of the personae can be called structural only in the sense that it concerns the interplay between the two. It is not closely related to the problems of "poetical architecture," of developmental versus static organization, or (except superficially) of the relation of the extra-poetic to the poetic situation. However, this successful aspect of the poem deserves examination because Milton resolved the poetic difficulties arising from this interplay with greater skill than he had shown before. In no other poem, before or after, does he adopt such a posture of humility. "Charta ista" ("this paper") is "exiguum opus" ("a poor attempt"). His gratitude to his father is "arida" because his words are futile. He uses the honorific "donum" (8, 10, 112)[7] for his father's gifts to him, while his own possible repayments are merely "munera" (8) and "factis" (112). He concludes by deprecating his work as "my juvenile verses and amusements."

The poem must make the elder Milton an attractive figure (the biographical considerations here are obvious and need not delay us), in part because the poet's own persona depends on that of his father and the two emerge through their interactions. If the elder appears as merely a grumpy old man, the younger will appear, in trying to appease and persuade him, as either comic or servile. Yet an inevitable and central element of the poem is the clash between the young poet's lofty concept of poetry and the old man's deprecation of it. Milton solves this aesthetic problem essentially by the use of two ideas: the repeated praise of the old man's "dona," and the emphasis on his accomplishments as a musician and therefore a protégé of Phoebus:

> Nunc tibi quid mirum, si me genuisse poëtam
> Contigerit, charo si tam propè sanguine juncti
> Cognatas artes, studiumque affine sequamur:

Ipse volens Phoebus se dispertire duobus,
Alter dona mihi, dedit altera dona parenti.
Dividuumque Deum genitorque puerque tenemus.

$$(61-66)$$

Now, since it is my lot to have been born a poet, why does it seem strange to you that we, who are so closely united by blood, should pursue sister arts and kindred interests? Phoebus himself, wishing to part himself between us two gave some gifts to me and others to my father; and, father and son, we share the possession of the divided god.

Instead of refuting his father Milton includes him, and the old man appears not as a dominating, insensitive boor (a role into which the poem could easily have pushed him), but simply as mistaken about the artistic bond which actually unites them. Milton's address thus establishes his father as a generous, permissive lover of learning who is partly responsible for his son's knowledge of Greek, Latin, Hebrew, and philosophy. By showing his father as a man of breadth and depth, Milton makes his own self-deprecation appear in the poem as appropriate, attractive, and free from any traces of fawning subservience. The diffident and humble Milton of "Ad Patrem," who occurs nowhere else in his poetry, is a charming person because the poem very skillfully makes him so.

VI

Comus as a Multi-Dimensional Poem

But now my task is smoothly don,
I can fly, or I can run.

During the spring or summer of 1634, perhaps two years after the writing of the Companion Pieces and three years before "Lycidas," Milton turned to the writing of *Comus,* which was the longest and most complex poem he had so far attempted.[1]

Comus is as firmly affixed to an extra-poetic pattern as any poem Milton ever wrote, and it is his first poem of any length which successfully integrates its extra-poetic pattern with the structure of the poem itself. There are two extra-poetic aspects which help to explain this successful integration. One is set forth on the title-page of the first (1637) edition—"A Maske Presented at Ludlow Castle, 1634: On Michaelmasse night, before the Right Honorable, Iohn Earle of Bridgewater, Vicount Brackly, Lord Praesident of Wales ..." The other relevant aspect is the fact that the Earl's children had come up from London for the Earl's investiture as Lord President and at least three of them took part in the masque.

Comus is therefore at once a fictive drama in honor of the Earl and a re-enactment of the family reunion which was actually taking place. Lady Alice Egerton, the Earl's fifteen-year-old daughter, was to play the part of the Lady, supported by her two brothers, John Lord Brackley, aged eleven, and Thomas Egerton, aged nine. Lady Alice's music master, Henry Lawes, was commissioned to write the music, direct the performance, and act the part of the Attendant Spirit (or "Daemon," in the 1637 edition). Milton had written his "Arcades" for presentation to the Egerton family two years before, and Lawes arranged for him to write the words. Clearly the ties among the performers and the audience at this presentation were very close.

But before we can look at these matters in detail, three main cruces which have recurred in the criticism of *Comus* demand discussion: (1) the poem's title; (2) its genre; and (3) its "center." The first of these is, I think, of little importance, but the other two are key problems.

The first edition of the poem, as we have seen, calls itself "A Maske Presented at Ludlow Castle," and the name *Comus* was not given to the work until John Dalton's edition of 1738. Stephen Orgel argues that Dalton's title is as inappropriate as if we were to call *Paradise Lost* by the name of its antagonist, Satan.[2] G.W. Whiting, likewise objecting to *Comus* as a title, proposes that it should be known as the *Masque of Chastity* or the *Masque of Virtue*.[3] And yet these titles would presumably be objectionable to the large number of critics who argue that the poem, or poetic drama, is not a masque at all, in spite of its title page. But it is late for these changes of title; most readers, critics, and editors call the poem *Comus* and I shall follow the custom simply because the dispute is not important.

The question of the genre, however, is quite relevant to the business of this discussion. The two extremes of position on the question are best typified by Enid Welsford on the one hand, who flatly denies that *Comus* is a masque: "The masque is a dramatised dance," she says. "*Comus* is a dramatised debate."[4] On the other hand, Marjorie Nicolson is no less definite: "*Comus,* I insist, was a masque. A masque was what Lawes had commissioned, and he would have been the first to know if a masque had not been what he received."[5]

To summarize here the 407 pages of Welsford's *The Court Masque* would be unfair to her position and would lead us far from the main line of this discussion of Milton's development. But to put her argument in its simplest terms, she establishes the limits of the masque as a genre and then finds *Comus* outside those limits. In opposition, Marjorie Nicolson merely defines "masque" as that which Henry Lawes meant when he used the term. If Lawes called *Comus* a masque, then the genre includes *Comus*.

One advantage of Welsford's argument is that it underlines some of the important differences between *Comus* and, for example, *The Masque of Blackness* or *Coelum Britannicum*. But an advantage of Nicolson's position is that it enables us to keep our eyes on Milton's poem and its place in his development, and not lose ourselves in such (for our purposes) irrelevancies as the characteristics of Daniel's *Vision of the Twelve Goddesses* or Jonson's *The Hue and Cry after Cupid*. William Riley Parker supplies us with a useful middle ground from which to consider the genre of *Comus*: "*Comus* was never once intended to be a part of the adult masque tradition. It is instead a lovely off-spring, with a 'genius' of its own."[6] Parker's metaphor is useful; *Comus* surely derives from the masque tradition, however strictly one defines the tradition, and however much it differs at times from "true masques."

To understand the place of *Comus* in Milton's literary development it is more enlightening to discuss the masque as a tradition rather than to reify it as an entity with fixed characteristics. It is true that Renaissance literary criticism was strongly and often rigidly generic; the questions of whether works were "proper" epics or "proper" tragedies vexed many of these critics. But to avoid these difficulties and digressions and get back to *Comus,* the most useful position is this: *Comus* derives from the masque tradition by possessing countless characteristics which resemble those of *The Masque of Blackness, The Masque of Beauty, Chloridia,* and so on. Likewise, *Comus* differs from these in important ways. But we must also remember that the masque tradition, even at the height of its flowering, was never a fixed, established genre, as indicated by the quarrels between such experienced practitioners as Ben Jonson and Inigo Jones over what a masque ought properly to be.

The question of the "center" of *Comus* is much more complex than those of its title and its genre, and perhaps two things have led some critics astray. The first is the geometric metaphor of the "center": *Comus* has a multi-dimensional quality, which we shall explore later, such as has not been present in Milton's poetry prior to 1634, and this makes the question of the "center" a difficult one. The second aspect of *Comus* which confuses the question of the "center" is the quality that *Comus* has of being simultaneously what Mazzoni calls a "phantastic imitation" (fictive) and at the same time an "icastic imitation" ("composed of true matter").[7] And this has embroiled critics in the question of whether they are talking about one complex of meanings in the poem and their center, or another complex with quite a different center.

Let us take the opening lines of the poem as an example:

Structure in Milton's Poetry

The first Scene discovers a wilde Wood.

The attendant Spirit descends or enters.
Before the starry threshold of *Joves* Court
My mansion is, where those immortal shapes
Of bright aereal Spirits live insphear'd
In Regions milde of calm and serene Air,
Above the smoak and stirr of this dim spot,
Which men call Earth ...

. . . .
　　　　　　　　　　　　　　　　　... but this Ile
The greatest, and the best of all the main
He quarters to his blu-hair'd deities,
And all this tract that fronts the falling Sun
A noble Peer of mickle trust, and power
Has in his charge, with temper'd awe to guide
An old, and haughty Nation proud in Arms:
Where his fair off-spring nurs't in Princely lore,
Are coming to attend their Fathers state,
And new-entrusted Scepter, but their way
Lies through the perplex't paths of this drear Wood.
　　　　　　　　　　　　　　　　(1-6, 27-37)

This passage is multi-dimensional in the sense that it embodies simultaneously a "phantastic" and an "icastic" imitation. In the phantastic imitation one of the dramatis personae "descends or enters" to tell us who he is and whence he comes. Later this "attendant Spirit" or "Daemon" will disguise himself as a shepherd and come to help the two brothers. He will supply them with the magic herb haemony, and he will guide the two brothers to Sabrina, who will release the Lady from her enchantment. The drama closes with the Attendant Spirit's final speech, "To the Ocean now I fly ...." It would not be worthwhile to insert even these few words of summary if it were not for the tendency of some critics to insist on one, and only one, level of meaning in *Comus.*

Taken from the viewpoint of the phantastic action, Tillyard is right in seeing the center as the scene in which Comus offers the captive Lady his glass "which she puts by and goes about to rise."[8]

Comus. Nay Lady sit; if I but wave this wand,
Your nerves are all chain'd up in Alablaster,

74

And you a statue, or as *Daphne* was
Root-bound, that fled *Apollo*.
　　Lady. Fool do not boast,
Thou canst not touch the freedom of my minde
With all thy charms, although this corporal rinde
Thou haste immanacl'd, while Heav'n sees good.
　　　　　　　　　　　(658-64)

　　But, to return to the opening lines, the Attendant Spirit who entered
the hall of Ludlow Castle on Michaelmas Night, 1634, was, in icastic
terms, Henry Lawes, music master to the Earl's daughter Alice, the
Lady of the drama. And the fact that Lawes was the Attendant Spirit is
much more relevant to *Comus* than, for example, the fact that it was
Richard Burbage who entered as Hamlet in the second scene of
Shakespeare's play. Since the music for *Comus* was composed by
Lawes, it was Lawes who literally, icastically, brought music to the
Egerton household. Thus when he refers to himself later (1020) as from
"the Spheary chime," the phrase is meaningful in two dimensions.
The "tract that fronts the falling Sun" (30), to which he refers, is of
course Wales, of which the Earl is now Lord President; and the "noble
Peer of mickle trust, and power" (31) was the Earl himself, in whose
honor this performance was being staged. Consequently, when the Attendant Spirit makes his exit a few lines later, Milton stresses this
icastic dimension—the extra-poetic fact of the Attendant Spirit's
position as the Egerton's household musician. The Attendant Spirit
says that he will

　　　　　　　　put off
These my skie robes spun out of *Iris* Wooff,
And take the Weeds and likenes of a Swain,
That to the service of this house belongs,
Who with his soft Pipe, and smooth dittied Song
Well knows to still the wilde winds when they roar.
　　　　　　　　　　　(82-87)

Shortly after this Lawes will return to the stage disguised as the shepherd Thyrsis—or, to keep in mind this interlocking of the phantastic
and icastic dimensions, one might better say that he will be "Lawes-
disguised-as-Attendant-Spirit-disguised-as-Thyrsis." And one must
realize that "disguise" has a special meaning here: the essence of
this disguise is not that it mislead the audience but that it not mislead

them. Here as usual in the masque tradition, the very transparency of the disguise is essential to the performance.

For example, Jonson's *Masque of Blackness* presents a "phantastic" drama involving Oceanus, twelve nymphs, sea monsters, and so on. But the masque also, in icastic or historic terms, concerns the union of the Scottish and English crowns under James VI and I; and part of its meaning involves the fact that the performance was attended by the King, with the Queen acting one of the parts. The following thoroughly icastic speech turns to the real world as it introduces one of the dances:

> BRITANIA, which the triple world admires,
> This Isle hath now recouered for her name;
> Where raigne those beauties, that with so much fame
> The sacred MUSES sonnes haue honored,
> And from bright HESPERUS to EOVS spred.
> With that great name BRITANIA, this blest Isle
> Hath wonne her ancient dignitie, and stile,
> *A world, diuided from the world:* and tri'd
> The abstract of it, in his generall pride.
> For were the world, with all his wealth, a ring,
> BRITANIA (whose new name makes all tongues sing)
> Might be a Diamant worthy to inchase it,
> Rul'd by a SVNNE, that to this height doth grace it:
> Whose beames shine day, and night, and are of force
> To blanch an AETHIOPE, and reuiue a *Cor's*.
> His light scientiall is, and (past mere nature)
> Can salve the rude defects of euery creature.[9]
>
> (241-57)

In a fashion similar to these lines from *The Masque of Blackness,* the opening lines of *Comus* are both phantastic and icastic; they refer both to a poetic situation (the entry of the Attendant Spirit) and to an extra-poetic situation (the entry of the Egerton family's music master). In this fusion of the two situations *Comus* is directly in the tradition of the court masque: *Comus* is not only a fiction about a Lady, the Two Brothers, Comus, and others, but a poem actually about the Earl of Bridgewater, his daughter Alice (fifteen), his two sons John (eleven) and Thomas (nine), their music master, and others whose names we can only wish that we knew. It is quite possible that our ignorance of some of these other facts conceals from us meanings that were quite clear to the audience that night. In its icastic sense the poem relates to the children's actual journey from London to Ludlow, probably an unpleasant 150-mile journey over seventeenth-century roads. The poem also relates to the real perils ahead in the children's lives and to the Earl's concern with these perils.

The importance of keeping the actual situation at Ludlow in mind is never more obvious than in the scene where the two brothers are frightened by the sound of the approaching Attendant Spirit:

> *Eld. Bro.* List, list, I hear
> Some far of hallow break the silent Air.
>   *2. Bro.* Me thought so too; what should it be?
>   *Eld. Bro.* For certain
> Either som like us night-founder'd here,
> Or els som neighbour Wood-man, or at worst,
> Som roaving Robber calling to his fellows.
>   *2. Bro.* Heav'n keep my sister, agen, agen, and neer,
> Best draw, and stand upon our guard.
>   *Eld. Bro.* Ile hallow,
> If he be friendly he comes well, if not,
> Defence is a good cause, and Heav'n be for us.
>
>   (479-88)

What we readers, who were not members of the audience at Ludlow Castle, can easily forget is the age and situation of the two brothers. The Achilles-figure who staunchly says "Best draw, and stand upon our guard" is nine years old, and his companion who responds "Defence is a good cause, and Heav'n be for us" is two years his senior. If we visualize the scene that autumn evening, with the proud father of these two warriors seated opposite them in the hall of the castle, the effect is funny and endearing. It is also structurally unifying in that the lines help to unite two aspects of the poem: the lines carry the story forward, but they also tie the story to the Egerton family, their home, and the family celebration. And to comprehend *Comus* properly we must see the relation of the poem not only to its story but, among other things, to the social structure which was the occasion for its being written.

Thus *Comus,* looked at purely from the dimension of the actual situation in Ludlow Castle in 1634 (as opposed to the phantastic situation of Comus and his magic rod), centers very importantly on the passage beginning at line 965, after the freeing of the Lady through the intercession of Sabrina. The stage direction says, "This second Song presents them [the three children] to their father and mother," and Milton gives Lawes, the family music master, these lines addressed to the Earl and Countess:

> Noble Lord, and Lady bright,
> I have brought ye new delight,
> Here behold so goodly grown
> Three fair branches of your own,
> Heav'n hath timely tri'd their youth,
> Their faith, their patience, and their truth.
> And sent them here through hard assays
> With a crown of deathless Praise,
>   To triumph in victorious dance
> O're sensual Folly, and Intemperance.
> (965-74)

The Egerton family has been allegorically and physically reunited. The "family ritual"[10] is reaching its completion, and now the poem ends with Lawes's closing song, "To the Ocean now I fly ...."

In the sense, then, that *Comus* faces a definite extra-poetic situation and ends with a resolution of the situation, it resembles "Elegia Tertia," "On the Death of a Fair Infant," and "Lycidas" rather than, for example, the Companion Pieces. The Nativity Ode is not relevant here because, while it commemorates the historical event of Christ's birth, it is a poem of celebration rather than one which faces a major problem and seeks a solution.

But *Comus* represents a major advance in poetic technique over "Elegia Tertia" and other early poems; "Elegia Tertia" was structurally flawed by Milton's inability to get from the beginning of the poem to the end except by an awkward leap. The extra-poetic problem of Bishop Andrewes's undeserved death received no help toward a solution from anything inherent in the structure of the poem.

Comus develops an inherent, "poetic" solution to its extra-poetic problem by placing both the phantastic and the icastic action against, or interweaving them with, an ideological universe on which both the phantastic and icastic events depend for their meaning. This is a universe not only of the Attendant Spirit and Henry Lawes, the Lady and Alice Egerton, and so on, but also a universe of good and evil, of virtue, temperance, and chastity, of licentiousness and foulness. And the unifying elements of this universe are to be found in Renaissance neo-Platonism.

As Sears Jayne points out,[11] *Comus* is a story not only of the journey of the Lady and her two brothers, it is also a dramatization of the life of the soul which, in Ficino and other neo-Platonists, went through three stages: (1) a descent from Heaven into the flesh; (2) a struggle, while in the flesh, against the demands of the flesh; (3) a victorious return to Heaven:

> Insofar as the *Mask* is about the life of the soul, it is about the middle stage only, the stage in which the soul reaches the turning point of its *circuitus spiritualis,* rejects the love of the body, and recalls its love of God.[12]

The Lady, her brothers, Comus, and Sabrina not only play their roles in the narrative of the drama, they also fulfill allegorical functions: the Lady as Reason, the Elder Brother as Faith, the Younger Brother as Patience, Sabrina as Mens (the higher part of the soul that leads the soul back to Heaven), and Comus as Passion, which is ultimately conquered by Reason but not destroyed by it. Thus at the end the Lady and her brothers reach their father; the soul completes its *remeatio* and arrives in Heaven. This is too brief a summary of the Platonic base of *Comus* to do it justice, and one should properly go to Jayne's complete exposition. But to do so here would be to lose the main direction of this already complicated chapter.

Going back, then, to the opening lines of *Comus* quoted before, the Attendant Spirit or "Daemon" enters not only as a persona of the drama, he also serves the function of intermediary spirit between God and man in the allegory—between "Jove's court" and "the smoke and stir of this dim spot." Ficino tells us that it is the proper function of daemons to

> mix agreeably and eagerly in the governing of lower things, but especially of human affairs, and from this friendly service

they all seem good; but some Platonists and Christian theologians claim that there are also bad daemons.... The good daemons, our protectors, Dionysius the Areopagite usually calls by the name angels, the governors of the lower world, and this differs little from the interpretation of Plato.[13]

Thus reading *Comus* not merely as a drama and a family ritual, but also *sub specie aeternitatis,* one can see a turning point ("center" is not an appropriate term) in the passage already quoted where "Comus appears with his rabble, and the Lady set in an inchanted Chair." He waves his magic wand so that she is "all chain'd up in Alablaster," and the soul is in its second state of capture *(raptio)* by the body, and must now face Comus's question:

> Wherefore did Nature powre her bounties forth,
> With such a full and unwithdrawing hand,
> Covering the earth with odours, fruits, and flocks,
> Thronging the Seas with spawn innumerable,
> But all to please, and sate the curious taste?
>
> (709-13)

The Lady is able to answer this question properly and retain her virtue because, as the Elder Brother earlier predicted,

> A thousand liveried Angels lacky her,
> Driving far off each thing of sin and guilt,
> And in cleer dream, and solemn vision
> Tell her of things that no gross ear can hear,
> Till oft convers with heav'nly habitants
> Begin to cast a beam on th'outward shape,
> The unpolluted temple of the mind,
> And turns it by degrees to the souls essence,
> Till all be made immortal.
>
> (454-62)

The resolution of the poem, in its neo-Platonic aspect, lies in the soul's liberation from the bonds of passion and ultimate ascendancy to its true Heavenly home to complete its *circuitus spiritualis.*

To return to the relation of *Comus* to the earlier "Elegia Tertia" and the later "Lycidas": "Elegia Tertia" fails partly because it embodies a transition in ideas and attitudes similar to "Lycidas," but the transition comes about by haphazard means. "Lycidas" succeeds because it builds into its poetic structure—by means of its imagery, its development of appropriate psychological stages, its prosody, and so on—the struggle, the spiritual pilgrimage which unites its extra-poetic resolution with its poetic resolution. *Comus* is clearly a forerunner of "Lycidas" in that it succeeds in some of the very ways wherein "Elegia Tertia" fails. The Lady ultimately reaches her father's house but not merely because she happens to have helpful friends like the Attendant Spirit and Sabrina. She arrives because she and her friends exist simultaneously in the physical and metaphysical world. So also, looking at the poem icastically, Alice Egerton will find her Heavenly destination because she is virtuous and because she understands that one must

> Love vertue, she alone is free,
> She can teach ye how to clime
> Higher then the Spheary chime;
> Or if Vertue feeble were,
> Heav'n it self would stoop to her.
>
> (1018-22)

And this simultaneity of existence on the part of the Attendant Spirit/Lawes, the Lady/Alice Egerton, and the others is not merely a trick to motivate an otherwise random plot: this is a poetic expression of the total world-view which gives form to the physical world—the wild wood, the adventures of the Lady and her Brothers, and the family of the Earl of Bridgewater.

It has been argued that such readings of the poem are needlessly esoteric and that the poem lacks this profundity.[14] But it is not in the multiplicity of its levels of meanings that *Comus* is unusual or even (in a sense) profound. This quality of meaning several things simultaneously is a commonplace in the masque tradition and occurs in masques which are quite trivial.

An example of this is Aurelian Townshend's *Tempe Restor'd*. Townshend's text is silly, but it was "presented by the Queene and foureteene Ladies, to the King's Maiestie at *Whitehall* on Shrove-Tuesday, 1631."[15] The story can be briefly summarized as follows: Circe transforms a young man with whom she is enamored into a lion, and then, preferring him in human shape, she changes him back. He flees in fright, comes upon the King (Charles), the sight of whom frees him from all fear. Circe is grief-stricken, and all the beasts who are voluntarily under her subjection try to entertain her. Then Harmony, Beauty, and fourteen stars "of happy constellation" (one of the stars was Alice Egerton) descend, accompanied by the music of the spheres. Circe voluntarily delivers her golden wand to Minerva, and Tempe, who had been possessed by Circe's beasts, is restored to the true followers of the Muses.

In order that no reader of the printed text might miss the allegory, Townshend explicitly states it at the conclusion:

The Allegory

In the young Gentlemen, who Circe had first enamored of her Person, and after, through Iealousie conceiued, Transformed into a *Lyon*. And againe remembring her former Love, retransform'd into his former shape, is figured an incontinent man, that striving with his affections, is at last by the power of reason, perswaded to flye from those Sensuall desires, which had formerly corrupted his Iudgement.... Circe here signifies desire in general ... The Nymphs ... figuring the Vertues, and the bruite Beasts, denoting the Vices.... The happie retreat of the Muses and their followers, is meant, the inchantment of vitious impostures, that by false meanes, seek to extirpate the true Louers of *Science* and *Vertue,* to which of right only that place belongs.[16]

Townshend took no chances on any reader's missing the Platonic overtones of his masque:

In Heroick vertue is figured the Kings Maiestie, who therein transcends as farre common men, as they are above *Beasts,* he being truly the prototipe to all the Kingdomes vnder his Monarchie, of Religion, Iustice, and all the *Vertues* ioyned together.

So that Corporeall *Beauty,* consisting in simmetry, colour, and certaine vnexpressable Graces, shining in the Queenes Maiestie, may draw vs to the contemplation of the *Beauty* of the soule, vnto which it hath Analogy.[17]

With Inigo Jones's staging, *Tempe Restor'd* may well have been a grand spectacle, although Townshend's text is a paltry thing. But his masque is helpful in understanding *Comus* for several reasons. First, of course, there are numerous superficial resemblances to *Comus*—the presence of Lady Alice Egerton in both casts, the use of the Circe myth, and the opposition of reason and incontinence.

But for purposes of this discussion, the importance of *Tempe Restor'd* is that it not only operates at several levels of meaning, it does this in the most blatant fashion. Like so many masques of the period, it manages to be multi-dimensional without in any sense being profound. Townshend's allegory and his Platonism are so explicit in the masque itself that his recapitulation of them is ludicrously redundant. The difference between Townshend's allegory in *Tempe Restor'd* and Milton's in *Comus* lies not in the fact that Townshend is complex where Milton is simple but lies in the fact that Townshend is clumsy and obvious where Milton is skillful and subtle. Townshend refuses to permit even the dullest reader to miss his allegorical meanings; Milton assumes in *Comus* as so often elsewhere that the audience that matters will discover his subtleties and profundities by themselves. The Platonism in *Comus* is much more complex than that in *Tempe Restor'd;* but the multi-dimensional structure of each is quite usual in the masque.

This multi-dimensional quality of the masque tradition so suited Milton's poetic needs at this point in his career that one is tempted to make some conclusions which are difficult to support. Either Milton chose to write *Comus* because he could see that the often simple-minded Platonic allegory of the traditional masque supplied the kind of structural unity and dialectic impetus which his earlier poems lacked; or, having been commissioned by Lawes to write a masque for his friends the Egertons, he discovered in this trivial and dying tradition the opportunity to give a poem both the unity and the dynamic progression which had heretofore been lacking in his longer poems. We have no way of knowing, of course, why Milton accepted Lawes's invitation to write a masque, but we can see that *Comus* gave him the opportunity to develop structural techniques which prepared him for "Lycidas" and the other great poems which were to follow.

VII

"Mansus" and the Panegyric Tradition

At non sponte domum tamen idem, & regis adivit
Rura Pheretiadae coelo fugitivus Apollo.

After *Comus,* Milton was ready for the great poems of his maturity, al-
though it was to be another three years before the first of these,
"Lycidas," was written. In perhaps the two years between 1637 and
1639 he produced "Lycidas," "Mansus," and "Epitaphium
Damonis." All three poems were outgrowths of the techniques
Milton had been developing, at least since the writing of "Elegia
Prima," and all three were preparations for the massive creations of
his later years, *Samson Agonistes, Paradise Lost,* and *Paradise
Regained.*

"Lycidas," "Mansus," and "Epitaphium Damonis," although
they obviously differ in important ways (not the least of which is
the fact that the first was written in English and the latter two in Latin),
at the same time have important similarities. One of the most obvious of
these similarities is the beatific vision that concludes each poem; another is the pastoralism, which pervades "Lycidas," emerges occasionally in "Mansus," and in "Epitaphium Damonis" moves
through the poem with such complexity that no brief phrase here can do
justice to it.

Since this study has made such extensive use of "Lycidas" as a
terminus ad quem for the early poems, it would be needlessly repetitive
to discuss the poem in detail again here. And Miltonic criticism has
long passed the point where it is necessary any longer to refute G.
Wilson Knight's remark that "Lycidas" is "an accumulation of
glittering fragments."[1] Critics have stopped worrying about pos-

sible digressions in the poem and have begun to concentrate on the intricate organization whereby Milton fuses the diverse elements of the poem into a single whole.

But Milton's use of the pastoral tradition in "Lycidas"—in fact in all three poems—has a relation to the structural aspects of the later poems and illuminates the direction that his poetic development was taking. In an obvious way, "Lycidas," "Mansus," and "Epitaphium Damonis" make use of the pastoral tradition in a fashion similar to the use of the epic tradition in *Paradise Lost*. But like *Paradise Lost,* these three poems also use the tradition in a less obvious way—as a means of stepping outside themselves generically to comment on the relation between the poetic tradition in which they exist and the extra-poetic situation with which they are concerned. As we have seen in the case of the multi-dimensional quality of *Comus,* this is a direction toward which Milton had been tending. In fact, if one considers the fact that "Elegia Prima," written eleven years before "Lycidas," is in a sense an exile-poem built of, and standing in a self-conscious relation to, the most famous of all collections of exile poems, Ovid's *Tristia* and *Epistulae ex Ponto,* one can see "Elegia Prima" as foreshadowing in an important way these three poems of the late 1630s, as well as *Paradise Lost* and *Paradise Regained.*

In the pastoral tradition this self-reflective quality appeared so many centuries back that it is only natural that "Lycidas" should embody at least one aspect of it: for centuries before Milton, pastoral poems—like masques in the seventeenth century—had been poems characterized by an inherent transparent disguise. The "Daphnis" whose death is lamented by Vergil in the fifth eclogue was almost certainly not someone named Daphnis; as already mentioned, it has been proposed by some, and denied by others, that "Daphnis" was the recently-assassinated Julius Caesar. And while the "Gallus" of Vergil's tenth eclogue was indeed C. Cornelius Gallus, still the rural costumes and the Arcadian scene serve similarly as nominal disguises. Likewise in Renaissance pastorals, Petrarch's eclogues are so laden with double meanings that they are really enciphered satires; and Castiglione's "Alcon," the influence of which is very great on both "Lycidas" and "Epitaphium Damonis,"[2] concerns itself, in terms of the extra-poetic situation, not with a shepherd named Alcon, but with the poet's dead friend Falcone. "Disguise" is really the wrong term; it is with a complex, extended metaphor that we are dealing. Vergil, Petrarch, Castiglione, Milton, and other pastoral poets using this part of the pastoral tradition are implying, in an intricate way, the relation between the situation at hand and that in the earlier poems in the tradition. To push the idea further, the poems of these pastoral poets are concerned not only with the explicit subject (for example, Castiglione with the death of a shepherd named Alcon) but with the relation of the explicit subject to the pastoral context as a way of seeking solutions to the extra-poetic situation—the death of one's friend. A poem making use of the pastoral "disguises" or metaphors is of necessity a poem which is in part about pastoral poetry, a self-reflective poem. And "Lycidas" of course fits into this category.

Beyond this, "Lycidas" is self-reflective, as we have seen, in its concern, particularly in the first fourteen lines, with the conflict involved in writing the poem. The reluctance of these opening lines and the sullen resignation of "Begin then, Sisters of the sacred well ... Begin, and somewhat loudly sweep the string" (15, 17) are on another plane from the grief for Lycidas; they are part of the poem about the poem. And they are part of the conflict which is resolved in the final paragraph—"Thus sang the uncouth Swain ..." (186). We need not review here the ways in which the dual conflict at the beginning of the poem is united and resolved at the conclusion. The important point is to see the connection between "Lycidas" as a pastoral poem and "Lycidas" as a poem about pastoral poetry, anticipating in a less complex way the manner in which *Paradise Lost* is an epic poem about epic poetry. To a large extent, "Lycidas," like *Paradise Lost,* derives both its unity and its impetus from this technique. "Lycidas" works out the resolution of its extra-poetic problems (the death of King, to state things briefly and simply) by means of existing, struggling, and finding tranquility through the use of the tradition built up in pastoral poetry. So *Paradise Lost* faces its extra-poetic problems (again, to be brief and simple, to "justifie the wayes of God to men") and comes to its complex of "answers" not only by using the conventions of epic poetry, but by self-consciously examining them and ultimately breaking through them to a concept of the higher heroism and the true Paradise.

To turn from "Lycidas" to "Mansus" is to drop to a considerably lower poetic level, although E.M.W. Tillyard thought that

"Mansus" was the best of Milton's Latin poems[3] and Walter Savage Landor praised it highly.[4] But our concern here is not with its quality as a poem so much as the degree to which it illuminates Milton's developing technique in the use of poetic structure as an integral part of the extra-poetic subject of the poem. "Mansus" is an important example of this aspect of Milton's development, but it is a difficult one to deal with because the poem makes use of an almost forgotten poetic tradition, that of the panegyric. The traditional conventions of the panegyric have almost disappeared, but "Mansus" makes important use of them in a fashion which casts light on Milton's similar but more skillful use of the better-known traditions of the pastoral and the epic.

Very little has been written on "Mansus," as opposed to the torrents of commentary on, for example, "Lycidas": its structure, its imagery, its relation to the pastoral tradition, and so on. Therefore it would seem wise to explore "Mansus" at some length. This exploration is necessary not only because the formalized panegyric tradition in itself is dead, but also because without an awareness of the tradition the reader misses the fact that Milton, time and again in the poem, negates or inverts the tradition in order to make his poem something unique and not merely an inert gesture of conformity.

In its most obvious aspect, "Mansus" is a poem in praise of Giovanni Battista Manso, the old Neapolitan nobleman and patron of poets whom Milton met on his Italian journey in 1638-39. But "Mansus," like so many of Milton's mature poems, refuses to rest passively within its genre as a panegyric. It combines praise with contemplation of death, it turns poetic conventions upside down, and it creates not merely an encomium of Manso but a celebration of the harmony of things. And by refusing to be a conventional panegyric, it makes use of the panegyric tradition to create its own structure and to generate its own momentum.

"Mansus" gathers together *topoi* that have come down through centuries of stylized adulation, but the poem also weaves these *topoi* into a fabric which establishes a continuity of the poetic tradition. And then it uses this continuity as a means of expanding "Mansus" to a significance beyond that of the simple occasion of its composition. The poem stresses not only Manso's assistance and spiritual kinship with Marino and Tasso; it also points out Manso's resemblance to Herodotus, Gallus, and Maecenas and then relates

Manso to this honorable line of patrons by both direct and inverse use of devices occurring in the poems of countless other panegyric poets for centuries. The conventions of the panegyric are not merely devices used to praise Manso; they are also the means by which the poem carries itself forward from the specific occasion of its composition— Milton's visit to Manso—to its final vision of a harmonious universe in which both poet and patron joyfully fulfill their proper functions.

The first thread of the panegyric tradition occurs in the middle of the little prose preface to "Mansus," introducing the Marquis to the reader. A *praefatio* was quite usual with those indefatigable panegyrists, Sidonius Apollonaris and Claudian, although theirs were always in elegiac distichs and never in prose. Here Milton touches momentarily on the prowess of Manso in both war and peace: "Joannes Baptista Mansus Marchio Villensis vir ingenii laude, tum literarum studio, nec non & bellica virtute apud Italos clarus in primis est" ("John Baptista Manso, Marquis of Villa, is one of the first men in Italy alike for the renown of his intellect and his literary pursuits and no less for his martial prowess"). Milton is here repeating a cause for praise which was not new to the old man. Manso's own collection of poems, *Poesie Nomiche,* had appended to it more than a hundred poems in his praise written by his friends. And time and again his friends praised him for prowess "nella militia e nella dottrina."[5]

But the literary forebears of this passage were much older than this collection of poems praising Manso; a *topos* stressing specifically this pair of virtues went back in Latin poetry more than fifteen hundred years. For example, Statius's "Epistula ad Vitorium Marcellum" praised Marcellus as a lawyer and civilian administrator and then continued, "nec enim tibi sola potentis / eloquii virtus: sunt membra accommoda bellis" ("For it is not only the gift of powerful eloquence that is thine: thou hast limbs that are made for war").[6] In a similar fashion the unknown author of "Ad Messallam" (or "Panegyricus Messallae") praised Messalla for his prowess in both war and peace: "Nam quis te maiora gerit castrisve forove?" ("For who doth greater things than thou, whether in the camp or forum?"),[7] he asked—and then devoted the next sixty-six lines of the poem to answering his question with examples and metaphors stressing Messalla's two-fold achievements.

Another poem which helped to shape the panegyric tradition is the "Laus Pisonis" (or "Ad Pisonem") attributed to Ovid, but almost certainly not by him. "Ad Messallam" and "Laus Pisonis" seem to have been important enough in establishing the poetic panegyric tradition, at least for the sixteenth century, to be the prime examples cited by J.C. Scaliger in his *Poetics* under the heading "Genus τῶν ἐγκομίων." Piso's panegyrist seems to have felt the pressure of the tradition. Piso apparently had had no military career so the poet had to do the best he could. First he pointed out that virtue does not decline merely because there are no wars—the deeds of peace are just as heroic (19-36). Then he praised Piso for his skill in mock combat (177-89), and finally he had to resort to pointing out Piso's skill in the battles of *ludus latrunculorum,* a game resembling checkers (190-208).[8]

Milton himself, in *Of Education,* published about five years after the writing of "Mansus," prescribed training that would give legitimate cause for this *topos:* "I call therefore a compleat and generous Education that which fits a man to perform justly, skilfully and magnanimously all the offices both private and public, of Peace and War."[9]

The rest of Milton's preface faces the subject of the poem, the praise of Manso, with no further concern with tradition. But in the opening lines of the poem itself he again merges his subject with the tradition:

> Haec quoque Manse tuae meditantur carmina laudi
> Pierides, tibi Manse choro notissime Phoebi,
> Quandoquidem ille alium haud aequo est dignatus honore,
> Post Galli cineres, & Mecaenatis Hetrusci.
> Tu quoque si nostrae tantùm valet aura Camoenae,
> Victrices hederas inter, laurosque sedebis.

(1-6)

These verses also, Manso, the Pierides are meditating in your praise—in yours, Manso of the wide acquaintance among the choir of Phoebus, for since the death of Gallus and Etruscan Maecenas the god has granted to hardly any one else honors equal to yours. If my Muse has breath sufficient, you too shall sit among the victorious ivy and laurels.

Milton's stress here on the extent of Manso's fame is another traditional panegyric *topos* which this poem weaves into its overt statements of praise. The pseudo-Tibullus, in praising his patron Messalla, similarly centered much of his poem on the extent of Messalla's fame:

> Sed generis priscos contendis vincere honores,
> quam tibi maiores maius decus ipse futuris:
> at tua non titulus capiet sub nomine facta,
> aeterno sed erunt tibi magna volumina versu,
> conveniuntque tuas cupidi componere laudes
> undique quique canent vincto pede quique soluto.
> quis potior, certamen erit: sim victor in illis,
> ut nostrum tantis inscribam nomen in actis.
>
> (31-38)

> But thou strivest to surpass the olden honours of thy line, thyself a greater lustre to posterity than ancestry to thee. For thy exploits no legend underneath a name has room. Thou shalt have great rolls of immortal verse; and, in eagerness to write thy praises, all will assemble who compose in rhythm, whether bound or free. They will strive who shall be first. May I be the conqueror among them all, that I may write my name above the great story of those deeds.

Fifteen hundred years later George Buchanan, at that time a schoolmaster in Bordeaux, was still keeping the *topos* alive by reassuring the Emperor Charles V that his reputation extended through Italy, Spain, Germany, Portugal, the Danube, and Africa.[10] When James's queen, Anne, died in 1619, Patrick Hannay announced that the grief was so extensive that

> *Thames* trembles, *Forth* doth feverize for fear,
> Both roar to see their sovereign thus appear:
> Their billows break their hearts against the shore.
> Their fishes faint (yet cannot tell wherefore),
> But when they float upon the water crop,
> And see the tears from eyes and oars which drop,
> They think them all too few, and add their own
> And swim in proper *waters* (erst unknown).[11]

Rarely has Universal Nature lamented with greater bathos than in Patrick Hannay.

When Vincenzo Carrafa praised Manso in the collection in the *Poesie Nomiche* he pointed out that the sonorous trumpet proclaimed Manso's name from the Ganges to the Tagus.[12] But when the *topos* recurs in "Mansus," its very conventionality is, for Milton's purposes, not a fault but a useful poetic technique: just as "Lycidas" fuses the poetic tradition of pastoralism with the extra-poetic problem of death, so "Mansus," the poem, unites the conventions of the panegyric with the praise of Manso, the old Neapolitan nobleman, who is carrying on the traditions of Maecenas and Gallus.

The opening section of a panegyric (lines 1-6 in "Mansus") is called the *principium* in Roman rhetoric, and the anonymous author of *Ad Herennium* urges, "Ab eius persona de quo loquemur, si laudabimus: vereri nos ut illius facta verbis consequi possimus" ("When we draw our Introduction from the person being discussed: if we speak in praise we shall say that we fear our inability to match his deeds with words).[13] *Ad Herennium* had the prestige resultant from being attributed (incorrectly) to Cicero; as one of the standard textbooks at St. Paul's and other grammar schools of the sixteenth and seventeenth centuries, it deeply influenced the English rhetorical tradition.[14] Milton's fifth and sixth lines—"Tu quoque, si nostrae tantùm valet aura Camoenae / Victrices hederas inter, laurosque sedebis"—are probably a tenuous reflection of this tradition. The actual tenuousness of the reflection is probably a small but significant part of the poem Milton is making, but we shall return to this point in a moment. The confession of inadequacy is a common and well-developed *topos* in panegyrics.[15]

The great reason for praising Manso, Milton tells us, is his friendship and helpfulness to poets—specifically to Tasso, to Marino, and now to Milton himself. Milton embodies his praise of the old man in a series of metaphors and similes involving figures from Greek and Roman literature and mythology. In his *principium* he has compared Manso with Gallus and Maecenas; then in lines 22-23 he compares him with Herodotus. And later in a long metaphor in the middle of the poem he likens Manso to the centaur Chiron:

> Dicetur tum sponte tuos habitâsse penates
> Cynthius, & famulas venisse ad limina Musas:

At non sponte domum tamen idem, & regis adivit
Rura Pheretiadae coelo fugitivus Apollo;
Ille licet magnum Alciden susceperat hospes;
Tantùm ubi clamosos placuit vitare bubulcos,
Nobile mansueti cessit Chironis in antrum,
Irriguos inter saltus frondosaque tecta
Peneium prope rivum: ibi saepe sub ilice nigrâ
Ad citharae strepitum blandâ prece victus amici
Exilii duros lenibat voce labores.
Tum neque ripa suo, barathro nec fixa sub imo,
Saxa stetere loco, nutat Trachinia rupes,
Nec sentit solitas, immania pondera, silvas,
Emotaeque suis properant de collibus orni,
Mulcenturque novo maculosi carmine lynces.

(54-69)

It shall be said that of his own free will Apollo dwelt in your
house and that the Muses were familiar attendants at your
doors. Unwillingly that same Apollo came, when he was an
exile from heaven, to the farmstead of Admetus, although Admetus had been host to the great Hercules. When he wished to
get away from the clamorous ploughmen, he retreated to the
renowned cave of the gentle Chiron, among the moist
woodland pastures and verdurous shades beside the river
Peneus. There, under the dark ilex, persuaded by his
friend's soft entreaty, he would lighten the hard labors of
exile by singing to the accompaniment of the cithara. Then
neither the banks nor the rocks fixed in the lowest depths of
the chasm stood fast in their places; the Trachinian cliff
swayed and no longer felt the vast weight of its familiar
forests; the trees were moved and hastened down from their
hills and the spotted lynxes became gentle at the unfamiliar
song.

The sources in Greek and Roman literature for this passage are interesting and they cast an important light on a central element of the
poem; Milton draws most obviously on Homer, Pindar, Euripides,
and Ovid. Presumably Manso would not have been overawed by the
breadth of Milton's references—having one's hospitality favorably
compared with the heroes and gods of antiquity would undoubtedly

have pleased, but not surprised, any educated Italian of the seventeenth century.

But the Greco-Roman comparisons such as those in this passage, the Maecenas-Gallus passage, and the Herodotus passage also have interesting roots in the panegyric tradition. Messalla, the pseudo-Tibullus told his readers, was greater than Nestor or Ulysses (48-51). Piso's eloquence, according to the "Laus Pisonis," outdid the strength of Ulysses, the conciseness of Menelaus, or the sweetness of Nestor (61-64). In fact, Piso's eloquence surpassed that of the poet himself just as the swan outdoes the little bird of Pandion, the swallow (77-80). Piso's ability to play the lyre was so like that of Achilles that one could think that Phoebus himself had been Piso's teacher (166-68). And as a patron of poets, Piso would (the poet hoped) be as generous as Maecenas, without whom Vergil, Varius, and Horace would have remained unknown (246-51).

In Greek rhetoric the term for these comparisons is σύνκρισις, and Aristotle urged it as an important element in speeches of praise. A very common type of σύνκρισις for panegyric poets is that which concerns the relation of the giver (the poet) to the receiver (the patron being praised); the two becoming metaphorically the poet/host and the patron/guest. In this *topos* the humility of the poet/host and the majesty of the patron/guest appear as a σύνκρισις involving one or another of the humbler figures in Greek legend who received a god or hero into his home. So the pseudo-Tibullus, in offering his poem to Messalla, likened himself to the Cretan Icarus offering a gift to Apollo; he went on to compare himself to Icarus also in Icarus's reception of the god Bacchus as a guest. So too the poet resembled the peasant Molorchus, who was Hercules's host (7-13).

In keeping with this tradition Sidonius, in the fifth century A.D., compared himself to the humble Chiron, while the Emperor Anthemius was like Jove.[16] Chiron, the lesser figure who teaches the greater, appeared also in a panegyric by Claudian which said that the relation of Claudian's patron, the Emperor Honorius, to Honorius's father Theodosius was like that of Achilles to Chiron.[17] The *topos* still had vitality in the sixteenth century when George Buchanan, similarly using the host-guest figure in his panegyric to the Emperor Charles V, compared the emperor to Theseus, Hercules, and Jupiter, while likening himself and his colleagues in Bordeaux to Hecale, Molorchus, and Tethys.[18]

Mansus

But in this long metaphor involving Manso and Chiron, Milton has made a radical break with the tradition that he is using by reversing the traditional panegyric relation. Instead of presenting a noble patron/guest who resembles Apollo, Achilles, Hercules, or Jove, served by a humble poet/host who resembles Chiron or Molorchus, Milton uses the metaphor the other way around. It is Milton, the poet, who is the guest, who is like Apollo or Hercules, and who graciously expresses his gratitude for the hospitality of patron/hosts like Manso and Chiron. Milton even goes so far as to tie Manso's very name to Chiron's by a pun: "Nobile mansueti cessit Chironis in antrum" ("He retreated to the renowned cave of the gentle Chiron").

The atmosphere that Milton creates by giving the lowly role of Chiron to the patron rather than to the poet boldly pervades much of the poem. It is the poets who summon back native kings into our songs (80); the "choro Phoebi" (2) are the poets themselves, while a patron like Manso is only "of wide acquaintance" among the poets. It is significant that the fawning poet of the "Laus Pisonis" called Piso "Pierii tutela chori"—"protection" or "tutor" of the Pierian choir (244). For Milton, Manso is no "tutela"—his value is as an assistant to poets.

In Milton's poem it is the poets who in after-life dwell with the gods and look with serene spirit on the patrons below (95-100). In this passage and elsewhere, "Mansus" embodies a clear class distinction: of primary importance are the poets—Homer, Vergil, Horace, Tasso, Marino, and Milton; of secondary importance are those who help poets by patronage or by preserving their fame—Gallus, Maecenas, Herodotus, and Manso.

This probably explains why Milton's remark referred to earlier—"Tu quoque si nostrae tantùm valet aura Camoenae, / Victrices hederas inter, laurosque sedebis" (5-6)—reflects only faintly the panegyric "inadequacy *topos*." In many of the earlier panegyrics this *topos* stretched out for ten or fifteen lines.[19] In Milton's poem the *topos* is only vestigial for the simple reason that Milton did not feel inadequate with regard to Manso. The poem is centrally concerned with Milton's idea of the proper relation of a patron toward a poet, with the patron acting as the poet's devoted and loyal supporter. In return for these services the poet should praise him.

There is a Vergilian tag in lines 49 and 70 of "Mansus" which reinforces this relation—"Fortunate senex," Milton addresses

Manso, "ergo quacunque per orbem ..." and later "Diis dilecte senex ...." The source of these lines is Vergil's first eclogue— "Fortunate senex, ergo tua rura manebunt," and later in the same poem, "Fortunate senex, hic inter flumina nota." In Vergil's poem a character named Meliboeus, with some condescension, spoke the lines in addressing an old man living on a poor farm. It would be an overstatement to say that Milton's attitude toward Manso is as condescending as that of Meliboeus toward the old man, but the tone of Vergil's poem, and by reflection of Milton's poem, is worlds away from the servility which is prevalent in the panegyric tradition. The poets who recorded their praise of Messalla, Piso, the later Roman emperors, and Roberto Sanseverino would never have dared to arouse these Vergilian overtones by addressing their majestic patrons as "fortunate senex."

This reversal of the panegyric tradition, whereby the poet occupies the hierarchical position normally held by the patron, and the patron is reduced to the position usual to the grateful, humble poet (one cannot help wondering what Manso thought of the poem!) is a more intricate form of the reversal found in "Elegia Prima," where the relation of the exile-poet and his feelings toward his place of exile are reversed. Here in "Mansus" it is the role of the poet and his patron which are reversed. But this technique has its connections with the structure of *Paradise Lost* as well: Satan, the traditional epic hero who is driven forth, endures hardships, fights wars, and wins a new realm for his people, is set off against Adam, who learns the higher epic virtues of suffering, patience, and an exile which will gain the Paradise within. As we shall see later, this technique is in an important way carried even further in the structure of *Paradise Regained.*

Returning to "Mansus," Milton now speaks of the old man's birth:

> Diis dilecte senex, te Jupiter aequus oportet
> Nascentem, & miti lustrarit lumine Phoebus,
> Atlantisque nepos; neque enim nisi charus ab ortu
> Diis superis poterit magno favisse poetae.
>
> (70-73)

Old man, beloved of the gods! At your birth Jupiter must have been favorable, Phoebus and the grandson of Atlas must have

shed their gentle light upon you, for no one, unless from his
birth he were dear to the gods, could have befriended a great
poet.

Intrinsically these lines develop nothing of great significance in the
poem, but they do help to establish the relations of the poem with its
ancestors, and without these links to the tradition, the poem would be
unable to develop the juxtapositions and differentiations necessary to
its existence. The Greco-Roman rhetorical tradition called this section of a panegyric the γένεσις , its function being to refer to any
noteworthy fact preceding or attending the birth of the man being
praised—any omens or significant dreams. Quintilian, for example,
said, "Other topics to be drawn from the period preceding their birth
will have reference to omens or prophecies foretelling their future
greatness, such as the oracle which is said to have foretold that the
son of Thetis would be greater than his father."[20] And
Quintilian's *Institutio Oratoria,* like "Cicero's" *Ad Herennium,* helped establish the models for panegyrics at sixteenth- and
seventeenth-century grammar schools, including St. Paul's. In this
context Milton's subjunctive "lustrarit" (71) is perhaps symp-
tomatic: he does not actually propose that Phoebus did this for Manso
but he implies that it would be in keeping with the panegyric tradition
to have it said.

As Milton draws to his conclusion he again turns to the traditional
topoi and again he reverses them. The two *topoi* that will be relevant
here are the vision and the closing prayer. The vision-*topos* concluded
"Ad Messallam," and like Milton, the pseudo-Tibullus saw himself
as dead and experiencing a new life. However, the after-life that he
foresaw was not lofty and beatific like Milton's, but rather reincarna-
ted even lower in the scale—as a bird, a bull, or a plowhorse (207-9).
But even after this literally harrowing experience he hoped to become a
man again and renew his praise of Messalla. It is hard to imagine a
greater contrast than that between the servility of this poet and the
sublime self-assurance of Milton.

There are of course several elements in "Mansus" that are not
purely panegyric. Milton writes at some length not only about
Manso's admirable traits but also about the quality of English poetry,
the customs of the Druidic religion, and his own plans for poetry. For
example, woven into the *topos* of the closing prayer (for a friend such as
Manso in future years) Milton says:

O mihi si mea sors talem concedat amicum
Phoebaeos decorâsse viros qui tam bene nôrit,
Si quando indigenas revocabo in carmina reges,
Arturumque etiam sub terris bella moventem;
Aut dicam invictae sociali foedere mensae,
Magnanimos Heroas, & (O modo spiritus adsit)
Frangam Saxonicas Britonum sub Marte phalanges.

(78-84)

O, if my lot might but bestow such a friend upon me, a friend who understands how to honor the devotees of Phoebus—if ever I shall summon back our native kings into our songs, and Arthur, waging his wars beneath the earth, or if ever I shall proclaim the magnanimous heroes of the table which their mutual fidelity made invincible, and (if only the spirit be with me) shall shatter the Saxon phalanxes under the British Mars!

E.M.W. Tillyard, who thought "Mansus" was "the best of all Milton's Latin poems (the *Epitaphium Damonis* included)," said of this passage, "There is great power in the crash of *frangam* after the hushed parenthesis of *O modo spiritus adsit*."[21] And Walter Savage Landor in his *Imaginary Conversations* called the line "a glorious verse" and had Southey object only that it overrated the early Britons: " 'Was the whole nation [of Britons] ever worth this noble verse of Milton? It seems to come sounding over the Aegean Sea and not to have been modulated on the low country of the Tiber.' "[22]

One might argue that this passage is a digression in a poem devoted to the praise of Manso, but the panegyric has customarily been a widely digressive genus. All sorts of irrelevancies find their way into panegyrics, just as panegyric *topoi* occur in all sorts of poems, and if Milton is digressive he violates no accepted precepts. When the pseudo-Tibullus compared Messalla with Ulysses, he then diverged for thirty lines (52-81) to recount the adventures of Ulysses; later he stopped his praise of Messalla and for twenty-four lines (151-74) discussed the five zones of climate that encircle the earth, making some parts habitable and others uninhabitable. The "Laus Pisonis" likewise digressed to the subject of the cycle of the seasons (145-54). And Mantuan's vision of the Virgin, which occupied 448 lines of his 822-line poem praising Roberto Sanseverino, contained sections on the motions of the tide, on original sin, and on the logic underlying the doctrine of God's omnipresence.

Milton's praise of Manso is, as we have seen, much more restrained than that of some of his predecessors, who grovelled in servility. But he was not an innovator in keeping his praise of Manso within reasonable bounds. Statius, who was probably contemporaneous with the author of the "Laus Pisonis," praised the youthful Crispinus in a credible and restrained fashion.[23] In the sixteenth century Fracastorius praised Danielus Rainerius, the prefect of Verona, for faithful and honest discharge of his duties, but always with moderation.[24]

As we have seen, Milton builds into his panegyric a significant reversal of an important part of the panegyric tradition—for Milton it is the function, almost the duty, of patrons to honor such poets as Vergil, Tasso, Marino, and Milton, rather than the function or duty of the poets to honor their patrons. Much of the friendly charm of the best parts of Milton's poem arises from its air of companionship, as opposed to the servility of most of the poems in the panegyric tradition. And this artful dissonance between Milton's "Mansus" and the tradition derives its force not only from the reversed metaphor of Chiron, Apollo, and other mythological figures, but also from the closing vision. Milton's predecessors had visions of their patrons smiling down on poor mortals such as the poet, but Milton, with a self-confidence unusual even in him, envisages himself smiling down with satisfaction at the assistance of patrons like Manso. It would be difficult to defend the tone of these closing lines, especially the last line where Milton is so exalted by his own apotheosis that he bursts into applause for himself. But the passage does have important connections with the panegyric tradition and with the happy relation of poet and patron, which is at the heart of the poem.

This concluding section of "Mansus" (85-100) resembles both directly and inversely not only the traditional panegyric vision but also the visions which concluded some of the earlier epicedia such as "Elegia Tertia" and "In Obitum Praesulis Eliensis," as well as the beatific vision at the conclusion of "Lycidas," and the as yet unwritten "Epitaphium Damonis" on Charles Diodati.[25] One important difference of course is that in all the other poetic visions Milton is alive, and it is the subjects of his poems who are dead, blissful in the company of the saints. In "Mansus," in a mood of self-assurance that one can only envy, Milton's vision is of himself having died, happily receiving his just Heavenly rewards.

But another important difference between this concluding vision and that in the early epicedia (excluding "Lycidas," of course) is the extent to which the whole structure of "Mansus" has led toward the scene in which the poet receives the immortal honors which are his due, the patron playing a suitably subordinate part in assisting with the ritual. The flaws in "Mansus" lie in the incredible self-admiration Milton shows in the closing lines. But the structure of the poem, whereby it uses the panegyric tradition to establish the appropriate relation of poet and patron and thus builds a coherent organization which leads to a vision of the true rewards of true greatness, is far more unified than anything we find in the early epicedia. "Mansus" is far from being one of Milton's great poems, but its weaknesses are not structural. Furthermore the strength of the structure is evidence of the progress Milton has made between the awkward epicedia of 1626 and these carefully built poems of the late 1630s. Because "Mansus" is closely linked in its structural sophistication with "Lycidas" and "Epitaphium Damonis," it helps, in spite of its flaws, to clarify the achievement of the other two poems.

The similarities and differences of "Mansus" and these other two poems cast light on another important aspect of "Mansus." In the other two poems of this period—"Lycidas," written a year before "Mansus," and "Epitaphium Damonis," a year after—the world of mortals is tainted. Lycidas received no proper reward here below and death came too soon; Damon's death also, from a purely human point of view, was senseless and, until the closing vision, it was in many ways worse than that of the animals. Each poem progresses from the polluted natural world to the Christian supernatural community which resolves the earlier dilemmas by surmounting and abandoning the natural world.

"Mansus" is significantly different and becomes a considerably richer poem if, while we read it, we keep in mind what Milton had just done in "Lycidas" and what he would soon do in the "Epitaphium." This is not, of course, to urge that the three poems form a unified trilogy, but only to suggest that certain inherent qualities of "Mansus" appear in sharper outline when we contrast it with the other two poems.

"Mansus" represents the natural world as having its own logic, rewards, and happiness. The result of Manso's help to Tasso is "felix concordia." The "pia officia" of Manso continue after Tasso's death, and it is important that they should. On the other hand, in "Lycidas" the question "... What boots it with uncessant care / To tend the homely slighted Shepherd's trade?" (64-65) implies (at this point in the poem, and in the natural world) quite a different answer.

"Mansus" also presents a different world-view from that in "Epitaphium Damonis," where the "certa praemia" (36) for Damon leave the world's essential dilemma unsolved and insoluble except by supernatural means. But in "Mansus" the picture of human society is one of harmony and happiness. Manso's acts bring satisfaction to Marino not only while Marino is still alive, but even when he is dead: "Nec manes pietas tua chara fefellit amici" (15) ("And your affectionate devotion has not disappointed your friend's spirit"). Therefore Milton is confident of his own happiness after death partly because of the hope for the support of patrons like Manso who will preserve his fame—the "praemia certa bonorum" (94) he calls this support in a phrase that anticipates the "certa praemia" of "Epitaphium Damonis."

The death-theme on which "Mansus" concludes is not simply tacked on as a kind of self-flattering ending to a poem which began in praise of someone else. Death pervades the whole poem—Tasso is dead, so is Marino, and the name of Manso, who is an old man, is linked with the ashes of Gallus and Etruscan Maecenas. Manso's great service has been to rescue the dead poets from oblivion in the tomb:

> Nec satis hoc visum est in utrumque, & nec pia cessant
> Officia in tumulo, cupis integros rapere Orco,
> Quá potes, atque avidas Parcarum eludere leges.
>
> (17-19)

> But you were not content to do merely this much for either poet, and your loving fidelity did not end at the tomb. As far as lies within your power, you labor to snatch them uninjured out of Hades and to cheat the voracious laws of the Fates.

And the fame of the long-dead kings of Britain will, Milton hopes, find life again through his own poetry.

The connections between the panegyric and the elegy are of course close; elegies are so naturally panegyric that the portmanteau word "elogy," as a combination of "elegy" and "eulogy," is not rare in the seventeenth century.[26] But while elegies are commonly panegyric, panegyrics are not necessarily elegiac and especially not, as in "Mansus," when the person praised is still alive, with the traditional *topos* of the concluding Heavenly vision involving the poet himself, rather than his patron or friend, blissfully smiling at his own happy circumstances.

These two genres are ultimately fused in "Mansus" because of the concept of death and after-life embodied in the poem. In "Mansus" the after-life is far from other-worldly in the way that the after-life of "Lycidas" and "Epitaphium Damonis" is. Poets like Horace, Vergil, Tasso, Marino, and Milton have enjoyed the friendship of Gallus, Maecenas, and Manso in this world; and after death, "Mansus" implies, they derive a very human pleasure from knowing that they are still honored here below. The universes of "Lycidas" and "Epitaphium Damonis" are tragically fractured: true justice and true bliss come about only in Heaven by the uniquely Christian miracle and not in the world of mortals. But the universe of "Mansus" is unified across the grave—a community of achievements, homage, and happiness, both here and hereafter.[27]

A key factor which integrates the universe of "Mansus" and defeats death and time is art—the art of Homer, Vergil, Horace, Tasso, and Marino—the art of Apollo, whose songs moved even the rocks and trees:

> Tum neque ripa suo, barathro nec fixa sub imo,
> Saxa stetere loco, nutat Trachinia rupes,
> Nec sentit solitas, immania pondera, silvas,
> Emotaeque suis properant de collibus orni,
> Mulcenturque novo maculosi carmine lynces.
>
> (65-69)

Then neither the banks nor the rocks fixed in the lowest depths of the chasm stood fast in their places; the Trachinian cliff swayed and no longer felt the vast weight of its familiar forests; the trees were moved and hastened down from their hills and the spotted lynxes became gentle at the unfamiliar song.

The art of Milton will defeat death and time by summoning back "invictae sociali foedere mensae, / Magnanimos Heroas" (82-83) ("the magnanimous heroes of the table which their mutual fidelity made invincible"). The fidelity of the Arthurian knights unified their world; the art of the poets and the appropriate fidelity of patrons to the poets unify the world of Milton and Manso.

Thus generically "Mansus" is a panegyric, and its use of the tradition is essential to what it is as a poem. By using and at the same time defying the tradition, by consciously reversing the traditional roles of the personae of the poem, and by producing a functional dissonance between the poem and its panegyric predecessors, Milton creates something which is simultaneously both conventional and unique. It is a poem which praises Manso, but also one which expands beyond an encomium of the old man to a vision of a universe in which such good men live. And in doing so it embodies what it speaks of: it helps to transmit the continuity of the historic community of panegyric poems through the traditions of its generic ancestors in the same fashion that the old man has carried on the customs of his spiritual ancestors, Herodotus, Gallus, and Maecenas. Ultimately the poem finds its integrity not only in the extra-poetic relation of Milton and Manso, but also in the poem's unified structure which imparts dynamic force to a vision of a universe brought into harmony by mutual trust, respect, and affection transcending human mortality.

VIII

"Epitaphium Damonis" as the Transcendence over the Pastoral

Vos cedite silvae

"Epitaphium Damonis" in some ways marks the end of a period in Milton's career. It was the last of the three long pastoral poems that followed *Comus*; it was, in fact, his last poem in the pastoral tradition. With the exception of the ad hoc verse letter to John Rouse and some tags in his prose, "Epitaphium Damonis" was Milton's last poem in Latin. It was also the last poem of any length to appear until the publication of *Paradise Lost*.

In some ways "Epitaphium Damonis" is intentionally and explicitly a terminal point in Milton's career. The poem states that he is now turning away from Latin and from pastoral poetry; and it is one of the purposes of this chapter to explore how Milton embodies these ideas not only in the words, but in the very structure of the poem. The fact that Milton was about to abandon the writing of poetry and turn his attention chiefly to prose and to matters of church and state is neither explicit nor implicit in the poem. Quite the contrary, "Epitaphium Damonis" looks as if it were a self-conscious prelude to the writing of an epic poem. It openly discusses the idea of writing an Arthurian epic in lines 162-78, although of course the Arthurian epic was never written. Instead, the story of "Adam Unparadis'd," begun shortly after the completion of "Epitaphium Damonis," eventually evolved from a tragedy into the epic form.

But "Epitaphium Damonis" is, nevertheless, a prelude to *Paradise Lost* in some ways, as well of course as being a first-rate poem in its own right. "Epitaphium Damonis" looks forward overtly to an Arthurian epic which never appeared, but it also embodies structural techniques which will characterize both of Milton's great epics. Like both *Paradise Lost* and *Paradise Regained*, "Epitaphium Damonis" is written not merely within a traditional form; it also steps outside the form, at times accepting and at times rejecting the tradition. And it uses this acceptance/rejection to impart a directional thrust to the organization of the poem. In the second chapter we saw the operation of this technique in *Paradise Lost*, and in the poems preceding "Epitaphium Damonis," we have seen Milton working his way in the direction of this kind of structure. "Elegia Prima" showed early signs of this and "Mansus" used this technique as a major organizing principle. In "Epitaphium Damonis" Milton has at last arrived at the full development of the poetic method which organizes, unifies, and gives structural impetus to the great epics which follow—*Paradise Lost* and *Paradise Regained*. In a sense "Epitaphium Damonis" is a prelude to *Paradise Lost*, but it is not a hesitant attempt; it is a fully developed poem which, in a little more than two hundred lines, integrates the same kind of dynamic unity which will shape the ten thousand lines of *Paradise Lost*.

Nominally, and especially in the opening lines, "Epitaphium Damonis" makes obvious use of the continuity of the pastoral tradition. In fact, the verbal tags from his Greek and Latin predecessors make up an almost endless list stultifyingly similar to the list of sources for the conventions in "Mansus."[1] An important element, however, of Milton's dependence on the pastoral tradition is that, like Theocritus, Moschus, Vergil in the eighth eclogue, and countless other pastoral poets, Milton uses a refrain. The wording of the refrain, "Ite domum impasti, domino jam non vacat, agni" ("Go home unfed, for your master has no time for you, my lambs") recalls line 44 in Vergil's seventh eclogue: "Ite domum pasti, si quis pudor, ite iuvenci" ("Go home, my well-fed steers, if you have any shame, go home!"). In that eclogue Vergil gives the line to a shepherd named Thyrsis, which is of course the pastoral name that Milton assumes in "Epitaphium Damonis." Milton's wording in his refrain also resembles the last line in Vergil's tenth and last eclogue: "Ite domum saturae, venit Hesperus, ite capellae" (77) ("Get ye home, my full-fed goats—the Evening-star comes—get ye home!").

Traditional though Milton's refrain may be, however, his treatment of it is not traditional. He follows the convention by the insertion of a recurring line, but the line, instead of being repetitious as is conventional in the pastoral, develops quite different meanings at different points in the poem, and these progressive changes of meaning are among the most important structural elements of the poem. Even after the refrain's final recurrence, forty lines from the end of the poem, it returns in a significantly transmuted form: "Ite procul lacrymae, purum colit aethera Damon" (203) ("Begone, my tears! Damon dwells in the pure aether"), as Thyrsis at last achieves his ecstatic vision of the transfigured Damon. This transmuted form is significant because it now makes explicit the changes which have been implicit in the refrain as it has returned with identical wording but a progressively developing context.

The refrain actually gives the poem much of its structure; the repetitions within different contexts mark the poem's progress and give it the impetus by which it moves from one state of mind to another. And the ultimate absence of a refrain, in the last forty lines, is as significant as its repeated presence in the beginning and middle of the poem.

Now to examine the structure of the poem in detail. The first thirty-four lines constitute a segment that can be separated and examined in isolation. After the usual plea[2] of the pastoral elegy to the nymphs and a slight account (9-13) of the physical circumstances of Damon's death, the poem glides gently among the flocks, and Thyrsis "simul assuetâ sedítque sub ulmo" (15) ("sat down under the accustomed elm") in sibilant calm, only to burst out passionately, "Tum verò âmissum tum denique sentit amicum" (16) ("then truly, then at last, he felt the loss of his friend") with a depth of feeling that startles us in this landscape of stereotypes. Thyrsis continues, angered at the responsibilities which intrude themselves upon his grief:

> Coepit & immensum sic exonerare dolorem.
> Ite domum impasti, domino jam non vacat, agni.
>
> (17-18)

And he began to pour out his tremendous sorrow in words like these: "Go home unfed, for your master has no time for you, my lambs."

And we have the refrain for the first time.

But the poem quickly subsides into competent pastoralism; no one would feel disgraced at being memorialized by lines 19-25:

> Hei mihi! quae terris, quae dicam numina coelo,
> Postquam te immiti rapuerunt funere Damon;
> Siccine nos linquis, tua sic sine nomine virtus
> Ibit, & obscuris numero sociabitur umbris?
> At non ille, animas virgâ qui dividit aureâ,
> Ista velit, dignumque tui te ducat in agmen,
> Ignavumque procul pecus arceat omne silentum.
> > Ite domum impasti, domino jam non vacat, agni.

Ah me! what deities shall I profess in earth or heaven, now that they have torn you mercilessly away in death, O Damon? And do you leave us in this way and shall your virtue go down without a name to be numbered with the company of the unknown dead? But he who divides the souls with his golden wand would not wish this, for he would lead you into a company worthy of you and would warn off the whole brutal herd of the silent dead. Go home unfed, for your master has no time for you, my lambs.

At the same time, however, no one would expect immortality from such a monument. For an instant the poem hints at its orientation toward the heavenly company by its passing contempt for the "obscuris umbris" and the "ignavum pecus." As Keightley points out,[3] "*Pecus* is a strange term to use for the dead," and he notes that Milton's line reflects Vergil's "Ignavum fucos, pecus a praesepibus arcent,"[4] where "pecus" has its normal meaning.

Of course Keightley is right: "pecus" is indeed a strange term, with its strangeness in Milton's poem underlined by the resemblance to the line in Vergil. It is of course the kind of word that Milton wants at this point. As the "Argumentum" to the poem states, Thyrsis "suamque solitudinem hoc carmine deplorat" ("bewailed himself and his loneliness in this song"). Thyrsis is searching for love and companionship. The difference between the instinct of the herd and the love of true friends is the very conflict which the poem explores more fully in lines 94-111:

Epitaphium Damonis

Hei mihi quam similes ludunt per prata juvenci,
Omnes unanimi secum sibi lege sodales.

(94-95)

How like one another are the steers at play in the meadows,
all mutually companions together.

It is only resolved at the very end of the poem, in the beatific vision ·
of the "coelicolae" joined in harmonious and eternal ecstasy. This
theme of friendship as opposed to gregariousness pervades the whole
section (19-25), and when the refrain occurs for the second time, at
line 26, it is no mere mechanical repetition. The context of the poem
has changed the meaning of the refrain by stressing ideas of love and
loneliness, and the "agni" of the refrain have become not merely
part of the pastoral furniture but integral elements in the patterning of
the poem. Thyrsis, deprived by death of true companionship, brushes
away the insensitive herd that distracts him.

In lines 27-34 the poem comes to a pseudo-conclusion as Thyrsis
predicts pastoral and pagan immortality for Damon, who will be
honored "post Daphnin," but nevertheless honored.[5] Daphnis,
mentioned in the first line of the poem, is of course a usual inhabitant
of pastoral poems.[6] Thus by line 34 Thyrsis has promised Damon a
measure of fame, but of course this is only a trifle compared with the
eternal bliss Damon will achieve in the scene described in the
concluding lines of the poem.

This is an important pivotal point in the poem (lines 27-34) and the
fact that Milton's grief is deep and sincere should not distract us from
perceiving the skill with which he manages his structure: a conflict
seems to have been resolved because Damon will not be forgotten
among the dim shades. This is as it should be; but the intercalated "Ite
domum impasti" (35), the third occurrence of the refrain, immediately destroys the momentary calm. For Damon, "Haec tibi certa
manent" ("For you these rewards are certainly in store"), but
what of Thyrsis, left with his loneliness—"At mihi quid tandem fiet
modò?" ("But what at last is to become of me?"). That is the
problem with which he began—"suamque solitudinem"—and now
the poem wrenches itself around to face this dilemma of love and
death:

109

> quis mihi fidus
> Haerebit lateri comes, ut tu saepe solebas
> Frigoribus duris?
>
> (37-39)

What faithful companion will stay by my side as you always did when the cold was cruel?

For an instant we glimpse a depth of personal emotion (as so often in the Latin poems and so rarely in the English poems) that is almost too painful. But the poem immediately resumes its pastoral wrappings:

> Sive opus in magnos fuit eminùs ire leones
> Aut avidos terrere lupos praesepibus altis?
>
> (41-42)

Whether the work were to chase the lions to close quarters or to frighten the hungry wolves away from the high sheepfolds?

It is unlikely that Diodati and Milton ever encountered any lions or wolves in London, and surely it was passages such as this that led Dr. Johnson to dismiss the whole poem with the remark that it was "written in the common but childish imitation of pastoral life." But within this ancient garment of pastoralism the poem leaps to life with the cry "Pectora cui credam?" ("To whom shall I confide my heart?"), a plea more poignant when placed in the midst of these bucolic conventions. Now the poem rushes on: there is "quis me lenire docebit / Mordaces curas?" ("Who will teach me to alleviate my mordant cares?") the echo from Horace[7] with great compression linking what must have been Milton's and Diodati's schoolroom reading; there is "quis longam fallere noctem / Dulcibus alloquiis?" ("shorten the long night with delightful conversation"), another echo from Horace[8] which also prepares for the section to come on the plans for the epic, lines 162-78, surely one of the subjects of the long nights' talks had Diodati lived; then there are the "L'Allegro"-like details of their friendship, "grato cùm sibilat igni / Molle pyrum, & nucibus strepitat focus" ("While the ripe pear simmers before the grateful fire and nuts burst on the hearth"). Now when the refrain interrupts at line 50 ("Ite domum impasti") it intrudes almost as abruptly into the warmth of the fireside scene as the sheep break into the reverie of Thyrsis, and once again the refrain is functioning structurally to move the poem ahead.

In the midst of this rustic realism, which continues with a description of the snoring peasant, "stertit sub sepe colonus" ("the ploughman snores under the hedge"), the pitiful loneliness creeps in again:

> Quis mihi blanditiásque tuas, quis tum mihi risus,
> Cecropiosque sales referet, cultosque lepores?
>   Ite domum impasti, domino jam non vacat, agni.
> At jam solus agros, jam pascua solus oberro,
> Sicubi ramosae densantur vallibus umbrae,
> Hic serum expecto.

$$(55-60)$$

> Who then will bring back to me your mirth and Attic salt, your culture and humor? Go home unfed, for your master has no time for you, my lambs. Alone now I stray through the fields, alone through the pastures, wherever the branches make dense shadows in the valleys, there I wait for evening.

Milton's mastery of onomatopoeia, by the way, was of course not limited to his English verse, and the next line, "Triste sonant, fractaeque agitata crepuscula silvae" (61) ("Over my head the rain and the southeast wind make their sad sound in the restless twilight of the wind-swept trees"), will stand with any of his more famous passages in English. The line has further implications to which we shall return later.

The entry of the conventional shepherds, Tityrus, Alphesiboeus, Aegon, and Amyntas, annoys Thyrsis so much that he slips away as the refrain recurs more frequently and the poem summons up what Mark Pattison calls "the dilapidated debris of the Theocritean world"[9]—Mopsus and the nymphs Hyas, Dryope, Aegle, and Chloris. But Thyrsis is no more assuaged by the nymphs and shepherds than the critics have been—"Nil me blanditiae, nil me solantia verba," ("No flattery and words of comfort move me")—and by the time the poem again interjects its "Ite domum impasti" at line 93, we are hearing not only the irritation of Thyrsis with pastoral duties, but also the restlessness of a deeply emotional poem within its pastoral garments.

It is within this context therefore that we ought to read the shepherd's speech a few lines earlier:

> Hîc gelidi fontes, hîc illita gramina musco,
> Hîc Zephiri, hîc placidas interstrepit arbutus undas.
>
> (71-72)

Here are cool springs, here are lawns soft with moss, here are zephyrs, and here the arbutus and the quiet streams whisper together.

This speech, as Milton's editors have pointed out, reflects Gallus's speech in Vergil's tenth eclogue:[10]

> Hic gelidi fontes, hic mollia prata, Lycori,
> Hic nemus; hic ipso tecum consumerer aevo.
>
> (42-43)

Here are cold springs, Lycoris, here soft meadows, here woodland; here, with thee, time alone would wear me away.

On being told this, one could wish that Milton's editors had devoted more time to the function of these resemblances. For the reader to be reminded of the passage in Vergil is not enough; he must also be aware of the countless thousands of pastoral poems, some like "Lycidas" very good and some others very bad, which have intervened between the tenth eclogue of Vergil and the "Epitaphium Damonis." The time for pastoralism, attractive though it once was in Vergil's hands and as echoed by Milton's shepherds in calling to Thyrsis, has passed. Thyrsis replies, "Ista canunt surdo, frutices ego nactus abibam" ("They sing to deaf ears, for I slip away into the thickets and am gone"). He is rejecting the charms of the cool waters and of Vergil's pastorals. He is saying, with words repeated but the meanings new, "Ite domum impasti, domino jam non vacat, agni" (74). He is saying that it is not enough to reward Damon, as Thyrsis did in lines 30-32,

> Illi tibi vota secundo
> Solvere post Daphnin, post Daphnin dicere laudes
> Gaudebunt.

To you, next after Daphnis, it shall be their delight to pay their vows, and sing praises of you next after Daphnis.

He is saying that it is Diodati who is dead; the old rituals have no power on such an occasion.

The poem returns its attention (94-111) to the central dilemma: we human beings are not content to be like the herd; we are not bulls, wild asses, or sparrows; but we pay a price for being above the herd—"aeternum ... in saecula damnum" (111). The refrain, entering again at line 112, is never more effective. Thyrsis's rejection of his sheep has grown from an expression of annoyance early in the poem to what at this point is an anguished realization of the tragedy of being human. And it is the refrain which functions both to unite the structure of the poem and to give impetus to the structure.

The dilemma of love and loss which seemed half-solved at line 34 now drives Thyrsis's spirits to their lowest point in lines 113-23 as he berates himself for having gone to Italy, with the result that he was absent when Damon died. But of course the poem cannot rest there, any more than "Lycidas" could have concluded with the image of Lycidas's bones being washed beyond the stormy Hebrides. As Thyrsis recalls his Italian stay he remembers the excitement of life there; but even while he was there his thoughts were on Damon and (although, unknown to him, Damon was already dead) he imagined what Damon might be doing, the long talks they might have had concerning the medicines and herbs of which Damon had expert knowledge. But these recollections can lead nowhere—"pereant herbae, pereant artesque medentum" ("let the herbs and simples perish, let all the arts of the doctors perish")—if they are useless in saving Damon.

As for Thyrsis, he was trying something "grande" on his pipes, something whose grave notes were too much for his pastoral flute. Self-consciously calling himself somewhat turgid, Thyrsis pushes away his pastoralism in a phrase of considerable intricacy:

> dubito quoque ne sim
> Turgidulus, tamen & referam, vos cedite silvae.
> Ite domum impasti ...
>
> (159-61)

I am afraid that I am in vain, yet I will relate it. Give way, then, O forest. Go home unfed ...

The phrase "vos cedite, silvae," as countless editors have noted, echoes Vergil's "concedite silvae," in the tenth eclogue, the eclogue from which Milton derives his refrain. But Milton is using the phrase "vos cedite silvae" to reinforce the stages of progression through which the whole poem has been moving. Likewise, Milton echoes what was Vergil's farewell to the eclogues. He does this in a phrase which picks up his own title to this section of his Latin poems: in a convention originating with Statius in the first century A.D., poets frequently called their collections of brief or minor poems "silvae" (literally "timber" and then metaphorically "rough or unpolished verses")—"sketches" is perhaps the best English equivalent.[11]

This meaning also underlies line 61 of "Epitaphium Damonis"—"fractaeque agitata crepuscula silvae." This is not merely onomatopoetic pastoralism: for Milton, twilight, "crepuscula," has come for the worn-out time of "fractae silvae." By now Milton has written his seven Latin elegies and eleven poems in Greek and Latin which he called, in the 1645 publication of his poems, "Sylvarum Liber." Milton is leaving pastoral poetry, and similar "silvae," for epic poetry; and he is leaving behind these brief poems of his youth for "something so written to aftertimes, as they should not willingly let it die ..." written "to God's glory, by the honour and instruction of my country."[12]

When the refrain recurs in the next line (161), for the next-to-last time, it is no mere rote repetition of a pastoral convention; it is a challenging reminder of how the poem has developed generically from its early obedience to the old poetic rituals to a farewell which takes the poem beyond the conventions of pastoralism into a genus of its own.

This technique of using the organization of the poem as a means of commenting on, and therefore giving structure to, the poem, is fully developed in "Epitaphium Damonis." And this technique is the reason for seeing the poem as a pivotal point in Milton's career. It is not only a poem about Diodati. In not only being itself, but in being about itself and what it is, by its structural progressions and its use of its poetic tradition, it acts as the major link between Milton's early poems and his last masterpieces: the dynamic thrust of *Paradise Lost,* as we saw in chapter II, derived in part from the juxtaposition of Adam and Satan with the epic tradition. And in chapter X we shall examine how Milton carries this use of traditional form as a structural force to its ultimate limits in *Paradise Regained.*

Epitaphium Damonis

Thus, to return to "Epitaphium Damonis," Thyrsis is led to the subject of the projected epic. This passage is one which Tillyard found digressive and a lapse of taste. But the justification for Milton's structure lies in the fact that Thyrsis's interests turned to poetry just as Damon's turned to medicine; quite logically their conversations, the cessation of which the poem lamented in line 47, would have turned to these things. Woodhouse, who as usual reads Milton with great understanding, says this section is

> a digression, indeed, only in appearance, for it has its own justification—and it is as skilful as bold.... It is bold because it *seems* to carry us away from Diodati; skilful because Diodati is ever and anon recalled, and justified because there is nothing arbitrary about it. *For in fact the seeming digression is the turning-point of the poem:* the shadows fall back and a subtle but perfectly recognizable train of associations leads us to the triumphant close.[13]

With increasing excitement Thyrsis sets forth his plans and repeats that his shepherd's pipe is no longer adequate. Whether "fistula" (169) means Latin verse or pastoral verse is the subject of some dispute;[14] but it is not an important dispute in this context because whichever of the two it may mean, the lines say in substance what the whole poem has been saying through its structure: that the tradition of Theocritean/Vergilian pastoralism, which the early part of the poem embodies, has worn too thin, that the ritual of nymphs and shepherds is threadbare. Biographically considered, the poem is predicting what was in effect to be true: that this will be Milton's last Latin and/or pastoral poem (except for the poem to Rouse seven years later).

But biographical considerations operate outside the structure of "Epitaphium Damonis"; within the structure this section acts as an instrument for increasing the excitement which has replaced the melancholy of the lines preceding it. Also, for reasons we shall explore in a moment, it begins the turning point of the poem, of which Woodhouse spoke in the passage quoted above. It is turning the poem toward the realm of art. Now the poet is ready to sing of epic heroes:

Ipse ego Dardanias Rutupina per aequora puppes
Dicam, & Pandrasidos regnum vetus Inogeniae,

Brennùmque Arviragúmque duces, priscùmque Belinum.
(162-64)

> I, for my part, am resolved to tell the story of the Trojan ships
> in the Rutupian sea and of the ancient kingdom of Inogene,
> the daughter of Pandrasus, and of the chiefs, Brennus and Ar-
> viragus, and of old Belinus.

Speaking now in the tones of an epic poet, he looks for fame not in
Latin but in English:

Et Thamesis meus ante omnes, & fusca metallis
Tamara, & extremis me discant Orcades undis.
Ite domum impasti, domino jam non vacat, agni.
(177-79)

> And before them all my Thames, and the Tamora, which min-
> erals discolor, and if the Orkneys in their distant seas will
> learn my song. Go home unfed, for your master has no time
> for you, my lambs.

Now this last repetition of the refrain brushes aside the flocks, but not
with annoyance, anger, despair, or anguish. He dismisses them
resoundingly, for the last time in the poem. He lifts up his eyes from
the pastoral to the epic, and from the Latin language to the English,
and the meaning of the refrain has now changed almost totally. Pastoral poetry is something inferior, something to be surmounted.

"Epitaphium Damonis" differs markedly from "Lycidas" in
its pastoralism; for, though "Lycidas" is a pastoral, it is also a
poem concerned with the pastoral tradition and, in a sense, moves out
of its pastoralism to look back at it, always, however, remaining pastoral. While it manages a structural progression from one set of positions—both poetic and extra-poetic—at the beginning to another set
at the end, the progression is always embodied in the pastoral metaphor. "Epitaphium Damonis" disengages from pastoralism even
further: as the poem progresses, it derives part of its impetus by
spurning pastoralism. The vacuity and misguidance of Mopsus, Tityrus (who seems to stand for Vergil himself in line 117), Aegon, and
the others is a technique for using the total pastoral tradition (or
rejecting that tradition) to carry the poem forward to its resolution.
This is not to say that a poem is somehow better for not being pasto-

ral; it is simply to say that, in "Epitaphium Damonis," when Milton follows the pastoral tradition strictly, he does so to suit his structural ends. When he flagrantly breaks with the tradition, it is because that is what the poem must do to be the effective, dynamic unity that it is.

The pastoralism of "Epitaphium Damonis" has important connections with the Renaissance idea of the hierarchy of literary genres, which placed epic poetry highest of all, hymns, psalms, and odes as the loftiest types of lyric poetry, and pastoral poetry lowest. This critical concept becomes, in "Epitaphium Damonis," a poetic device for giving structure to the poem—that is, for imparting a logic and direction to the progression of the poem toward the vision of the transfigured Damon in Heaven. The early parts of "Epitaphium Damonis" drew some of their impetus from clothing the deeply personal outcries ("Pectora cui credam") in the diguises of pastoralism, much as if there were a poem within the poem, swaddled by the ancient tradition. Thus the poem derives a great part of its vigor, its upward surge, from using the pastoral metaphor as something to burst through. The ecstatic hymn emerges triumphantly at the end of the poem not only in terms of ideas and images, but also in terms of poetic structure.

Milton is making use of a tradition scattered all through Renaissance literary criticism. J.C. Scaliger, for example, condescendingly calls pastoral poetry "antiquissimum idem, et mollissimum, et simplicissimum, et ineptissimum."[15] George Puttenham, in *Of Poets and Poesy,* speaks of pastoral poets who "in base and humble stile by maner of Dialogue, vttered the priuate and familiar talke of the meanest sort of men, as shepheards, heywards, such like: such among the Greekes *Theocritus,* and *Virgill* among the Latines."[16] Sir Philip Sidney, in defending pastoral poetry, asks, "Is it then the Pastorall *Poeme* which is misliked? (For perchance where the hedge is lowest they will soonest leape over) is the poore pipe disdained, which sometimes out of Mælibeus mouth, can shewe the miserie of people, under hard Lords?"[17] Milton is moving beyond pastoralism in "Epitaphium Damonis," and he not only uses the poem to say this, he makes the saying of it a means of imparting structure and impetus to the poem.

Further, the poem uses language in a fashion somewhat similar: "Epitaphium Damonis" is written in Latin, the language of Vergil's eclogues, but it is written about the abandoning of Latin as the language of poetry. This theme of dynamic emergence is not only part of the theology and psychology of the poem, but pervades almost every element. And its connections with the structure of *Paradise Lost,* where the higher concept of epic heroism replaces the lower as the poem progresses, are very close. The manner in which "Epitaphium Damonis" manages pastoralism is a logical predecessor of the way that *Paradise Lost* manages the epic form. And after *Paradise Lost, Paradise Regained* is a further extension of the direction in which Milton is developing—it is the logical conclusion to Milton's use of poetic structure.

In the concluding section of "Epitaphium Damonis" Milton supports this theme of dynamic emergence with an image which leads the poem to its final vision: the extremely complex images of the trophies brought from Italy, the "bina pocula," concerning which there has been so much controversy:

> Haec tibi servabam lentâ sub cortice lauri,
> Haec, & plura simul, tum quae mihi pocula Mansus,
> Mansus Chalcidicae non ultima gloria ripae
> Bina dedit, mirum artis opus, mirandus & ipse,
> Et circùm gemino caelaverat argumento:
> In medio rubri maris unda, & odoriferum ver
> Littora longa Arabum, & sudantes balsama silvae,
> Has inter Phoenix divina avis, unica terris
> Caeruleùm fulgens diversicoloribus alis
> Auroram vitreis surgentem respicit undis.
> Parte alia polus omnipatens, & magnus Olympus,
> Quis putet? hic quoque Amor, pictaeque in nube pharetrae,
> Arma corusca faces, & spicula tincta pyropo;
> Nec tenues animas, pectúsque ignobile vulgi
> Hinc ferit, at circùm flammantia lumina torquens
> Semper in erectum spargit sua tela per orbes
> Impiger, & pronos nunquam collimat ad ictus,
> Hinc mentes ardere sacrae, formaeque deorum.

(180-97)

These things I was keeping for you in the tough-barked laurel. These and more also—and in addition the two cups which Manso gave me—Manso, who is not the least glory of the Chalcidian shore. They are a marvellous work of art, and he is a marvellous man. Around them goes an engraving with a double motif. In the middle are the waves of the Red Sea, the perfumed springtime, the far-stretching shores of Arabia, and the groves that distill balsam. Among those trees the Phoenix, the divine bird which is unique on earth, gleams cerulean with parti-colored wings, and watches Aurora rise over the glassy waters. In another part are the wide-spreading sky and mighty Olympus. Who would suppose such a thing? Here is Cupid also, his quiver painted against a cloud, his gleaming arms, his torches and his darts of bronze tincture, the color of flame. From that height he does not wound frivolous spirits or the ignoble hearts of the rabble, but—looking around him with flaming eyes—he tirelessly scatters his darts aloft through the spheres and never points his shots downward. That is why the minds of the elect and the essences of the gods themselves are enkindled.

This is probably the most difficult passage in what is, in so many other ways as well, an extremely difficult poem. And the intricacies of Milton's poetic structure have been obscured by a scholarly controversy which is not of the first order of importance. The controversy is, of course, over whether the cups mentioned in the poem refer to actual cups given by Manso to Milton, or whether they refer perhaps to something else. Milton's editors note that the first idyll of Theocritus introduces a cup—offered to Thyrsis—which is wrought with elaborate carvings; and Vergil mentions a pair of cups in his third eclogue. Therefore Keightley thinks that Milton's *pocula* were merely a poetic fiction.[18] But Masson, Jerram, and MacKellar[19] think they were "an actual pair of cups or chased goblets which Milton received" (Masson). John Black, on the other hand, suggests that these are not real cups but rather a pair of books which are not only from Manso but also by Manso.[20] And De Filippis, agreeing with him, points out that Manso's *Erocallia* and *Poesie Nomiche* fit neatly as gifts to John Milton and therefore as the cups given to Thyrsis.[21]

In any case, and the question may be as insoluble as that of the two-handed engine, the cups do have functions, both major and minor, within the poetic structure. For example, they are decorated with such inevitable resurrection symbols as the sea, springtime, the Phoenix,[22] and Aurora rising from the waters. But more important to the structure of the poem is the beauty of the cups and of the engraved figure of Amor, and here the poem arrives at its second pivotal point. It is here that "Epitaphium Damonis" manages its transition from the beautiful things of this world—poems of the deeds of heroes and cups wrought with great skill—to the eternal beauties of Heaven; the transition turns, of course, on the figure of Amor.

To understand the structural function in the poem of the cups and the figure of Amor we need to turn briefly to the Platonic and neo-Platonic tradition and to read the poem against this background. Love, to Plato[23] and the neo-Platonists, was the agency whereby one made the ascent to absolute Goodness, Beauty, and Truth. Marsilio Ficino puts it this way: Love unites the mind more quickly, more closely, and more stably with God than does knowledge, because the force of knowledge consists more in distinction, that of love in union."[24] This ascent by means of Love begins with the physical world:

> The splendor of the highest Good itself shines in individual things, and where it shines more fittingly, there it especially allures him who contemplates it, excites him who looks at it.... There it is apparent that the Soul is inflamed by divine splendor, glowing in the beautiful person as in a mirror, and secretly lifted up as by a hook in order to become God.[25]

"This metaphor of the hook," Kristeller notes, "shows the real meaning of Ficino's theory of beauty. The beauty of things is the lure by which the Soul of the lover is led back to God."[26]

Milton comes close to saying the same thing in a letter to Charles Diodati dated 23 September 1637:

> What besides God hath resolved concerning me I know not, but this at least: He hath instilled in me, if into anyone, a vehement love of the beautiful. Not with so much labour, as the fables have it, is Ceres said to have sought her daughter Proserpina as it is my habit day and night to seek for this idea of the beautiful, as for a certain image of the supreme beauty, through all the forms and faces of things (for many are the shapes of things divine) and to follow it as it leads me on by some sure traces which I seem to recognize.[27]

For Ficino this love of beauty was a Daemon, because just as daemons (like the Attendant Spirit in *Comus*) are intermediaries between heaven and earth, so Love holds a mean position between beauty and lack of beauty.[28] This angelic figure of Love, as Merritt Hughes points out,[29] occurs in English poetry as "Spenser's Celestial Cupid," the

> Lord of truth and loialtie
> Lifting himselfe out of the lowly dust
> On golden plumes up to the purest skie.
> (*An Hymne in Honour of Love,* 176-78)

For Milton, Amor serves a very complex function here. First and simplest, Amor is the figure on the cups which Thyrsis received from Mansus (whether the cups are actual, imaginary, or symbolic is irrelevant here). Secondly, as lines 194-97 tell us, Amor, the neo-Platonic force of Love, enkindles the "mentes sacrae" such as Damon, making possible for Damon the Heavenly union which the closing section describes. And this same Amor, operating through the physical beauty of the cups, lifts Thyrsis's eyes to the metaphysical, eternal beauty of his final vision.

But more important, Amor functions to resolve the central dilemma of the poem—that of reconciling man's lofty spirit to the grief that death inflicts. This is of course the dilemma posed again and again by the epicedia, dating back to "Elegia Tertia" thirteen years earlier. And while that early poem was unable to find a poetic structural resolution congruent with the extra-poetic vision of divine bliss, by now, in "Epitaphium Damonis," the structure of the poem becomes one of the main means by which the vision is attained. In "Epitaphium Damonis," Thyrsis envies the lower animals their mindless associations but scorns the "agni" and the "ignavum pecus" (25), so Amor, as the poem emerges to its resolution, passes over the "pectus ignobile vulgi" (193). And this divine Love, which the beauty of the carved physical figure of Amor embodies, inspires the human spirit to achieve a truer and higher union than the physical world permits. So also the regal figure of the divine Amor now towers in a neo-Platonic fashion over the same "amor" (78) which Mopsus suggests as the cause of Thyrsis's sorrow. The pastoral Mopsus is typically wrong: it is not "amor" which caused the sorrow, but "Amor" who will lift the poet beyond his sorrow. And in like fashion the ecstatic hymn which "Epitaphium Damonis" has become soars beyond the conventional pastoralism with which it began.

At last this extremely complex poem achieves its goal, the vision of the transfigured Damon in Heaven, where love is eternal. And now the last vestiges of pastoralism drop away, just as the refrain has by now been left behind; up to now Diodati has been clothed in the pastoral name of Damon, according to the conventions of the pastoral in using "disguises." But now, as the poem approaches its neo-Platonic vision of Truth, Damon casts aside his shepherd garments like the Earl's children in the closing moments of *Comus*. Now (210) he assumes his true (in several senses) name, his "divino nomine," Diodatus, a "gift of God," even though "silvísque vocabere Damon" (211), a phrase which adroitly reminds us of the structural progression of the poem. Now the earthly dilemma of love and death, of the need for companionship that is not merely gregariousness, finds its solution in the true and eternal Love of the celestial marriage feast, Bacchic in its ecstasy and divine in its dedication.

As for Thyrsis, he has surmounted the pseudo-conclusion which led him to ask, "At mihi quid fiet modò?" (37). As the intricate structure of the poem reaches its culmination, what remains for him now as a solace for the agony of his loneliness is the glimpse of divine and eternal Love, and also (and this is part of the poem too) the creation of this pastoral-elegiac hymn to celebrate the eternal joy of his friend—this work of art which, like the cups of Mansus, both embodies and makes possible, through the transcendent direction of its poetic structure, the extra-poetic vision of triumphant bliss which it creates.

IX

Samson Agonistes
and the Tragic Justice of God's Ways

I with this Messenger will go along

Let us now assume that the next major poem that Milton wrote was
Samson Agonistes. For some readers this is almost like asking them to
assume that Marlowe wrote *Hamlet,* so some justification for the assumption is surely necessary. Perhaps the best justification is that of
despair: learned and intelligent readers for years have disagreed over
the date of *Samson Agonistes,* have changed their minds, and at this
point (1974) have produced no real unanimity as to the date of the play.
In a study such as this, a full-blown investigation of all the evidence
would be digressive, and a conclusion based on arguments that are at
some obvious points weak will still be more useful to the subject at hand
than an exhaustive but inconclusive argument which unnecessarily ob-
scures our understanding of the direction of Milton's poetic development.

The disagreements concerning the date of *Samson Agonistes* may be
reduced to the question of a choice among four main periods in
Milton's life: (1) the mid-1640s, shortly after Milton listed the five
suggested titles for plays in the Trinity College manuscript;[1] (2) 1647-
53;[2] (3) 1660-61;[3] (4) 1666-70.[4] The first of these positions places
the play before Milton became totally blind; the second, during the
time he was losing his sight but had at least some hope of its restoration. The first three positions date the play before the publication of
the first edition of *Paradise Lost* in 1667; the last places it after the
completion of *Paradise Lost* and either before or after the writing of
Paradise Regained. None of these positions, however, should force us
to the neat but perhaps false assumption that *Paradise Lost, Paradise*

Regained, and *Samson Agonistes* were written consecutively.[5] If we consider the fact that both Milton's personal life and his professional life were, to put it mildly, tumultuous between the completion of "Epitaphium Damonis" in 1639 or 1640 and the publication of *Paradise Lost* in 1667, it is not difficult to imagine that many of Milton's poems, some perhaps no longer extant, were begun, put aside, taken up again, and if at last completed, then completed in a sequence which has no bearing on the order of their beginning. It is even possible that a forgotten croquet-box in some Irish castle still contains an Arthuriad that Milton never brought to the point of completion.

But the precise date of *Samson Agonistes* is not crucial to this study. It seems to me, for reasons I shall explain, that *Samson Agonistes* bears the marks of a less sophisticated use of the tragic tradition than the use of the epic tradition in *Paradise Lost* and *Paradise Regained,* and for this reason I should prefer to think of *Samson Agonistes* as coming before the two epics. But we are dealing with Milton's only extant tragedy and there are very few fixed points for comparison. In the case of the two epic poems one would still be quite certain on innumerable grounds that *Paradise Lost* antedated *Paradise Regained,* even if there were no external evidence such as their titles or the Elwood anecdote concerning the genesis of *Paradise Regained.* But the relation of the date of *Samson Agonistes* to that of the two epics can only be called uncertain. Since it must be placed somewhere in the sequence of this study, let it be here—that is, before the publication of *Paradise Lost,* and before the composition, or at least the completion, of either of the epics.

The relation of *Samson Agonistes* to Greek tragedy was thoroughly and skillfully dealt with by William Riley Parker more than thirty years ago, and the main direction of Parker's study remains valid.[6] It does not need restating here. One of Parker's points, however, should be stressed: that while *Samson Agonistes* most closely resembles *Oedipus at Colonus,* "Milton's 'debt' to Greek tragedy is a fairly scattered one."[7] This contrasts with Milton's practice in his other mature poems, where his "debt"—"utilization" is a better word—is frequently precise and, as we have seen, highly functional. The question as to why the relation of *Samson Agonistes* to Greek tragedy is different from the relation of "Epitaphium Damonis" to the pastoral tradition, or that of Milton's two epics to those of Homer and Vergil, is not a question with a clear answer. But it is clear and important that the relation of *Samson Agonistes* to Greek tragedy is more modal than instrumental: Milton follows the Greek tradition in *Samson Agonistes,* but he never sets up the active interplay between his poem and the tradition that we find between his two epics and the epics of Vergil and Homer.

In earlier chapters we have examined Milton's use, or lack of use, of poetic means, particularly poetic structure, as a way of solving an extra-poetic problem such as the justification of the death of a good man. In the case of *Samson Agonistes,* an approach to the play from this point of view is complicated by the fact that Samson in the play and Milton after 1652 were totally blind. If one connects these two conditions and makes the connection central to the tragedy, then *Samson Agonistes* becomes a poetic means for Milton's coming to terms with his own physical handicap, just as "Epitaphium Damonis" was a way of coming to terms with his grief at the death of Charles Diodati.

But there are several difficulties with this approach to the play, the most obvious being that it assumes that Milton began the play after 1652, when he became blind; or if he began the play at an earlier date, that he later revised it to relate it to his own blindness. These conditions may have existed, but the proof is lacking.

A more serious objection to this autobiographical reading of the play is that Samson's condition resembles Milton's only in the fact of their blindness, even assuming that Milton was indeed blind at the time of the writing of the play. Samson's blindness was imposed on him by violence and by his enemies as a means of punishing him and leaving him impotent; it was a just punishment in that Samson had been foolish enough to allow himself to be betrayed by a woman.

Judged from his other writings, Milton viewed his own blindness in a totally different way. In his *Defensio Secunda* he speaks of his own blindness in some of the greatest prose he ever wrote, but in a way quite unrelated to the condition of Samson:

> Hence, when that office against the royal defence was publicly assigned me, and at a time when not only my health was unfa-vorable, but when I had nearly lost the sight of my other eye; and my physicians expressly foretold, that if I undertook the task, I should in a short time lose both—in no wise dismayed

at this warning, methought it was no physician's voice I heard—not the voice even of Aesculapius from the shrine of Epidaurus—but of some diviner monitor within; methought, that, by a certain fatality in my birth, two destinies were set before me, on the one hand, blindness, on the other, duty— that I must necessarily incur the loss of my eyes, or desert a sovereign duty.[8]

The personality that emerges from these lines may indeed be as heroic as Samson, but the situation, the problems, and the solutions are quite unrelated to those of Samson in the play.

If we return to Milton's poetry, the sonnet commonly called "On His Blindness" (Sonnet 19, "When I consider ...") closes with the line, "They also serve who only stand and wait." The emotive force of this last line is the subject of some disagreement,[9] but surely all readers will agree on one point with regard to the conclusion of *Samson Agonistes:* in destroying the temple Samson does not serve by standing and waiting. Likewise Sonnet 23 ("To Mr. Cyriack Skinner Upon His Blindness") shows little relation in its ideas, feelings, or development to *Samson Agonistes.* If there is anything of the blind Milton in *Samson Agonistes,* there is a great deal of the blind Milton that is not in the play, and the critic had best retreat to higher and safer ground.

A more productive way to view the play is to separate the author from the protagonist, then to examine the play itself and see what happens. Samson, we are told, is "a person separate to God, / Design'd for great exploits" (31-32). Yet as the play opens he is "Betray'd, Captiv'd, and both my Eyes put out, / Made of my Enemies the scorn and gaze" (33-34). But the Chorus assures us (293-94), "Just are the ways of God, / And justifiable to Men." The central extra-poetic problem here is quite similar to that of "Elegia Tertia," "On the Death of a Fair Infant," "Lycidas," "Epitaphium Damonis," and *Paradise Lost:* that of reconciling the seemingly unjust world in which we live to the justice which Milton believes is God's way. Housman recommends malt as the reconciling force; Milton uses the traditions of poetry—the epicedic, the pastoral, the epic, and in this instance the tragic.

One can see significant differences and similarities between *Samson Agonistes* and his previous poems such as "Elegia Tertia" and "On the Death of a Fair Infant": the early poems were also concerned with historic events, events which actually took place, such as the deaths of Lancelot Andrewes, Anne Phillips, Edward King, and so on. Milton's belief in the Bible as true history answers any objection that a twentieth-century skeptic may have to the differences between the factual basis of Bishop Andrewes's death and that of Samson. Likewise, these earlier poems all use the literary conventions as fictions or metaphors in which to clothe the historical facts. To ask if Milton really dreamed that he saw Bishop Andrewes in Heaven or if *Samson Agonistes* is a precise report of the events is as irrelevant to literary criticism as Dr. Johnson's objection that Milton and Edward King never herded sheep together.

What is more important is that all these poems attempt to move from the fractured, absurd world of human affliction in which death is without meaning to a universe of harmony in which even the greatest human losses have a justification in the Divine plan.

As we have seen, the early poems are marred by structural flaws in managing this transition from the ideas and attitudes at the beginning to those which suffuse the concluding resolution. Gradually Milton manages, by various organizational patterns, to learn the techniques, or to develop for himself the techniques, for the transition to the resolution. By the time Milton has completed *Paradise Lost,* of course, these transitions are no mere obstacles to be overcome; rather they have long since developed into ways of imparting structure to the poem. The dynamism of the transition is not only one of the most important structural elements of the poem, it is part of the "subject," part of the "matter" of the poem as well.

It is hardly surprising then that *Samson Agonistes,* whether it dates from the 1640s or the 1670s, has mastered these difficulties of the early poems. *Samson Agonistes* has the coherent, integrated structure which characterizes "Lycidas," "Epitaphium Damonis," and the other mature poems. And it is by means of its literary form, its "tragicness," that it moves from position to position, at last achieving the reconciliation implicit in its initial conflicts.

This is not, of course, the structure of *Samson Agonistes* that Dr. Johnson saw and attacked in his famous remark that "the poem, therefore, has a beginning and an end which Aristotle himself could not have disapproved; but it must be allowed to want a middle, since nothing passes between the first act and the last, that either hastens or delays the death of Samson."[10]

These remarks, as most critics since Johnson have agreed, result from a misreading of the play, but they are helpful nevertheless for several reasons. First of all, the faults that Dr. Johnson points to are quite marked, as we have seen, in some of Milton's early poems—"Elegia Tertia," "In Obitum Praesulis Eliensis," and others. In "Elegia Tertia" Milton's grief for Andrewes's death is an appropriate beginning, and his vision of the transfigured Andrewes is an appropriate ending, but here indeed the middle is missing.

Dr. Johnson's remark is useful also because, by making us look for and at the structural elements which serve as the middle of the play, we see more clearly the unique whole that the play is. But since the problem of Dr. Johnson's objections to the middle of *Samson Agonistes* has already been much discussed, this analysis need not be extensive. The main task here should be to see how Milton's solution to the structural problems of *Samson Agonistes* is related to his solutions to these problems in his other mature poems.

In brief, Samson appears to us at first faced with two problems. One is the external problem of his bondage to the Philistines, which Milton brings into a sharp focus first by Manoa's plea that Samson allow himself to be ransomed, then by Dalila's attempt to recapture him, then by the taunts of Harapha, and finally by the demand of the messenger that Samson be present to honor the feast of Dagon by a public display of his strength. That the Philistines intend this as Samson's ultimate degradation is clear from Manoa's speech to Samson:

> A worse thing yet remains,
> This day the *Philistines* a popular Feast
> Here celebrate in *Gaza;* and proclaim
> Great Pomp, and Sacrifice, and Praises loud
> To *Dagon,* as thir God who hath deliver'd
> Thee *Samson* bound and blind into thir hands,
> Them out of thine, who slew'st them many a slain.
> So *Dagon* shall be magnifi'd, and God,
> Besides whom is no God, compar'd with Idols,
> Disglorifi'd, blasphem'd, and had in scorn
> By th'Idolatrous rout amidst thir wine.
> (433-43)

Stated in greatly reduced terms, the play is organized around an external conflict between Samson and the Philistines, with the prestige of God and Dagon at stake. Samson is, it seems, physically in the power of the Philistines, and therefore he will lose and Dagon "shall be magnifi'd." The resolution comes, of course, by the ironic reversal wherein Samson complies with the order to attend but in doing so brings ruin on the Philistines and glory to God.

Looked at purely from this point of view, Dr. Johnson's attack seems to have some validity: one might argue that the structure of the play might as well have allowed for the entry of the Officer to remove Samson at, say, line 115 (when the Chorus in fact enters) rather than at line 1308, where Milton actually has the Officer appear. If Samson were immediately to agree—"I with this Messenger will go along"—at about line 200 instead of at line 1384, the tragedy might have proceeded forthwith to the destruction of the temple a thousand lines sooner. The play could have been reduced to four scenes—Samson in captivity, the demand that Samson appear at the feast, Samson's compliance, and finally the report by the messenger of the death of Samson and the Philistines. Thus Manoa, Dalila, and Harapha become structurally unnecessary, and the Chorus and the Messenger serve only to recount the off-stage destruction.

To state Dr. Johnson's argument in its extreme form, everything up to line 1300, where Samson is still refusing to go, is either "beginning" or irrelevant. And the ending of the play, in this reading, begins at line 1384 where Samson says, "I with this Messenger will go along." From that point, the organization of the play leads inexorably to the death of Samson and the Philistines. This leaves a minuscule middle consisting of three lines in a play of 1,758 lines:

> *Sam.* Be of good courage, I begin to feel
> Some rouzing motions in me which dispose
> To something extraordinary my thoughts.
> (1381-83)

If we read the play thus, *Samson Agonistes* leaps from its initial despair to its ultimate peace in as abrupt a fashion as the epicedion for Lancelot Andrewes.

But of course this reading will not do. To return to our so-called "middle" lines (1381-83): if we ask why Samson felt these "rouzing motions" at this point and not sixty lines earlier when he flatly says "I cannot come," a quite different structure to the whole play emerges. He cannot come for the same reasons that he could not come 1,300 lines earlier when he described himself:

> Scarce half I seem to live, dead more than half.
> O dark, dark, dark, amid the blaze of noon,
> Irrecoverably dark, total Eclipse
> Without all hope of day!
>
> (79-82)

God being omnipotent, if Divine inspiration had come to Samson in those first hundred lines, the resolution would have come then. But Milton is not a naive poet, and the resolutions he seeks will come only through a complex structure which follows the tragic tradition.

Samson's struggle, however, is not merely external; it is also internal, and in fact the internal, spiritual struggle is far more important. It is this internal struggle which establishes the structure of the play. Critics have objected to the "marmoreal" quality of Samson's personality, as if he remained unchanged throughout the play. Therefore let us take a closer look at the changes which do take place in Samson. Samson at line 1426, when he leaves with the Officer, is different from, but developed out of, the Samson we see at the beginning, lying

> at random, carelessly diffus'd,
> With languish't head unpropt,
> As one past hope, abandon'd,
> And by himself given over.
>
> (118-21)

The Chorus accurately says to him, "Thou art become (O worst imprisonment!) / The Dungeon of thy self" (155-56). The structure of the play is organized around Samson's freeing himself from this dungeon, and his realization that the physical dungeon is not his most important prison.

At the same time that the beginning of the play is showing us the degraded Samson, it keeps before our eyes the picture of the victorious Samson, chosen by God for great deeds:

> O wherefore was my birth from Heaven foretold
> Twice by an Angel, who at last in sight

> Of both my Parents all in flames ascended
> From off the Altar....
>
> . . . .
>
> Why was my breeding order'd and prescrib'd
> As of a person separate to God,
> Design'd for great exploits....
>
> (23-26, 30-32)

Samson speaks of himself with an unconscious double irony:

> Yet stay, let me not rashly call in doubt
> Divine Prediction; what if all foretold
> Had been fulfilld but through mine own default,
> Whom have I to complain of but my self?
>
> (43-46)

The irony is double in that Samson, seemingly deceived by the prophecy of his high destiny, is actually deceived by the fact that he thinks the prophecy is a deception, while in fact it is a true prophecy.

This double irony is not merely an exercise in rhetorical grammar; Milton is interweaving Samson's triumphant death, which will occur 1,700 lines later, with the picture of his degraded life at the beginning. We have seen the same kind of structural reinforcement in the opening lines of "Lycidas." Interwoven with the image of Lycidas's untimely death are fertility symbols, images of resurrections, and a prosodic pattern which is not random but meticulously distorted. All of these elements act as links with the balanced, harmonious resolution of "Lycidas," and in the early poems, it is the absence of this kind of organization which makes the poetic structure weak.

One of the clearest steps in Samson's advance from despair at the beginning of the play occurs in his dialogue with Manoa. Manoa "comforts" Samson (340-72) by regretting that he ever had a son, and by blaming God for mistreating Samson. Samson's response ("Appoint not heavenly disposition, Father ...") absolves God of the blame and is again self-accusatory, but with a significant difference. Samson's vigorous defence of God's ways is quite different here from his own self-pitying lament in his opening soliloquy ("Why was my breeding order'd and prescrib'd / As of a person separate to God?"). Further, Samson now refuses to admit that his present position is one of total degradation:

> The base degree to which I now am fall'n,
> These rags, this grinding, is not yet so base
> As was my former servitude, ignoble,
> Unmanly, ignominious, infamous,
> True slavery, and that blindness worse then this,
> That saw not how degeneratly I serv'd.
>
> (414-19)

The progress of the play toward Samson's ultimate spiritual redemption has already begun and is surely obvious if we compare his speech here with what he said in his soliloquy only 350 lines before:

> O loss of sight, of thee I most complain!
> Blind among enemies, O worse then chains,
> Dungeon, or beggery, or decrepit age!
>
> (67-69)

In what might be called a miniature Platonic dialectic, Samson has risen, in the first four hundred lines, to an awareness of higher values; the impetus toward his triumphant death has already begun.

This structural linkage of Samson's despairing entry with his victorious exit to bring about the death of himself and his enemies depends on the reintegration of his personality, and this takes place as he faces successive challenges, the first being Manoa's attempt to reinforce Samson's self-pity. And we shall see more clearly the progressive integration of Samson from a dispirited, self-pitying slave to the heroic avenger of his people if we concentrate on what it is that brings about Samson's rejuvenation. In short, it is the challenges themselves that save him; pity and words of comfort are useless or worse. Inactivity is not restful but debilitating; Samson himself says:

> This day a solemn Feast the people hold
> To *Dagon* thir Sea-Idol, and forbid
> Laborious works, unwillingly this rest
> Thir Superstition yields me; hence with leave
> Retiring from the popular noise, I seek
> This unfrequented place to find some ease,
> Ease to the body some, none to the mind
> From restless thoughts, that like a deadly swarm
> Of Hornets arm'd, no sooner found alone,

> But rush upon me thronging, and present
> Times past, what once I was, and what am now.
>
> (12-22)

The reason that some critics have found Samson marmoreal is this characteristic that Milton builds into Samson's personality: Milton repeatedly shows Samson as either flaccid or decisive, but he never lets us see Samson deliberating. Samson never resembles Hamlet, agonizing as he weighs the advantages of two courses. When Samson is given an opportunity to choose, he is not only decisive, he is invigorated by the chance to decide. It is when he is left to himself, inactive, that "restless thoughts ... like a deadly swarm / Of Hornets arm'd, no sooner found alone, / But rush upon me thronging."

Thus Manoa's proferred help to Samson is doubly ironic:

> But for thee what shall be done?
> Thou must not in the mean while here forgot
> Lie in this miserable loathsom plight
> Neglected. I already have made way
> To some *Philistian* Lords, with whom to treat
> About thy ransom: well they may by this
> Have satisfi'd thir utmost of revenge
> By pains and slaveries, worse then death inflicted
> On thee, who now no more canst do them harm.
>
> (478-86)

The irony is double in that Manoa presents a remedy which Samson immediately finds abhorrent and which tends to exacerbate his wounds by emphasizing his impotence. But Samson's revulsion from Manoa's offer—Samson's opportunity to choose a passive escape and therefore his opportunity to reject this passive escape—helps to strengthen him. This occasion for alternatives assists in reconstituting his personality, with the result that the play is carried forward to its tragic/victorious resolution. Manoa means well; Samson takes it ill; but ultimately Manoa's advice has been restorative in its effect.

We see this un-Hamlet-like quality in Samson most clearly in his meeting with Dalila. One might expect the protagonist to waver, to feel the pangs of remembered love, however dead now because of her treachery; but this is not the character of Milton's Samson. As in the meeting with Manoa, the chance to choose is the opportunity to be decisive: "My Wife, my Traytress, let her not come near me" (725) are his first words to her, and then, "Out, out *Hyaena;* these are thy wonted arts" (74). Again, the irony is double. Dalila feigns help, intends harm, and actually benefits Samson by giving him an alternative on which to act, an escape from the "deadly swarm of Hornets" which rush upon him not when he is challenged, but when he is alone and "at rest."

Furthermore, as Parker points out, Samson emerges from his encounter with Dalila close to the renewed hero which he will become. When she enters, Samson greets her with roars of rage, and his dislike for her never wavers. But as he talks to her he becomes more reasonable and perceptive:

> At distance I forgive thee, go with that;
> Bewail thy falshood, and the pious works
> It hath brought forth to make thee memorable
> Among illustrious women, faithful wives:
> Cherish thy hast'n'd widowhood with the gold
> Of Matrimonial treason: so farewel.
>
> (954-59)

Dalila leaves him in a burst of self-congratulation:

> Nor shall I count it hainous to enjoy
> The public marks of honour and reward
> Conferr'd upon me, for the piety
> Which to my countrey I was judg'd to have shewn.
>
> (991-94)

But Samson's reflections on this hostile encounter are those of a man looking for rational answers:

> *Sam.* So let her go, God sent her to debase me,
> And aggravate my folly who committed
> To such a viper his most sacred trust
> Of secresie, my safety, and my life.
>
> (999-1002)

Samson is mistaken because of the double irony; her attempt to debase him is actually restorative. But it would no longer be accurate, as it was early in the play, to describe him as

> vast, unwieldy, burdensom,
> Proudly secure, yet liable to fall
> By weakest suttleties, not made to rule,
> But to subserve where wisdom bears command.
>
> (54-57)

Samson is rapidly gaining wisdom as the result of his opportunities to behave unwisely. When the Chorus vacuously refers to the powers of "inward passion" and the "secret sting of amorous remorse," Samson's laconic answer now shows a detachment that he lacked when Dalila entered:

> *Sam.* Love-quarrels oft in pleasing concord end,
> Not wedlock-trechery endangering life.
>
> (1008-9)

One must not, of course, identify blind Samson with blind Milton (if Milton was blind at this point); but the response to Samson to this series of challenges is typically Miltonic, and Samson's rehabilitation in the face of, indeed as a result of, outward opposition cannot help but remind us of Milton's disparagement of "cloistered virtue" in *Areopagitica* and his image of the Hercules-like Christ-child in the Nativity Ode. Likewise, the closing lines of "Lycidas" are not contemplative but anticipatory of a return to the world of activity; and similarly, at the end of his career, Milton's epic on Christ turns to Christ's active resistance to temptation rather than to "Christ bound, crucifi'd, Christ risen," or "Christus patiens," as the Trinity College manuscript suggests. For Milton, as for Aristotle, virtue was not a state of being, but a free, deliberate action. And the Samson he gives us has a greater inner consistency of personality, as well as a gradual but well-marked development toward the vigorous, decisive kind of virtue which is so characteristically Miltonic.

Samson's encounter with Harapha resembles the other two challenges except that by now Samson has fully recovered his spiritual strength and integrity. We need only compare a few of Samson's responses to Harapha with his soliloquy at the opening of the play to see the extent of Samson's spiritual rehabilitation. When Harapha says he has "come to see of whom such noise / Hath walk'd about" (1088-89), Samson's answer is terse but hardly feeble—"The way to know were not to see but taste." And when Harapha suggests that

Samson's strength has depended on "black enchantments, some Magicians Art," Milton uses the occasion to show Samson at last self-renewed, spiritually strong, ready for whatever virtuous act God offers as an opportunity:

> *Sam.* I know no Spells, use no forbidden Arts;
> My trust is in the living God who gave me
> At my Nativity this strength, diffus'd
> No less through all my sinews, joints, and bones,
> Then thine, while I preserv'd these locks unshorn,
> The pledge of my unviolated vow.
> For proof hereof, if *Dagon* be thy god,
> Go to his Temple, invoke his aid.
>
> (1139-46)

Parker points out that Harapha's response to Samson's speech,

> *Har.* Presume not on thy God, what e're he be,
> Thee he regards not, owns not, hath cut off
> Quite from his people, and delivered up
> Into thy Enemies hand.
>
> (1156-59)

restates Samson's own lament at the opening of the play—"O wherefore was my birth from Heaven foretold / Twice by an Angel" (23-24).[11] But Samson is now able to respond to what had once been his own attitude by renouncing despair and proclaiming his faith in God's mercy:

> *Sam.* All these indignities, for such they are
> From thine, these evils I deserve and more,
> Acknowledge them from God inflicted on me
> Justly, yet despair not of his final pardon
> Whose ear is ever open; and his eye
> Gracious to re-admit the suppliant;
> In confidence whereof I once again
> Defie thee to the trial of mortal fight,
> By combat to decide whose god is god,
> Thine or whom I with *Israel's* Sons adore.
>
> (1168-77)

The impetus of the play has been to take Samson from the early despair, which Harapha attempts to revive, to this confidence in his own powers and the powers of God.

After Harapha's departure, Samson faces one last challenge—a subtler one than any before. The Messenger orders him to attend the Feast of Dagon, and Samson, consistent with his new-found strength, refuses: "Return the way thou cam'st, I will not come" (1332). Challenged again by the Messenger he reaffirms the integrity he has now found:

> Can they think me so broken, so debas'd
> With corporal servitude, that my mind ever
> Will condescend to such absurd commands?
> Although thir drudge, to be thir fool or jester,
> And in my midst of sorrow and heart-grief
> To shew them feats and play before thir god,
> The worst of all indignities, yet on me
> Joyn'd with extream contempt? I will not come.
>
> (1335-42)

At last, in the ensuing dialogue with the Chorus, Samson now lifts the dispute to its proper plane; the Samson who has raised himself from moaning degradation to a martial offensive now brings himself one stage higher. He is now able to see that the real opposition is not between Samson and the Philistian lords, but between God and Dagon. Samson is God's champion, but he is not God:

> *Sam.* Where outward force constrains, the sentence holds
> But who constrains me to the Temple of *Dagon*,
> Not dragging? the *Philistian* Lords command.
> Commands are no constraints. If I obey them,
> I do it freely; venturing to displease
> God for the fear of Man, and Man prefer,
> Set God behind: which in his jealousie
> Shall never, unrepented, find forgiveness.
> Yet that he may dispense with me or thee
> Present in Temples at Idolatrous Rites
> For some important cause, thou needst not doubt.
>
> (1369-79)

The Chorus's bewilderment ("How thou wilt here come off surmounts my reach") reflects the fact that the tragedy has abruptly shifted to a higher set of values.

And now Samson, having recreated his own will by enduring the challenges and temptations, having raised up Samson, makes the ultimate step of putting Samson aside and subordinating his new-found will to the will of God:

> *Sam.* Be of good courage, I begin to feel
> Some rouzing motions in me which dispose
> To something extraordinary my thoughts.
> I with this Messenger will go along,
> Nothing to do, be sure, that may dishonour
> Our Law, or stain my vow of *Nazarite.*
> If there be aught of presage in the mind,
> This day will be remarkable in my life
> By some great act, or of my days the last.
>
> (1381-89)

Having conquered his friends, his enemies, and at last himself, Samson now goes forth to accomplish the "great act" for which he had been intended by God. The victorious catastrophe which follows, the death of Samson and the Philistian lords, is now the logical structural outcome of the successive steps which have raised Samson from a slave to a hero. And these successive steps closely resemble the organizational techniques which unified "Lycidas" and "Epitaphium Damonis" and (as we saw in chapter II) are important characteristics of *Paradise Lost.*

But to explore fully the ways in which Milton brought *Samson Agonistes* as a poem to bear on the extra-poetic problem of the justice of God's ways, one major question must be faced: What is the nature of the poem? To be specific, is the play indeed, as Milton himself calls it, a tragedy? To reduce the problem to some simple elements, we must consider Manoa's closing speech:

> *Man.* Come, come, no time for lamentation now,
> Nor much more cause, *Samson* hath quit himself
> Like *Samson,* and heroicly hath finish'd
> A life Heroic.
>
> (1708-11)

And we must take into account the response of the Chorus:

> *Chor.* All is best, though we oft doubt
> What th'unsearchable dispose
> Of highest wisdom brings about,
> And ever best found in the close.

> (1745-48)

The mood of the Nazarites is triumphant; the "choice nobility and flower" of the Philistines have been killed; "the vulgar only scap'd who stood without" (1659). God has been vindicated and Dagon discredited. Although Samson is dead, at the same time he has triumphed. Is this tragedy?

With some reservations, the answer must be yes. The similarities of *Samson Agonistes* to the tragedies of Aeschylus, Sophocles, and Euripides are too numerous and well known to recount here. The problem in answering the question is not to show the ways *Samson Agonistes* resembles the tragedies of the Greeks, but to account for the differences.

The difficulty raised by the triumph of Samson is discussed by Una Ellis-Fermor, who points out "the steady psychological progression from despair through heroic conflict upwards to exultation and the final assumption into beatitude."[12] She concludes that the play is not a "miscarried tragedy" but rather a play of another sort which she categorizes as "religious drama"—"a major work of this rare but distinctive kind, among the finest of that kind in our experience." Miss Ellis-Fermor's discussion of *Samson Agonistes* is in the main very helpful, although her phrase "final assumption into beatitude" is either mistaken or misleading. *Samson Agonistes,* unlike "Lycidas" and "Epitaphium Damonis," closes with no hint of the spiritual survival of the dead protagonist; there is no mention of life after death or Heavenly rewards for Samson.

Parker handles the problem of the triumphant ending by relating it to Aristotle's concept of the final cause of tragedy—"through pity and fear affecting the purgation of these emotions." Samson, Parker points out, arouses our pity for his plight and our fear for what may happen to him. And the purgation of these emotions, he argues, results from these exalted closing speeches by Manoa and the Chorus.[13] Woodhouse agrees with Parker that *Samson Agonistes* is a tragedy.[14] He argues that, just as *Paradise Lost* resembles but does not attempt to reproduce the spirit and effect of Homer and Vergil, so *Samson Agonistes* is patterned on Greek tragedy, but with the aims of achieving an effect both similar and different.

The question of course is how, or how rigidly, one defines tragedy. If one accepts a definition such as that of I.A. Richards, *Samson Agonistes* is clearly not a tragedy:

> Suppressions and sublimations alike are devices by which we endeavour to avoid issues which might bewilder us. The essence of Tragedy is that it forces us to live for a moment without them.... Tragedy is only possible to a mind which is for the moment agnostic or Manichean. The least touch of any theology which has a compensating Heaven to offer the tragic hero is fatal. That is why *Romeo and Juliet* is not a Tragedy in the sense in which *King Lear* is.[15]

While Milton's play does not offer Samson an afterlife in Heaven, it clearly compensates him in that he dies knowing that he has Heaven's approval. And Richards is of course right in implying that *Samson Agonistes* is a very different sort of play from *King Lear*.

But the question of what tragedy "really" is constitutes a jungle so vast that it would be foolish to enter it here. The point at issue with regard to *Samson Agonistes* is whether a tragedy must end in the utter defeat of the protagonist, and for sixteenth- and seventeenth-century playwrights and critics, there was no unanimity. Even Aristotle's *Poetics* did not give them a clear answer. Aristotle says:

> Now, the best tragedies are founded on the stories of a few houses—on the fortunes of Alcmeon, Oedipus, ... and those others who have done or suffered something terrible.... In the second rank comes the kind of tragedy which some place first. Like the Odyssey, it has a double thread of plot, and also an opposite catastrophe for the good and for the bad. It is accounted the best because of the weakness of the spectators; for the poet is guided in what he writes by the wishes of his audience. The pleasure, however, thence derived is not the true tragic pleasure. It is proper to Comedy, where those who, in the piece, are the deadliest of enemies—like Orestes and Aegisthus—quit the stage as friends at the close, and no one slays or is slain.[16]

This passage in the *Poetics* caused endless controversy among Renaissance critics, especially since some of the tragedies of Euripides—*Electra, Ion,* and *Helen*—do not end with the protagonist defeated or dead.[17] Scaliger rightly comments that "it is by no means true, as has hither been taught, that the unhappy outcome is essential to tragedy—provided it contains horrible events."[18] Giraldi Cinthio agrees that the conclusion of a tragedy need not be unhappy:

> Of the two sorts of tragedy there is one that ends in sorrow. The other has a happy end, but in bringing the action towards its conclusion does not therefore desert the terrible and the compassionable, for without these there cannot be good tragedy. This type of tragedy, to which Aristotle gives the name mixed, is shown to us by Plautus in the Prologue of the Amphitryo.[19]

One Renaissance example of this kind of "mixed" tragedy is George Buchanan's *Baptistes,* written about 1540, and appearing in an English translation in 1642 under the title *Tyrannicall-Government Anatomized.*[20] The translation has been attributed to John Milton, but there is little basis for the attribution. The ending of *Baptistes* is "mixed," much as that of *Samson Agonistes;* the Nuncius enters to report John's beheading, and the reactions of the Messenger and the Chorus to John's death differ. The Chorus bewails the "horrible and most inhumane act," but the Nuncius answers, "Why weepe you? cease to pour out vaine complaints."[21] While John is dead, his assured resurrection, the Nuncius points out, makes death a short sleep before the beginning of another life.

But Milton's preface to *Samson Agonistes* is unequivocal; he quotes Aristotle's *Poetics* on the subject of tragedy, both in Greek and in Latin, and entitles the preface "Of That Sort of Dramatic Poem Which is Call'd Tragedy." He justifies his writing of a tragedy by citing, among others, *"Gregory Nazianzen* a Father of the Church [who] thought it not unbeseeming the sanctity of his person to write a Tragedy, which he entitl'd *Christ Suffering."*

It should be noted that *Christ Suffering* (or χρίστος Πάσχων) is not by Saint Gregory of Nazianzen (325?-390?), Bishop of Constantinople, but by a Byzantine Greek of about the twelfth century, and that Gregory's sixteenth-century editor, Ioannes Lewenklaius, had doubts about Gregory's authorship of the play.[22] Furthermore, he had doubts about the play's being a tragedy; "Tragoedia seu potius Tragicomoedia," he calls it. Be that as it may, Milton called *Christ Suffering* a tragedy, although its ending is even more triumphant than that of *Samson Agonistes*. When the weeping Mary approaches Christ on the cross, He asks why she should grieve:

> Quid, ô quid, ô mulier, tuos
> Sic spargis oculos lachrymis humentibus?
> Quid demittis os, triste tam longum ingemens?

> Why, o why, woman, have you thus wet your eyes with dewy tears? Why with sighs do you cast down a face so sad?[23]

And later He addresses his mother, "Esto bono animo, nam probè haec curavero" ("Be of good spirits, for I shall take care of this").

The play concludes with the resurrected Christ, "sine carne et osse," addressing Mary and Mary Magdelene:

> vos in omnes spargite
> Et me, & patrem ipsum, & spiritum sanctum, ite iam
> Vos ite chari buccinatores, sinus
> Per orbis omnes, regiasque per domos
> Canite epicenia & triumphi lauream,
> Davidis urbem rumor hic totam impleat.

> Carry forth to everyone concerning me and my Father, and the Holy Ghost, go now, go, trumpeters of grace, to all the corners of the earth, all the houses and the kingdoms, sing forth the triumph, this prophecy of David fills the whole city.[24]

The fact that a play ended with this victorious mood seems, from Milton's point of view, not to have disqualified it as a tragedy; one can only conclude therefore that Milton did not consider the triumphant aspects of the ending of *Samson Agonistes* deviations from the tragic tradition.

Thus for Milton, the tragic tradition, with its high seriousness, its grave morality, and its tight structural progression, is a highly appropriate means of working out the dilemma of the human condition. Pity and fear are emotions proper to the world Milton lived in, and to the poetic tradition in which he wrote *Samson Agonistes*. The purgation of these emotions through the poetic perceptions of God's ultimate justice, as embodied in the closing lines of *Samson Agonistes,* is the appropriate function of the play and its ultimate justification. Just as "Lycidas" and "Epitaphium Damonis" used the pastoral tradition, each in its own way, to work out the extra-poetic problems of the seemingly irrational death of a friend, so *Samson Agonistes* uses the tragic tradition to work out the larger problem concerning the ultimate justice and mercy of God. And just as those pastorals generated, by means of their structure, a force which carried them to their resolutions, so *Samson Agonistes,* from the first entry of the blind Samson to the peaceful closing speech of the Chorus, moves forward through structural progressions which unify the tragedy and at the same time give it an impetus which marks each scene as a step toward Samson's triumphant death.

The relation of *Samson Agonistes* to *Paradise Lost* and *Paradise Regained* is of course a close one; all three poems are concerned with the challenge of temptation and the virtues of restraint. We ought not therefore to leave the play without also noticing an important difference between *Samson Agonistes* and the two epics, beyond the obvious differences between epics and tragedies. As we have seen, *Paradise Lost* moves away from the conventional epic virtues of martial courage and skillful bloodletting toward the Christian virtues of love, endurance, suffering, and humility. *Paradise Regained,* of course, carries this progression further. *Samson Agonistes* differs markedly from this aspect of the two epics. It is true that the poem concludes on a peaceful note, its closing lines being, "With peace and consolation hath dismist, / And calm of mind all passion spent" (1757-58). But *Samson Agonistes* is not a poem in praise of patience and heroic martyrdom in the sense that *Paradise Lost* is. Manoa's closing speech is anything but forgiving toward Samson's enemies:

> *Samson* hath quit himself
> Like *Samson,* and heroicly hath finish'd
> A life Heroic, on his Enemies
> Fully reveng'd, hath left them years of mourning,
> And lamentation to the Sons of *Caphtor*.
>
> (1709-13)

"Heroism," in the context of *Samson Agonistes,* is violent, vengeful, and bloody, even if it does not actually involve the "gorgious Knights / At Joust and Torneament" that *Paradise Lost* spurns. Samson dies,

> straining all his nerves he bow'd,
> As with the force of winds and waters pent,
> When Mountains tremble, those two massie Pillars
> With horrible convulsion to and fro,
> He tugg'd, he shook, till down they came and drew
> The whole roof after them, with burst of thunder
> Upon the heads of all who sate beneath,
> Lords, Ladies, Captains, Councellors, or Priests,
> Thir choice nobility and flower.
>
> (1646-54)

And Manoa summons the Chorus in his final speech with the same stress on physical violence:

> Let us go find the body where it lies
> Sok't in his enemies blood, and from the stream
> With lavers pure and cleansing herbs wash off
> The clotted gore....
> . . . .
> Thither shall all the valiant youth resort,
> And from his memory inflame thir breasts
> To matchless valour, and adventures high.
>
> (1725-28, 1738-40)

This is strongly at odds with the spirit of Adam's last speech in *Paradise Lost:*

> Henceforth I learne, that to obey is best,
> And love with fear the onely God, to walk
> As in his presence, ever to observe
> His providence, and on him sole depend,
> Mercifull over all his works, with good
> Still overcoming evil, and by small
> Accomplishing great things, by things deemd weak
> Subverting worldly strong, and worldly wise

By simply meek; that suffering for Truths sake
Is fortitude to highest victorie.

(XII. 561-70)

The heroism that Adam learns is quite different from that which
Samson attains.

One may argue, of course, that Milton had no choice as to his ending
of *Samson Agonistes:* having chosen to dramatize Samson's destruction of the Philistines, he could hardly conclude the play with anything
but the downfall of the temple. But one must not ignore the fact that the
final struggle and victory in *Samson Agonistes* is purely physical; once
Samson has succeeded in conquering himself spiritually, his actions
bear a strong resemblance to the virtues that *Paradise Lost* scorned:

> the wrauth
> Of stern *Achilles* on his Foe pursu'd
> Thrice Fugitive about *Troy* Wall; or rage
> Of *Turnus* for *Lavinia* disespous'd,
> Or *Neptun's* ire or *Juno's,* that so long
> Perplex'd the *Greek* and *Cytherea's* Son.
>
> (IX. 14-19)

What does this mean with regard to the sequence of the writing of
Samson Agonistes and the two epics? No answer can be conclusive on
the basis of evidence such as this. As we have seen, there are too many
possibilities, and the evidence is open to too many interpretations. For
example, Stern argues that *Samson Agonistes* and *Paradise Regained*
are intended as companion pieces, the one portraying active vengeance
on God's behalf, the other passive resistance.[25]

Irene Samuel offers an interesting alternative reading of *Samson
Agonistes.* She points out the differences between the vengeful,
bloody ending of this play and Milton's attitudes toward violence
elsewhere, and argues that Samson's destruction of the temple and
the Philistines is not the result of true vision but of false:

> Given a Samson self-deluded earlier about his divinely
> inspired impulse to marry Dalila, his final impulse may be as
> little divine in its inspiration. True, the Chorus and Manoa
> take his last deed as proving God's renewed favor. And if we

credit them with wholly reliable views, with speaking for their author, their testimony would annul any construction other than theirs of the catastrophe. In fact the Chorus and Manoa have consistently been out of their depth with Samson, missing his point at every turn. And if in their dialogue with him, when he is there onstage, they do not fully understand him, and so speak not Milton's but their own limited vision, their final verdict on what happens offstage cannot speak Milton's.[26]

The catharsis, in this reading, is an experience which we as readers undergo at the end of the tragedy, but which the Chorus does not. "We are left with 'calm of mind, all passion spent' in a sense other than theirs."[27]

If indeed we are to read the ending of *Samson Agonistes* in this way, with true vision exclusively the achievement of the reader, and the view of Samson, Manoa, and the Chorus a distorted one, we have a decided departure from Milton's practice elsewhere; in "Elegia Tertia," *Comus,* "Lycidas," "Epitaphium Damonis," *Paradise Lost,* and *Paradise Regained,* the "protagonist" or persona struggles and achieves along with us an understanding of God's ways. Professor Samuel is right in saying that the gloating of the Chorus does not correspond to Milton's habit; but if she is right in saying that *Samson Agonistes* concludes with all the dramatis personae either dead or deluded, this also departs from Milton's habit.

We face a dilemma—that is, a departure from Milton's habit— either way. It is true, as Professor Samuel says, that Samson's "announced vocation was to deliver Israel, not to slay Philistines."[28] And she is right that "we need only read past chapter 16 in the Book of Judges to learn how much deliverance Israel gained."[29] But early in the play the Chorus affirms that "Just are the ways of God / And justifiable to men"; in *Paradise Lost,* as in poems as early as "Elegia Tertia," this justice ultimately becomes clear not only to us as readers, but to the personae as well. It is true that *Samson Agonistes* is purely a drama, not a narrative poem, and therefore lacks any "icastic" or non-fictive character to speak Milton's own point of view, as does the "epic voice" in *Paradise Lost* and *Paradise Regained.* Unfortunately we have no other "pure" drama by Milton (if we exclude *Comus* because of the masque conventions) for comparison; our only points of comparison are "dramatic" poems like "Lycidas," where the speaker is "the uncouth Swain," and "Epitaphium Damonis," where the speaker is the shepherd Thyrsis. In both of these poems there is no division between a false vision of the personae and a true vision which is not stated explicitly but only deduced by the reader; we as readers accompany the swain and Thrysis in their spiritual struggles and arrive at the same culminating vision.

In short, either Milton departs from his normal habit by finding "calm of mind," "justification," in bloody vengeance, or else he departs from his normal habit by leaving all the personae in *Samson Agonistes* unenlightened in a work concerned with the struggle for enlightenment. Perhaps there is no solution that will salvage the play as we might wish it to be: "true history" in the Book of Judges leaves Samson and his enemies dead from a vengeful, bloody act and the Israelites undelivered. Thus Milton must either in some way depart from his normal habit or else tamper with history. What we have at the conclusion of *Samson Agonistes* may well be Milton's incomplete solution to the dilemma. Professor Samuel with great critical subtlety and skill extricates *Samson Agonistes* from an ending contradictory to Milton's usual beliefs, but she leaves the play with an ending which is unsatisfactory in other ways, particularly in its deviation from Milton's usual practice of explicitly joining reader and protagonist in a culminating understanding of the justice of God's ways.

If Professor Samuel's otherwise excellent reading of *Samson Agonistes* is mistaken in this respect, one can make some tentative conclusions concerning a possible chronological sequence of these last poems. A logical progression would be that Milton developed from the conventional, warlike idea of heroism, mentioned as early as 1628 in "At a Vacation Exercise" and discussed as late as 1639 or 1640 in "Mansus" and "Epitaphium Damonis," to its explicit embodiment in Samson's death; that he then moved beyond this to the more spiritualized heroism of *Paradise Lost,* with its explicit rejection of martial heroism; and that his poetic-ethical development culminated in the complete renunciation of physical combat in *Paradise Regained.* At the same time, however, one must remember the lack of definitive evidence and the uncertainty of any argument based on a poet's developing along lines of completely logical progression.

A consideration which should not be ignored, however, is the relation of *Samson Agonistes* to its Greek prototypes. Parker has shown the extent to which *Samson Agonistes* resembles *Prometheus Bound* in some ways, and *Oedipus at Colonus* in many more ways. But if we compare Milton's use of Greek tragedy in *Samson Agonistes* with his use of the Homeric and Vergilian epics in *Paradise Lost* and *Paradise Regained*, we find important differences. In writing his tragedy, Milton adapts the Greek tradition to the Biblical story, fitting the life and death of Samson into a Greek mold with great skill. Yet the relation is always an adaptation and a fitting in; *Samson Agonistes* parallels the Greek tradition without ever making the vital, active use of the tradition that *Paradise Lost* and *Paradise Regained* make of the epic tradition.

Two examples from *Samson Agonistes* may suffice to clarify this point. As the play begins, Samson, blind, dejected, and enslaved, is led onto the stage by a boy. So also *Oedipus at Colonus* begins with the blind, dejected Oedipus led on by Antigone. The parallelism of the two scenes ends there; the boy disappears from *Samson Agonistes,* never to appear again, while Antigone is vital to the rest of Sophocles's play. As the scene in *Samson Agonistes* develops, his soliloquy and then his dialogue with the Chorus of Danites bear no important relation to the scene in *Oedipus at Colonus,* where a man from Colonus enters and tells Oedipus that he is now in the grove of the Eumenides. This is not to rebuke Milton for a fault in his play; it is simply to point out that the resemblances between the scene in Sophocles and the scene in Milton are no more than superficial, and the similarities are put to no use by Milton.

There is also a parallelism between Sophocles's scene involving Creon and Oedipus—where Creon tries first persuasion and then extortion to force Oedipus back to Thebes—and Milton's scene involving Samson and the threats first of Harapha and then of the Officer who comes to force him to the feast of Dagon. But here too the parallelism between Sophocles and Milton is merely superficial, and the differences are obvious. Milton of course knew *Oedipus at Colonus* but he was not using Sophocles's play in an active, functional way in the creation of his own play.[30]

In contrast, we have seen in chapter II the continuous functional use that *Paradise Lost* makes of the epic tradition. The parallelism, particularly with the *Aeneid,* is not merely the use of similar devices in similar situations, but the setting up of a dynamic interaction between specific ideas, characters, and actions in Vergil and similar ideas, characters, and actions in *Paradise Lost*. The result of the relation between the *Aeneid* and *Paradise Lost* is not merely parallelism but, as we have seen, the creation of a *tertium quid:* two similar poems in a relationship which operates by means of their similarities as well as their dissimilarities.

Chapter II contains several examples of this *tertium quid,* but perhaps one more example here will underline this important difference between *Paradise Lost* and *Samson Agonistes* in the use of their respective traditions. In Book IX of the *Aeneid,* after the famous episode in which Nisus and Euryalus attack the camp of the Rutuli,[31] with the resultant capture of the two Trojans, Nisus demands of the Rutuli that death fall on him rather than on his friend:

> "Me, me adsum, qui feci, in me convertite ferrum,
> o Rutuli! mea fraus omnis; nihil iste nec ausus
> nec potuit; caelum hoc et conscia sidera testor;
> tantum infelicem nimium dilexit amicum."

> (427-30)

> "On me—on me—here am I who did the deed—on me turn your steel, O Rutulians! Mine is all the guilt; he neither dared nor could have done aught; this heaven be witness and the all-seeing stars! He but loved his hapless friend too well."[32]

Echoes of Nisus's words resound through Eve's speech in her most heroic moment—her response to Adam's attack on her which begins "Out of my sight, thou Serpent, that name best / Befits thee with him leagu'd, thy self as false / And hateful" (X. 867-69). She answers in the fashion that *Paradise Lost* emphasizes is true heroism:

> Forsake me not thus, *Adam,* witness Heav'n
> What love sincere, and reverence in my heart
> I beare thee, and unweeting have offended.
> . . . .
>   ... On me exercise not
> Thy hatred for this miserie befall'n,
> On me alreadie lost, mee then thy self
> More miserable; both have sin'd, but thou
> Against God onely, I against God and thee,

And to the place of judgment will return,
There with my cries importune Heaven, that all
The sentence from thy head remov'd may light
On me, sole cause to thee of all this woe,
Mee mee onely just object of his ire.

(X. 914-16, 927-36)

Clearly the relation of the *Aeneid* to *Paradise Lost* here, the relation of Nisus to Eve, is not merely passive parallelism: Nisus and Eve are self-sacrificing heroes, but Nisus's heroism is that of the sword and serves Rome and Eve's heroism is that of the soul and serves God. The active quality of the relation between Nisus's heroism and Eve's creates this *tertium quid*—the concept that spiritual heroism is superior to physical heroism. Without this quality, *Paradise Lost* would not be the poem that it is.

This passage also indicates the endless complexities of discussing the structure of Milton's mature poetry. Eve's speech here has important links not only with the *Aeneid,* but also with the speech of Christ to the Father in Book III where He offers to come to fallen man "unimplor'd, unsought," and then foreshadows Eve's very words in Book X, as He too echoes Nisus—"on mee let thine anger fall," Christ says (III. 237), "on me let Death wreck all his rage" (241). It is Christ's phraseology which comes to Eve's lips almost 7,000 lines later, "unimplor'd, unsought," in her moment of greatness and humility.

It is revealing to contrast these intricate relationships between the *Aeneid* and *Paradise Lost* with Milton's use of a similar echo from Vergil forty years earlier in his "In Quintum Novembris," where Milton writes:

Subdolus at tali Serpens velatus amictu
Solvit in has fallax ora execrantia voces.

(90-91)

Dressed in such garb the Deceiver, the Serpent, lyingly shaped his execrable lips to these words.

And "Subdolus Serpens" summons the sleeping Pope:

Dormis nate? Etiamne tuos sopor opprimit artus?
Immemor O fidei, pecorumque oblite tuorum!

(92-93)

Do you sleep, my son? Does slumber weigh down your limbs? O heedless of the faith and neglectful of your flocks!

The seventeen-year-old Milton is clearly remembering Mercury's summons to the dilatory sleeping Aeneas:

"Nate dea, potes hoc sub casu ducere somnos,
nec quae te circum stent deinde pericula cernis,
demens, nec Zephyros audis spirare secundos?"

(IV. 560-62)

"Goddess-born, when such hazard threatens, canst thou still slumber, and seest thou not the perils that from henceforth hem thee in, madman! Hearest not the kindly breezes blowing?"

But beyond the verbal parallelism of "In Quintum Novembris" and the *Aeneid,* there is no significant relationship; the Vergilian residue in Milton's youthful Latin poem is inert. In Milton's mature epic he is making the Aeneas/ Satan relation and the Nisus/Eve relation a functioning part of the structure of the poem.

But let us return to *Samson Agonistes.* While the play clearly parallels Greek tragedy—uses the Greek tradition, and resembles *Prometheus Bound* in some ways and *Oedipus at Colonus* in many more—*Samson Agonistes* never makes the functional poetic use of the Greek plays in the same fashion that Milton's two epics use Homer and Vergil.

It would be too glib a conclusion to say that this metaphoric, functional use of the epic tradition in *Paradise Lost* unquestionably shows that *Paradise Lost* must be later than *Samson Agonistes.* The same logic would lead us to date *Samson Agonistes* even prior to "Epitaphium Damonis" and therefore some time in the 1630s because of the metaphoric use that "Epitaphium Damonis" makes of the pastoral tradition. In the long run we are forced to the cliché that internal evidence such as style or method of using sources is an insecure basis for dating poems. But if *Samson Agonistes* is indeed Milton's last poem, coming after the developing sequence of *Paradise Lost* and then *Paradise Regained,* we have a strange picture: that of an experienced, serious poet writing a tragedy, which he says is "the gravest, moralest, and most profitable of all other Poems," who then ignores a poetic technique which was relevant to the material at hand, and which had been magnificently successful in the two epic poems which he had just completed. After using the epic tradition in the active, functional way that he did in *Paradise Lost* and *Paradise Regained*, it is difficult to imagine that Milton then went back to the highly competent parallelism which characterizes the use of the tragic tradition in *Samson Agonistes*.

On the other hand, *Paradise Lost* fits easily as the next step after *Samson Agonistes* in the use of a major Greco-Roman literary tradition—a step which combines the functional use of the tradition, as in "Epitaphium Damonis," with the grand scale and loftiness of genre of *Samson Agonistes*— epic poetry and tragedy being competitors as the loftiest of genre in the eyes of seventeenth-century poets. After the progression from *Samson Agonistes,* with its passive parallelism, to *Paradise Lost,* with its functional interaction with the tradition, then (as we shall discuss in the next chapter) *Paradise Regained* is the logical ultimate step.

A reading of *Samson Agonistes* must not bog down in a controversy over dates; it is too great a play for that. In any case, if *Paradise Lost* and *Paradise Regained* had never existed, we can see *Samson Agonistes* as a mature, highly organized pondering and resolving of the problems of the human condition—problems that Milton tried to work on in "Elegia Tertia" and "On the Death of a Fair Infant." And now, at the height of his poetic powers, the flaws, the gaps, the false resolutions of those early poems are behind him. With Aeschylus, Sophocles, and Euripides as his poetic models, with the tragic tradition as he understood it as his method, Milton creates in *Samson Agonistes* a verbal embodiment that gives poetic structure and a resolution to the Chorus's hope that

> Just are the ways of God,
> And justifiable to Men.
> (293-94)

X

Paradise Regained as the Transcendence over the Epic

Tempt not the Lord thy God, he said and stood

Concerning *Paradise Regained,* Milton's nephew Edward Phillips remarked that it "is generally censured to be much inferior to [*Paradise Lost*], though he [Milton] could not hear with patience any such thing when related to him."[1] Not many of Milton's readers seem to have agreed with Milton; the poem has been more respected than liked, and Mark Pattison thought *Paradise Regained* "betrays the feebleness of senility."[2]

This is the result of a misreading of *Paradise Regained.* Rather than its being a feeble poem, it is in many ways a bold culmination of the direction that Milton's poetic development had been taking. In a sense it represents a step beyond *Paradise Lost* similar to Milton's earlier progression from "Lycidas" to "Epitaphium Damonis": *Paradise Regained* is "post-epic" in the same way that "Epitaphium Damonis" is "post-pastoral."

This is not to say that *Paradise Regained* is Milton's greatest poem; we may or may not like what *Paradise Regained* is, or does, but we underestimate the poem if we think it is feeble, fumbling, or merely drab. There are of course several reasons for the coolness of readers toward *Paradise Regained.* Some are obvious and need only to be mentioned before we move on—for example the tendencies of readers to look on *Paradise Regained* as if it were simply the next four books of *Paradise Lost.* The mistake is common and deplorable, but it has been so much discussed that we need say nothing further about it here. Two other reasons for this coolness are the nature of the style and the nature of the action. The vocabulary, the imagery, and the sentence-structure of *Paradise Regained* are far less florid than those of *Paradise Lost;* Milton's language is startlingly simple and direct. In fact its laconic brusqueness when we expect graceful elaboration shocks us and repels readers who look for the luxurious ornateness of much of *Paradise Lost.*

But if we give Milton credit for having some notion of what he was up to, rather than assuming that he was merely a tired old man, we shall find that the dry, ascetic style and the infrequency of the grand Miltonic similes are poetic devices as integral in their way to the achievement of this poem as the richness of *Paradise Lost* is to that poem's unique achievement.

A crucial point is the seemingly static nature of the plot of *Paradise Regained.* Milton limits himself to a situation in which almost nothing physical happens. While *Paradise Lost* sweeps through centuries and literally from Heaven to Hell, with battles, love scenes, spiritual crises, violence, and death, *Paradise Regained* essentially limits itself to an interrupted dialogue between two characters. There is almost no action—but this limitation is at the heart of the poem. Although Jesus is tempted by all the attractions of the world, there is practically no physical action because He wills that nothing physical should happen. It is essential to see that this lack of overt action, the apparently static quality of the poem, does not reflect the senility of the poet, as Pattison suggests, but instead is a key element in what the poem is really about.

The bold vigorous step, artistically speaking, is to refuse to write a work filled with wild adventures, but rather to write one that is empty of them, one that rashly renounces them as cheap tricks, and yet attempts to create a work of art out of this very renunciation. One may wish that Milton had not tried so strenuous a poetic experiment—that is the reader's privilege—but the reader would be unwise to think that Milton does this feebly or carelessly. Rather, it seems likely that, as so often happens in the mature years of a great artist, Milton consciously decided to concentrate on the nature of his artistic material, exploring its unique potentialities to their ultimate realization, allowing his audience to follow him or not according to their abilities. One is reminded here of Beethoven in his late quartets, or of Wagner in *Parsifal.*

In one sense *Paradise Regained* is static, as "Elegia Quinta" and the Nativity Ode were static, although for different reasons. At the same time *Paradise Regained* moves, but not as *Paradise Lost* moves. *Paradise Lost* progresses in some obvious narrative ways: Adam and Eve come into being, live their lives, eat the fruit, and go into exile. Likewise, as we have seen in chapter II, the structure of *Paradise Lost* carries the poem forward to a point in the closing lines of Book XII where Adam, divinely instructed, experiences the revelation of what true heroism is: that "suffering for Truths sake / Is fortitude to highest victorie" (569-70). This Adam is more profound, more conscious, even though fallen, than the Adam of Book IV. *Paradise Lost* has moved not only from one event to another and from one spiritual state (innocence) to another (sin, or sin and partial redemption). The poem has also moved inward on itself, from a lesser to a greater insight into the highest state of Man. Thus the dynamic progression of *Paradise Lost* must of course be seen not merely as a narrative of the physical adventures of Adam, Satan, and the others, but as an internal journey, a spiritual pilgrimage in the same sense that "Lycidas" and "Epitaphium Damonis" also are searchings and discoveries of the justification of God's ways.

In the case of *Paradise Regained* it is a mistake in a sense to look on the poem as a sequel to *Paradise Lost,* but paradoxically and in another sense *Paradise Regained* does indeed take up where *Paradise Lost* leaves off: *Paradise Regained* focuses on this progression toward insight into the nature of true heroism, which is only one element in *Paradise Lost,* and as much as possible, *Paradise Regained* makes this the center of the poem. In *Paradise Regained,* the narrative progression from event to event, or from one emotional state to another has been peeled away and discarded. In *Paradise Regained* only the self-discovery remains as the heart of the poem. Adam's self-discovery in *Paradise Lost* is a noble vision, but the self-discovery of Jesus, of the Christ who becomes man and then rediscovers his divine identity, is a far loftier thing.

As several critics of *Paradise Regained* have pointed out, this theme of self-discovery begins early in the poem;[3] Jesus is, in Book I, "obscure, / Unmarkt, unknown" (24-25), and while the Dove pronounces Him as God's beloved Son, the significance of this is hardly clear. Satan hears the proclamation but is not sure—"Who this is we must learn" (91)—and even Jesus is confused:

> O what a multitude of thoughts at once
> Awakn'd in me swarm, while I consider
> What from within I feel my self, and hear

> What from without comes often to my ears,
> Ill sorting with my present state compar'd.
>
> (I. 196-200)

When He goes into the wilderness He knows that it is with divine authority, yet He is led "by some strong motion ... to what intent I learn not yet" (290-92).

This theme dominates much of the poem. For example, it serves to explain the function of Andrew and Simon, who introduce Book II: they know that the Messiah has come, but the real significance, the real nature of the event and the real nature of the Messiah is not clear to them. Their partial knowledge and partial ignorance are way-stations in the progression of the poem toward the moment of illumination. We must see that progression toward true understanding as similar to, but a development beyond, the structure of *Paradise Lost*.

A few lines later the poem underlines this theme of concealment and discovery in Mary's speech—"O what avails me now that honour high / To have conceiv'd of God?" she asks (II. 66-67). There have been portents of her son's greatness:

> But where delays he now? some great intent
> Conceals him: when twelve years he scarce had seen,
> I lost him, but so found, as well I saw
> He could not lose himself; but went about
> His Father's business; what he meant I mus'd,
> Since understand; much more his absence now
> Thus long to some great purpose he obscures.
> But I to wait with patience am inur'd;
> My heart hath been a store-house long of things
> And sayings laid up, portending strange events.
>
> (II. 95-104)

The answer to Mary's question, the poem tells us, is

> The while her Son tracing the Desert wild,
> Sole but with holiest Meditations fed,
> Into himself descended.
>
> (II. 109-11)

This answer points to the structural progression which the poem will make: just as the speaker in "Elegia Tertia," more than forty years before, tried fumblingly to move toward an insight into the justice of Lancelot Andrewes's death, so now, in *Paradise Regained,* the structure of the poem organizes itself with complete mastery around Jesus's journey of descent into Himself in order to discover His true nature.

Thus the temptations of Satan are not merely challenges to which Jesus responds; they are explorations by both Satan and Jesus. As the temptations progress, the dialogue between Jesus and Satan becomes longer, more searching, and richer. Jesus's first curt answer to Satan (I. 335-36) is a line and a half long. His second answer, nine lines later, dismisses Satan in ten lines. But his last speech to Satan in Book III (387-440) is fifty-four lines long; and in Book IV, in answer to Satan's offer of "the schools / Of Academics old and new," Jesus speaks "sagely" for almost eighty lines (286-364). Then Satan, one of whose functions in the poem is likewise that of spiritual explorer, answers:

> Thenceforth I thought thee worth my nearer view
> And narrower Scrutiny, that I might learn
> In what degree or meaning thou art call'd
> The Son of God, which bears no single sence;
> The Son of God I also am; or was,
> And if I was, I am; relation stands;
> All men are Sons of God; yet thee I thought
> In some respect far higher so declar'd.
>
> (IV. 514-21)

Parenthetically one ought to note the relation of this spiritual journey by Satan in *Paradise Regained* to Satan's physical search, in *Paradise Lost,* for "another World, the happy seat / Of some new Race call'd Man" (II. 347-48).

One need not stop now to trace the succession of temptations in *Paradise Regained,* each leading both Satan and Jesus further on—not to physical adventures and explorations, but deeper into themselves. The end of this internal voyage, for Jesus, is of course the last temptation, Satan's placing of Him on the pinnacle (IV. 54 f.). This temptation may seem an inept break in the order of the temptations, in the structural progression of the poem, since the first two temptations appear to be subtle appeals to the spirit, while the third temptation appears to be a crude attempt at violence. But the third temptation, the moment on the pinnacle, is climactic not as an act by Satan but as a culminating response of self-revelation and self-discovery by Jesus: "Tempt not the Lord thy God." Jesus at last realizes and pronounces the nature of His divine character. The outcome of this attempt by Satan at seduction is not another fall but an inward journey which progresses to an ultimate revelation—Jesus's knowledge that He is both man and God.

This is what it means to say that the progression of *Paradise Regained* is related to, but a development beyond, *Paradise Lost: Paradise Regained* discards elements such as the degeneration of Satan's personality in *Paradise Lost,* or the physical journeys and struggles which are the necessary prefaces to the temptation before the Forbidden Tree. On the other hand, elements in *Paradise Lost* such as the spiritual growth of Adam toward self-knowledge, obedience, and suffering for Truth's sake have their fully developed counterparts in *Paradise Regained,* in which the structural impetus of the successive dialogues with Satan enable the poem to embody Jesus's "descent into himself." Thus the structure of *Paradise Regained* carries the poem forward to an internal culmination which is no less dynamic than that of *Paradise Lost,* and a resolution which is far more appropriate to the internalized poem which *Paradise Regained* is—a poem whose structural progression is metaphysical in the literal, Aristotelean sense of thrusting beyond the physical.

But there is another important way in which *Paradise Regained* goes beyond *Paradise Lost*—in its handling of the epic tradition. And it is here that Milton made some of his most startling and, artistically, his most dangerous innovations.

In some respects *Paradise Regained* is what Milton said in 1641 (in *The Reason of Church Government)* that he might write—a brief epic. The poem is divided into books, like the *Iliad,* the *Odyssey,* and the *Aeneid*; it is a long (2,070 lines) narrative poem with a semidivine hero who triumphs.

But it is so strikingly different from the traditional epic that one is brought up short—no love scenes, no real battles, no high adventure, no journeys to distant lands. It is interesting to note one of Milton's descriptions of epic poetry (in Book I of *Paradise Lost)* and to see how much it depends, for him, on poets like Pulci, Boiardo, and Ariosto; it is poetry of grand battles and far-flung places:

> and what resounds
> In Fable or *Romance* of *Uthers* Son

Begirt with *British* and *Armoric* Knights;
And all who since, Baptiz'd or Infidel
Jousted in *Aspramont* or *Montalban,*
Damasco, or *Marocco,* or *Trebisond,*
Or whom *Biserta* sent from *Afric* shore
When *Charlemain* with all his Peerage fell
By *Fontarabbia.*

(I. 579-87)

And of course this is the kind of poetry which the introductory lines
(13-41) of Book IX specifically reject:

Sad task, yet argument
Not less but more Heroic then the wrauth
Of stern *Achilles* on his Foe pursu'd
Thrice Fugitive about *Troy* Wall; or rage
Of *Turnus* for *Lavinia* disespous'd.

(IX. 13-17)

But while Milton explicitly rejects these epic traits in this and later passages in *Paradise Lost,* we must not forget that he included a great many
of these epic traits in the preceding parts of *Paradise Lost,* and he must
have been conscious that he compromised his position at many points.
The angels do battle in Book VI, the races and games are there (I. 531
f.), and Milton asks his muse for a catalogue of the forces in the field (I.
376 f.), which she gives him, for about 150 lines. As Milton Miller
points out:

> Though the super-heroic standard is that of patience and heroic
> martyrdom, the deeds described by Raphael as deserving me-
> morial among the heavenly host are not deeds of patience and
> martyrdom at all but of heroism in battle, and we remember
> that some of the fallen angels also sing the "partial" songs
> about "Thir own Heroic deeds and hapless fall" (II, 549).
> And the Son's thunder, if more potent, is not unlike Satan's
> in kind.[4]

In short, *Paradise Lost* at times wavers as it now uses and now rejects
the "tinsel trappings" of the epic form.

But *Paradise Lost* looks forward to *Paradise Regained* in one formal aspect which is relevant here, and that aspect is the conscious acceptance and rejection of the martial epic achieved by placing Satan repeatedly against the background of Aeneas and his deeds. As we have seen in chapter II, again and again Satan echoes Aeneas's speeches and re-enacts a debased form of Aeneas's heroic voyage to establish his nation. Thus at times *Paradise Lost* is able to include the adventures proper to an epic without condoning them as evidence of the highest virtue. But at other times *Paradise Lost* vacillates by condemning the very thing it attempts. *Paradise Regained,* on the other hand, succeeds in its own terms by reconciling Milton's ethical theory of the highest virtue with the structural demands of his poem and the conventions of the epic tradition.

What Milton has done in *Paradise Regained* is quite similar to what a twentieth-century composer might do in writing, for example, a sonata or a waltz: the composer creates a metaphoric dialogue between himself and Mozart, or himself and Johann Strauss or Franz Schubert. A composer today would be foolish to write an opera, for example, without being conscious of the fact that Rossini, Verdi, and Wagner were in the audience whether he wanted them there or not.

And *Paradise Regained* is, among other things, a vigorous dialogue with the epic tradition. Sometimes the poem accepts the epic form, sometimes it rejects it, but a large part of the poem is involved in this dialogue. One might answer that this is a truism, since everything is bound to be either an epic trait or not an epic trait, but this is to misunderstand Milton. Much of what happens in *Paradise Regained* is not merely non-epic; it is specifically anti-epic. John Steadman remarks that *"Paradise Lost* is to the tradition of heroic poetry what the 'anti-novel' is to the conventional novel."[5] But this is even more true of *Paradise Regained*. The poem brings up "epicness" and then renounces it—renounces it in a more inherent and effective fashion even than the explicit statement in Book IX of *Paradise Lost*.

Let us take an example: the second temptation, in which Satan offers Jesus worldly power:

> He [Jesus] look't and saw what numbers numberless
> The City gates out powr'd, light armed Troops
> In coats of Mail and military pride;
> In Mail thir horses clad, yet fleet and strong,

Prauncing their riders bore, the flower and choice
Of many Provinces from bound to bound;
From *Arachosia,* from *Candaor* East,
And *Margiana* to the *Hyrcanian* cliffs
Of *Caucasus,* and dark *Iberian* dales,
From *Atropatia* and the neighbouring plains
Of *Adiabene, Media,* and the South
Of *Susiana* to *Balsara's* hav'n.
He saw them in their forms of battell rang'd,
How quick they wheel'd, and flying behind them shot
Sharp sleet of arrowie showers against the face
Of thir pursuers, and overcame by flight;
The field all iron cast a gleaming brown,
Nor wanted clouds of foot, nor on each horn,
Cuirassiers all in steel for standing fight;
Chariots or Elephants endorst with Towers
Of Archers, nor of labouring Pioners
A multitude with Spades and Axes arm'd.

(III. 310-31)

One is of course reminded of passages such as the seventh book of the *Aeneid,* where Mezentius, Lausus, Turnus, and the other Italian chiefs are arrayed against Aeneas, and Milton could hardly have wished otherwise than that we should be so reminded. But the difference between this scene and its counterparts in the *Aeneid* are what make *Paradise Regained* the unique poem that it is. In the *Aeneid* (as in the sixth book of *Paradise Lost)* the battle is within the poem; the outcome of the central conflict of the poem depends on the outcome of the battle.

Paradise Regained is quite different. In the first place the combatants in this passage are not the protagonists and antagonists of the poem; they are only part of the furniture. And in the second place the furniture is not really there in the sense that Satan and Christ are. The battle is a scene conjured up by Satan's power as an attempt to subvert Christ, and it fails. Christ's rejection is explicit:

Much ostentation vain of fleshly arm,
And fragile arms, much instrument of war
Long in preparing, soon to nothing brought,
Before mine eyes thou hast set ...

. . . .
> ... that cumbersome
> Luggage of war there shewn me, argument
> Of human weakness rather then of strength.
> (III. 387-90, 400-402)

We should read this rejection of military power in the light of the epic tradition—as not merely an account of the extra-poetic events involving Satan and Christ, but as a crucial factor in the poetic tradition with which the poem works, and out of which the poem has developed. In this passage Milton is not ignoring the epic tradition; he explicitly points to it here and then turns his back on it. This is what I mean by an anti-epic element in the poem. By Milton's dialogue with the epic tradition I mean this artful acceptance and rejection of the epic tradition—the acceptance of the tradition when that suits the needs of the poem and the later (or simultaneous) rejection, either formally or materially, when the poem needs that.

It is in this respect that *Paradise Regained* resembles "Epitaphium Damonis"—or an extension of one of the techniques of "Epitaphium Damonis": *Paradise Regained* makes use of the epic tradition, but it does not use the tradition merely as a mode in which the events are presented. The epic tradition here is a poetic instrument which functions to give *Paradise Regained* its internalized progression—again, one needs the term "metaphysical" in its Aristotelean sense: the structural progression of *Paradise Regained* is, in this sense, metaphysical. Just as the inward, "beyond-the-physical" journey of Jesus results in His self-discovery, so other aspects of *Paradise Regained* use and at the same time reject the epic tradition to move the poem into spiritual profundities heretofore unrealized in the epic tradition.

As we have seen, this is also one of the directions *Paradise Lost* takes—a progression from the false, old-epic heroism of Satan to the true Christian heroism of suffering for Truth's sake. But the difference is that *Paradise Regained* faces this realization more immediately, directly, and constantly than *Paradise Lost,* and therefore *Paradise Regained* ultimately arrives at a more complete culmination of the trends which *Paradise Lost* only half-realizes.

It is usually the rejection of the epic tradition, rather than the acceptance of it, which gives *Paradise Regained* its chilly and forbidding quality. But it would be misunderstanding the poem to see this rejection as evidence that the aged Milton had become chilly and forbidding. He is simply making use of the epic form—here in a negative way—to embody his ethical concepts. These are ethical concepts which he stated in *Paradise Lost,* but which he never quite so boldly built into the very form of the earlier poem. We may argue, if we like, that we prefer the good old intrinsic blood and guts, that we like the battles of the *Aeneid* or the *Iliad,* and the falling pillars in *Samson Agonistes,* and that is our privilege. But let us not make the mistake of thinking that this odd handling of battles in *Paradise Regained* is a symptom of senile decay; the experiment may be too daring and hence unsuccessful—the general lack of popularity of the poem points that way—but the experiment is nothing if not bold.

This dialogue with the epic form is not a haphazardly recurring trait. The opening boldly places the poem up against the epic tradition—"against" it in both senses of the word: the opening is simultaneously opposed to and connected with the epic form. Milton uses the same four-part form with which he began *Paradise Lost:*[6]

1. *The Principium* (3-7), stating the large theme of the poem, "Recover'd Paradise to all mankind," just as *Paradise Lost* does in lines 1-26, where "Man's first disobedience" states the principal subject of the poem. In both *Paradise Lost* and *Paradise Regained* Milton echoes Vergil's *principium* (1-7) and Vergil's brief statement of the theme in line 1—"arma virumque." The pattern is one that Renaissance commentators on the epic pointed out as also occurring in the *Iliad* (1-7) and the *Odyssey* (1-11).

2. *The initium* (8-17), introducing the first scene and giving the causes of the action. *Paradise Lost* at this point (27-49) asks the muse "what cause / Mov'd our Grand Parents ... ?" echoing of course Vergil's "Musa mihi causas ... " (8). In *Paradise Lost* the *initium* also supplies the answer, "Th'infernal Serpent," just as Vergil does in his *initium* (8-11), pointing to the wrath of Juno. So Milton in *Paradise Regained* tells us of the coming clash between "this glorious Eremite" and "the Spiritual Foe" in the desert.

3. *The Exordium* (18-43), which is a description of the place of the opening scene. Here in *Paradise Regained* it is Satan's summoning of the council of devils. In *Paradise Lost* (50-83) it describes the devils rolling in the fiery gulf. So in the *Aeneid,* lines 12-33 ("Urbs antiqua fuit ... ") place the action soon to follow in the ancient city of Carthage.

4. *The Ianua Narrandi* (44), which resembles *Paradise Lost,* line 84, in being an address by "th'Arch-Enemy" Satan to his followers, paralleling the speech by the great adversary in the *Aeneid,* Juno, which begins at line 37 of that poem.

This is of course standard epic machinery and a good Renaissance epic poet usually followed this tradition; Sannazaro, Vida, Giles Fletcher, and Phineas Fletcher are among the well-known epic poets who followed this four-part opening pattern. In the hands of a bad poet the pattern becomes a slavish imitation; in the hands of a good one like John Milton this kind of formalism becomes, as we have seen, a gigantic metaphor whereby in *Paradise Regained* he can swiftly and implicitly compare Christ with Achilles, Odysseus, and Aeneas, as well as with his own Adam of *Paradise Lost.*

All this of course is to say that Milton is writing in the epic form. But we can now see that the mature Milton rarely wrote merely *in* a form. The form he used is one that he also transmuted into something uniquely fitted to the occasion and the poem. One is reminded of Gilbert Murray's remarks about Euripides:

> Every man who possesses real vitality can be seen as the resultant of two forces. He is first the child of a particular age, society, convention; of what we may call in one word a tradition. He is secondly, in one degree or another, a rebel against that tradition. And the best traditions make the best rebels.[7]

Euripides, says Murray, was such a man. So was Milton.

The first deviation from the epic form, the first "anti-epic" note, occurs in line 1 of *Paradise Regained.* Milton begins:

> I who e're while the happy Garden sung,
> By one mans disobedience lost, now sing
> Recover'd Paradise.

And of course this is a close echo of those opening lines of the *Aeneid* which traditionally precede the famous "arma virumque cano...." Prior to the well-known lines on arms and the man come four lines attested to by Donatus and Servius and occurring in many Renaissance editions, although rejected by many editors:[8]

Paradise Regained

Ille ego qui quondam gracili modulatus avena
Carmen, et egressus silvis vicina coegi
Ut quamvis avido parerent arva colono,
Gratum opus agricolis; at nunc horrentia Martis
Arma virumque cano.

I am he who once tuned my song on a slender reed, then, leaving the woodland, constrained the neighbouring fields to serve the husbandmen, however grasping—a work welcome to farmers; but now of Mars' bristling arms and the man I sing.

Vergil is telling us rather modestly that he is the poet who wrote the Eclogues and the Georgics, but that now he is turning to more important matters—"horrentia Martis / Arma virumque...." Put into this context, Milton's opening lines equate *Paradise Regained* with the *Aeneid*, which is hardly surprising; but what is surprising is that he implicitly equates his own *Paradise Lost* with the Eclogues and Georgics. It is dangerous to state in explicit prose what a poet creates through his implicit echoes; but I propose that these opening lines serve to imply that *Paradise Regained* surpasses *Paradise Lost* in maturity and high seriousness in the same fashion that the *Aeneid* towers over the Eclogues and the Georgics.[9]

Milton continues his acceptance/rejection of the epic tradition in line after line of the opening of *Paradise Regained*. Thus line 4 of *Paradise Regained* turns its back on the military epic just as firmly as the prologue to Book IX of *Paradise Lost*. This poem is not concerned with "Bases and tinsel Trappings, gorgeous Knights /At Joust and Torneament," but with

one mans firm obedience fully tri'd
Through all temptation, and the Tempter foil'd
In all his wiles, defeated and repuls't,
And *Eden* rais'd in the wast Wilderness.

(I. 4-7)

The great adventure in *Paradise Regained* is not a heroic journey but a stubborn, patient standing. The victorious field of battle is a desert, and instead of the traditional epic

wrauth
Of stern *Achilles* on his Foe pursu'd
Thrice fugitive about *Troy* Wall; or rage
Of *Turnus* for *Lavinia* disespous'd,
Or *Neptun's* ire or *Juno's.*

(PL IX. 14-18)

we have "this glorious Eremite" and "deeds / Above Heroic, though in secret done, / And unrecorded left through many an Age" (PR I. 8, 14-16).

Jesus's first appearance at lines 23-25—"the Son of *Joseph* deem'd / To the flood *Jordan,* came as then obscure, / Unmarkt, unknown"—is not unusual for the entry of an epic hero. What Milton does that is startlingly different is to leave Jesus at the end of the poem in physically the same state—still obscure, still unmarked—and while the structure of the poem has taken us inward, toward a "knowing," it is not toward Christ's fame but toward His self-knowing. The poem concludes not with Christ emerging victorious from the tomb (as for example in the conclusion of the *Christus Patiens* of Gregory of Nazianzen), but with Him returning in secret to His humble house.

The dynamic structure of *Paradise Regained,* following the directions toward which *Paradise Lost* was aiming, gives us a progression not through warfare and disobedience to the hope of a Paradise within, but through internal struggles and half-understood ideas of a filial relation to God onward to a true but completely internal revelation of the sonship of Jesus.

We can see this unique relation of the poem to the epic form in the chorus of angels in Book I:

Victory and Triumph to the Son of God
Now entring his great duel, not of arms,
But to vanquish by wisdom hellish wiles.

(173-75)

The traditional epic hero triumphed through force, and even the Christ of *Paradise Lost* is a warrior; with all respect for Raphael's explanation that the battles of Book VI of *Paradise Lost* are metaphoric, still, in terms of the poem and its imagery, Christ's battle against Satan and his army is as much physical warfare as those of

Achilles and Aeneas. But *Paradise Regained* explicitly rejects warfare entirely, much as it renounces other elements which mark the traditional epic. Christ the epic hero vanquishes Satan the epic enemy "by wisdom" (I. 175).

The poem even rejects the normal devices of suspense which we expect in a plot. When Satan appears in disguise at I. 314, the poem never for an instant pretends that the disguise is effective: "But now an aged man in Rural weeds, / Following, as seem'd, the quest of some stray Ewe." The scene is reminiscent of the encounter between Comus, who appears as a "gentle Shepherd," and the Lady (lines 265 f.); and of course the *topos* of the deity in disguise is common in countless other tales—in particular in Book I of the *Aeneid,* where Aeneas unknowingly encounters Venus. But Milton allows Comus's disguise to deceive the Lady for the remaining sixty-five lines of the scene, and they leave the stage with the Lady saying to Comus, "Shepherd, lead on." Vergil spins out the scene between Aeneas and Venus for almost a hundred lines while Aeneas begins to suspect that the maiden he has encountered is some goddess in disguise, but he does not know who. He half believes her denial, and only as she leaves does he discover the truth.

In *Paradise Regained* Milton creates quite a contrasting scene against this *topos* of the disguised god. The masquerading Satan gets out one speech:

> Sir, what ill chance hath brought thee to this place
> So far from path or road of men, who pass
> In Troop or Caravan, for single none
> Durst ever, who return'd, and dropt not here
> His Carcass, pin'd with hunger and with droughth?
>
> (I. 321-25)

And Christ cuts him off with a curt answer: "Who brought me hither / Will bring me hence, no other Guide I seek" (335-36). This is nothing less than an immediate stripping off of the disguise. When Satan wheedles,

> By Miracle he may, reply'd the Swain,
> What other way I see not, for we here
> Live on tough roots and stubs, to thirst inur'd
> More then the Camel.
>
> (I. 337-40)

Christ lays him bare in quite matter-of-fact tones:

> Think'st thou such force in Bread? is it not written
> (For I discern thee other then thou seem'st)
> Man lives not by Bread only, but each Word
> Proceeding from the mouth of God; who fed
> Our Fathers here with Manna....
>
> . . . .
>
> Why dost thou then suggest to me distrust,
> Knowing who I am, as I know who thou art?
>
> (I. 347-56)

Milton's method of picking up and tossing aside the *topos* of the deity in disguise is consistent with the mature sophistication of the whole poem. The method is not merely to ignore the potential suspense of the *topos;* it is first to call it up and then dismiss it, so that we are in no doubt as to what it is that he is doing because we see the alternative which he rejects. And this renunciation is part of the whole structure of *Paradise Regained;* the language, the action, and the arrangement are spare, direct, and undecorated. Milton's control is perfect.

When Christ triumphs over Satan in their first encounter (an "anti-epic" battle), His victory speech has this same pared-down bluntness:

> To whom our Saviour with unalter'd brow.
> Thy coming hither, though I know thy scope,
> I bid not nor forbid; do as thou find'st
> Permission from above: thou canst not more.
>
> (I. 493-96)

And that is all—none of the joy, rhetoric, or pride of a victorious epic hero; only three lines of laconic advice.

This exchange, this "anti-epic" battle, is also a logical development in the whole direction of Milton's poetic career: just as "Elegia Prima," more than forty years before, had been an exile-poem built out of—"against"—Ovid's exile poems, so *Paradise Regained* stands in relation to the epic tradition, only with far greater richness and complexity. And just as "Epitaphium Damonis," thirty years before *Paradise Regained,* both used and rejected pastoralism, so *Paradise Regained* makes the epic tradition not a model but an instrument for creating the unique kind of poem that *Paradise Regained* is.

This kind of conquest which Christ achieves over Satan must have been what *Paradise Lost* meant in Book IX by its scorn for tinsel trappings, although *Paradise Lost,* for all its progression toward a Paradise within, never approached this extreme. And it is hard to see how an epic poem could go much further than this toward making its conflict more spiritual or loftier. *Paradise Regained* thus becomes a poem not merely in keeping with the exalted nature of the epic tradition ("the best and most accomplished kindes of Poetrie," Sir Philip Sidney said[10]), but one which surpasses the tradition in embodying true, unobtrusive, spiritual heroism. Further, one should note the extent to which the poem has fused its extra-poetic pattern, the clash of Christ and Satan, with its poetic pattern, its epicness and its transcendence of even the epic, to create a poetic structure which uses the epic tradition as a foundation on which to build loftier pinnacles.

Satan's appearance in Book II is similarly managed. Like the traditional epic god he again uses his supernatural powers to disguise himself; but Milton, simultaneously accepting and rejecting the epic tradition, disdains to allow Satan to waste much of the poem's time. Christ enters the forest:

> he view'd it round,
> When suddenly a man before him stood,
> Not rustic as before, but seemlier clad,
> As one in City, or Court, or Palace bred.
>
> (II. 297-300)

And in one phrase, "not rustic as before," the poem dispenses with the traditional epic disguise.

Whatever Milton is doing, he is not fumbling. The potential suspense and the actual deflation of suspense are a sophisticated evolution arising logically out of the epic tradition, and again completely fusing the structure with the story, the poetic technique with the extra-poetic events.

The poem is not all as lean and boney as this. In Book II Satan tempts Christ with

> A Table richly spred, in regal mode,
> With dishes pil'd, and meats of noblest sort
> And savour, Beasts of chase, or Fowl of game,
> In pastry built, or from the spit, or boyl'd,

> Gris-amber-steam'd; all Fish from Sea or Shore,
> Freshet, or purling Brook, of shell or fin,
> And exquisitest name, for which was drain'd
> *Pontus* and *Lucrine* Bay, and *Afric* Coast.
>
> (II. 340-47)

This is, as David Daiches has pointed out,

> in the style of the richer passages of *Paradise Lost,* but instead
> of classical mythology being employed to build up a powerful
> and moving suggestion of ideal beauty (as it is in the first ac-
> count of Eden and of Eve), it is used almost ironically to sug-
> gest excess and exhibitionism. This effect is achieved partly
> by describing domestic objects and activities in high epic lan-
> guage as in
>
> > Beasts of chase, or Fowl of game,
> > In pastry built, or from the spit or boild,
> > Grisamber steam'd
>
> and partly by a note almost of parody in the exaggeration of
> such passages as those describing the two youths who stood by
> the sideboard or the nymphs under the trees. These are
> waiters and waitresses, and to describe the latter as
>
> > Ladies of th'*Hesperides,* that seemd
> > Fairer than feignd of old, or fabl'd since
> > Of Fairy Damsels met in Forest wide
> > By Knights of *Logres,* or of *Lyoness,*
> > *Lancelot* or *Pelleas* or *Pellenore*
>
> is a deliberate violation of decorum in order to achieve
> irony.[11]

It is a deliberate violation of decorum (as well as a deliberate gibe at
the Arthurian tradition which Milton had left behind him) because, in
this dialogue with the epic, Milton's form demands that these things
be said; by "these things" I mean not the poem's description of
the food, but the relation of this description of the waitresses to the
great narrative poems of the tradition. Pope does a similar, but

simpler, thing in "The Rape of the Lock." But Pope's parody, like most parodies, is comic; it is rare that a poem achieves some of its high seriousness by the direct use of parody.

As the temptations proceed through Satan's offer of worldly power we surely ought to see a reverse relation to the conventional epic; Aeneas proved his physical heroism by founding Rome; Christ proves His spiritual heroism by refusing Satan's offer of Rome. Readers may prefer the pomp and adventures of Homer and Vergil, or the vast cosmos and the rich language of *Paradise Lost;* but the flawless aesthetic integrity of *Paradise Regained* demands that Christ reject power over Rome with the words,

> Nor doth this grandeur and majestic show
> Of luxury, though call'd magnificence,
> More then of arms before, allure mine eye,
> Much less my mind.
>
> (IV. 110-13)

This context explains the peculiar formal appropriateness of the last temptation and Christ's victory. Satan places Christ on the pinnacle and says,

> There stand, if thou wilt stand; to stand upright
> Will ask thee skill; I to thy Fathers house
> Have brought thee, and highest plac't, highest is best,
> Now shew thy Progeny; if not to stand,
> Cast thy self down; safely if Son of God:
> For it is written, He will give command
> Concerning thee to his Angels, in thir hands
> They shall up lift thee, lest at any time
> Thou chance to dash thy foot against a stone.
>
> (IV. 551-59)

And now Christ achieves His triumph not by an epic adventurer's voyage or by heroic warfare but by anti-epic restraint. He conquers evil simply by being God. He does not march to victory, but rather refuses to act at Satan's command. His ultimate triumph over Satan and Satan's forces, and His climactic insight into His own true nature, after 1,900 lines of spiritual combat, are concentrated into just two laconic lines of the poem: "To whom thus Jesus: also it is written, / Tempt not the Lord thy God, he said, and stood" (IV. 560-61). And with this "act," if we can call it an act, the action is over. Any more expansive, "richer" account of the event, any sonorous Miltonic simile at this point would disintegrate this highest spiritual victory embodied in poetry which has renounced all but the barest, clearest language. The Milton who once planned an Arthuriad and who charmed countless readers of *Paradise Lost* with the splendors of Satanic rhetoric could surely have managed a passage involving a Christ who was "That glorious Form, that Light unsufferable, / And that far-beaming blaze of Majesty." But that effulgent image of the Nativity was appropriate to another poem over thirty years before. By now the old poet had won his triumphs in that style; now he is taking much the bolder course—culminating his poem with these spare lines which are exquisitely fitted to this moment in this poem. In a clear and important sense what is compressed into these two lines in *Paradise Regained* is a masterfully appropriate anti-climax to the anti-epic structure of the poem, an inward progression to an internal victory.

After these lines *Paradise Regained* moves quickly to its unobtrusive ending only seventy-five lines later. The angelic choir sings praises of Christ's victory. Then like so many epic heroes before Him, He returns home, but still unspectacularly stressing the unspectacular virtues of humility and obedience:

> Thus they [the Angels] the Son of God our Saviour meek
> Sung Victor, and from Heavenly Feast refresht
> Brought on his way with joy; hee unobserv'd
> Home to his Mothers house private return'd.
>
> (IV. 636-39)

and that ends the poem.

There is logic in Milton's impatience at hearing *Paradise Lost* preferred to *Paradise Regained*. This is a poem of over two thousand lines, but constructed with all the unified tightness of, for example, Milton's flawless sonnet to Edward Lawrence. *Paradise Regained* lacks the brilliance of *Paradise Lost* because brilliance would mar its steady gray restraint. It has no suspense, no physical combats or epic voyages, not only because they would clash with the poem's doctrinal foundations, but because the structure of the poem as a poem demands that the poet eliminate these elements—not that he ignore them, but that he raise them as possibilities and then reject them. The epic journey is into Himself; the structural progression is toward renunciation of the external glory of the epic tradition.

Only a poet who had already written a great epic poem could manage this kind of sophisticated dialogue with the tradition, this use of epic devices as a context within which (either simultaneously or at other times) to hold the epic devices up for consideration and deliberate rejection. If the poem has not attracted an enthusiastic audience, this is unfortunate. But surely Milton must have felt that it was the reader, not the poem, who was at fault.

XI

The Developing Concept
of Structure
in Milton's Poetry

Something so written to aftertimes,
as they should not willingly let it die.

When Milton was nineteen years old he said,

> I have some naked thoughts that rove about
> And loudly knock to have their passage out.

These are thoughts, he says,

> Such where the deep transported mind may soare
> Above the wheeling poles, and at Heav'ns dore
> Look in, and see each blissful Deitie
> How he before the thunderous throne doth lie.[1]

And when Milton was in his early thirties, shortly after the completion of "Epitaphium Damonis," he spoke of the function of a poet
"soaring in the high region of his fancies with his garland and singing
robes about him."[2] While some of Milton's poems are songs fit
best for singing on a May morning, Milton's chief concern
throughout his life was with poetry as a means of facing the way of
the world and coming to terms with it. After his return from Italy in
1639, he wrote,

> I began thus farre to assent both to them and divers of my
> friends here at home, and not lesse to an inward prompting

which now grew daily upon me, that by labour and intent
study (which I take to be my portion in this life) joyn'd with
the strong propensity of nature, I might perhaps leave something so written to aftertimes, as they should not willingly let
it die. These thoughts at once possesst me, and these other.
That if it were certain to write as men buy Leases, for three
lives and downward, there ought no regard be sooner had,
then to Gods glory by the honour and instruction of my
country.[3]

Poetry for Milton was in an important sense a dialectic, a mode of
working out, by patterns and techniques proper to the poem, such
problems as why death came to good old men like Lancelot Andrewes
and to innocent children like Anne Phillips. At first the poems did not
function very well. They stated the problem at the beginning of the
poem, sometimes bluntly, sometimes confusedly, rarely well, and they
came to their conclusion—that somehow God looked after His
own—by what was, in poetic structure, only an awkward leap. Only
after detours into poems that were largely celebratory rather than
dialectic, such as "Elegia Quinta" and the Nativity Ode, perhaps
by means of these detours, did Milton learn to integrate the dialectic
and the poem—to make the poem work toward truth and to make the
truth give structure to the poem. Woodhouse suggests that Sonnet 7
("How soon hath Time ..."), in 1632, was the turning point; that
here for the first time Milton makes the sonnet as a sonnet serve as an
instrument in solving the extra-poetic problem which the poem
proposes.[4] Certainly two years later, in 1634, when he wrote *Comus,*
Milton was on sure ground: *Comus* works with mature ease not only
as a celebratory masque but also as a unified poetic drama, and as a
neo-Platonic allegory on the progress of the soul toward truth. The
masque tradition which gives the poem form, the occasion and the
story which give it content, and the neo-Platonism which supplies the
basis for the structural unity all combine to constitute an entity of
greater complexity and integrity than anything Milton had previously
done.

Now Milton is ready for the masterpieces: first "Lycidas,"
which creates a pastoralism which is Greco-Roman, Celtic, and
Christian, and through its pastoralism, prosody, imagery, and highly
complex but unified structure, works its way to a vision of justice and

mercy. "Lycidas" resembles the early epicedia in the extra-poetic pattern it uses, but "Lycidas" surpasses them immeasurably in integrating that pattern with a poetic structure which carries the poem to a resolution inextricably interwoven with the totality of the poem.

"Mansus" intervenes here as a weak poem which must have served Milton well—it gave him a tradition to work with, to follow, to invert, and to move beyond. Few critics have praised it, but it is not difficult to imagine that "Mansus" was, for Milton, a useful step toward the structural innovations which lay ahead.

Then "Epitaphium Damonis" breaks through to a new level of poetic technique. Again, the problem is the death of a friend, a very close friend now. But the poem moves both within and beyond the pastoral tradition, and its resolution depends in part on its self-consciousness of its form, its awareness of moving dynamically beyond the poetic conventions within which it began, and the dynamism arising from the poetic conventions it surmounts.

Samson Agonistes brings the traditions of Greek tragedy to bear on the recurring question of the justice of God's ways. Whether it is Milton's last poem, the next-to-last, or earlier than that seems unanswerable on a basis of external evidence. Its conservatism in its use of the Greek tragic tradition, however, argues against its being a very late work. While it uses its Greek models skillfully and not slavishly, it tends to remain content within its tradition (unlike "Epitaphium Damonis," *Paradise Lost,* and *Paradise Regained*); it tends to use the Greek tragedies as general models, not as instruments for creating a new pattern adapted uniquely to this poem. Where "Epitaphium Damonis," *Paradise Lost,* and *Paradise Regained* repeatedly create functional dissonances between themselves and their respective traditions and then use these dissonances as instruments to arrive at extra-poetic resolutions, *Samson Agonistes* tends simply to use the tragic form as a vehicle for the Biblical story; and the tragic tradition in the play is more a generalized mode or vehicle than it is an implement whose function is to create the patterns of clashes and harmonies with the poem itself in order to arrive at a culminating insight.

But *Paradise Lost,* like "Epitaphium Damonis," refuses to rest within its tradition. It establishes itself again and again as an epic poem, yet at the same time it drives itself, somewhat like "Epitaphium Damonis," from more conventional epic positions early in the poem to concepts of higher virtue at the end, and to the explicit exaltation of the Christian virtues of patience and humility over the conventional epic virtues of physical courage and martial skill. Like "Epitaphium Damonis," *Samson Agonistes,* and many of the early poems, *Paradise Lost* is ultimately a dialectic poem; it seeks for the justification of God's ways. Like "Lycidas," "Epitaphium Damonis," and *Samson Agonistes,* it ultimately finds this justification, this answer to its extra-poetic problems, by poetic means: by its epic hero who learns to suffer for Truth's sake, and who journeys forth to seek the Paradise within.

Paradise Regained in many ways takes some of the unrealized implications of *Paradise Lost* to their logical conclusion and uses the epic tradition with even greater subtlety and sophistication than *Paradise Lost.* Its epic battles are all struggles of the spirit, and the conventional armies of epic poems are dismissed as merely "cumbersome luggage of war ... argument of human weakness rather then of strength." The pattern in *Paradise Regained* is not one of external conflict, although Satan is present, but of internal struggle: the journey is that of Christ who "into himself descended" and discovered His true nature. The discovery comes, like Aeneas's founding of Rome, through successive challenges; but the challenges presented by Satan are not those of war, and Christ's ultimate victory is not by physical violence but "By deeds of peace, by wisdom eminent, / By patience, temperance" (III. 91-92).

Thus the structure of the poem is as much anti-epic—a renunciation of the epic and a transcendence of the epic—as it is epic; but just as "Epitaphium Damonis" both uses and transcends pastoralism to achieve its poetic vision, so *Paradise Regained* uses both its acceptance and its rejection of the epic tradition to arrive at its ultimate extra-poetic resolution—the discovery of the self through the struggles of the spirit.

Paradise Regained stands far down the road from an early poem like "Elegia Prima," written over forty years earlier. In those youthful days, the rusticated undergraduate Milton turned not only to poetry to come to terms with his rustication, but to the literary tradition of Ovid and his exile-poems. So Milton turned his Ovid upside-down and wrote a poem on the joys of exile. At the other end of the road is that great, bare, boney epic, *Paradise Regained,* dictated by the blind, beaten old rebel. But he turned to poetry still though it now concerned the spiritual heroism of Christ and the coming to a self-knowing, rather than his own youthful problems. Of course Milton knows his Homer and Vergil as well as his Ovid, and now it is Homer and Vergil who are turned upside-down. He does not discard them—he uses them. He uses their traditions as building material when he needs these traditions as a foundation from which to rise. And from this foundation the poem develops its own structure, a structure which moves to its unique, spiritual, "metaphysical" resolution. What Milton achieves in *Paradise Regained* is immeasurably better than the Latin trifle of forty years before. But "Elegia Prima" bears the mark of the poet who was to write *Paradise Regained,* and *Paradise Regained* still retains a few traces of "Elegia Prima." After more than forty years and more than seventy poems, a great many naked thoughts had indeed knocked their passage out. In so doing they developed in Milton a concept of poetry in which extra-poetic experience, traditional form, and poetic structure fused themselves into one inseparable entity from the foundation to the pinnacles.

Notes

Note to Chapter I

1. Samuel Johnson. *The Rambler*, No. 139, Tuesday, 16 July 1751. *The Works of Samuel Johnson*, ed. W. J. Bate and Albrecht B. Strauss (New Haven: Yale University Press, 1969), 4: 371.

Notes to Chapter II

1. All quotations from Milton are from *The Works of John Milton*, ed. Frank A. Patterson (New York: Columbia University Press, 1931), hereafter cited as *Works*.

2. Arthur E. Barker, "Structural Pattern in *Paradise Lost*," *PQ* 28 (1949): 17-30; Geoffrey Hartman, "Milton's Counterplot," *ELH* 25 (1958): 1-12; H.V.S. Ogden, "The Crisis of *Paradise Lost* Reconsidered," *PQ* 36 (1957): 1-19; John T. Shawcross, "The Balanced Structure of *Paradise Lost*," *SP* 62 (1965): 696-718; A.S.P. Woodhouse, "Pattern in *Paradise Lost*," *UTQ* 22 (1952-53): 109-27. For key to abbreviations see Works Cited, p. 193.

3. Joseph H. Summers, *The Muse's Method: An Introduction to Paradise Lost* (Cambridge, Mass.: Harvard University Press, 1962), p. 114.

4. Barker, "Structural Pattern in *Paradise Lost*," p. 28.

5. Ibid., p. 30.

6. John Dryden, "Dedication to the Aeneis," *Works*, ed. Sir Walter Scott and George Saintsbury (Edinburgh: William Paterson, 1889), 14: 143-44.

7. Percy B. Shelley, *Shelley's Prose: The Trumpet of a Prophecy*, ed. David Lee Clark (Albuquerque: University of New Mexico Press, 1954), p. 290.

8. Lascelles Abercrombie, *The Idea of Great Poetry* (London: Secker, 1925), p. 141.

9. "[Milton's] design is the losing of our happiness; his event is not prosperous, like that of all other epic works." John Dryden, "Essay on Satire," *Works*, 13: 18.

10. D.W. Lucas, *Aristotle's Poetics* (Oxford: Clarendon Press, 1968), p. 140; in a footnote to chapter 13.52^b34-53^a5 (Aristotle's discussion of what sort of person experiences the tragic change of fortune) Lucas says, "It is a point of importance that A. does without the word which modern writers find indispensable in discussing the subject, namely 'hero.' In fact no such term existed until the sixteenth century when the Italian commentators on the *P*. made the transition from heroes, i.e. figures from the heroic age (ἡροικοὶ χρόνοι , *Pol.* 1285^b4) who are the normal subject of tragedy to the most conspicuous of them in any one play, the 'hero.' He was taken over from them in France by Boileau, and first appears in English in Dryden's Defence of the Epilogue in 1673."

11. Throughout this work I use the translations of Vergil by H. Rushton Fairclough in *Eclogues, Georgics, Aeneid, Minor Poems,* Loeb Classical Library (Cambridge, Mass.: Harvard University Press, 1946).

12. So John Steadman in *Milton and the Renaissance Hero* (Oxford: Clarendon Press, 1967), p. xiv, refers to "the three most prominent 'heroes' (Adam, Christ, and Satan)."

13. Trans. W.H.D. Rouse (New York: New American Library, 1937), pp. 132-33.

14. Milton was not, of course, the first epic poet to use this technique of setting off one epic hero against the background of another. R.D. Williams in "The Purpose of the *Aeneid,*" *Antichthon* 1 (1967): 34-35, points out that Vergil used Homer in this fashion by contrasting Aeneas with Oddysseus. "Odysseus is the great individualist, but Aeneas has to be the social man, *insignis pietate.*"

15. Similarly, Adam's visions of the future resemble the passages on the shields of Achilles and Aeneas in Homer and Vergil, as Lawrence D. Sasek points out in "The Drama of *Paradise Lost,* Books XI and XII," *Studies in English Renaissance Literature,* ed. W.F. McNeir, Louisiana State University Studies: Humanities Series, No. 12 (1962): 181-96.

16. See Mindele C. Treip, *N&Q* 203 (1958): 209-10.

Notes to Chapter III

1. See Walter MacKellar, *The Latin Poems of John Milton,* Cornell Studies in English 15 (New Haven: Yale University Press, 1930), p. 22, who dates the poem in the spring of 1626. Harris Fletcher in *The Intellectual Development of John Milton* (Urbana: University of Illinois Press, 1961), 2: 392-403, suggests that it may have been written in the spring of 1625. William Riley Parker in *Milton: a Biography* (Oxford: Clarendon Press, 1968), 1: 30 (hereafter cited as *Biography),* agrees with MacKellar. "Elegia Prima" may not actually be the first of the Latin elegies; Fletcher in *The Intellectual Development* and elsewhere argues that "Elegia Quarta" is earlier than "Elegia Prima." But the precise dates and even the sequence of the first and fourth elegies is not important to this discussion. I stress "Elegia Prima" not because it is the first of the elegies but because it is a skillful poem that exemplifies significant characteristics of Milton's early poetry.

2. Parker, *Biography,* 1: 29-30.

3. See Davis P. Harding, *Milton and the Renaissance Ovid,* University of Illinois Studies in Language and Literature, 30: 4 (Urbana: University of Illinois Press, 1946).

4. James Holly Hanford, "The Youth of Milton," *Studies in Shakespeare, Milton, and Donne* (New York: Macmillan, 1925), p. 109.

5. MacKellar, in *The Latin Poems,* pp. 190-200, lists a great many but there are many more that MacKellar does not mention.

6. *Tristia* I. i. 47-48.

7. Throughout this work I use the translations of the Latin poetry by Merritt Y. Hughes in his edition *The Complete Poems and Major Prose* (New York: Odyssey Press, 1957).

8. *Tristia* I. i. 39-42.

9. *Tristia* III. xiv. 37-38. Throughout this chapter I use the translations of Arthur Leslie Wheeler in the Loeb Classical Library (Cambridge, Mass.: Harvard University Press, 1962).

10. *Tristia* III. xii. 23-24. See also *Epistulae ex Ponto* I. viii. 35-36.

11. I use the translation of J.H. Mozley in the Loeb Classical Library (Cambridge, Mass.: Harvard University Press, 1962).

12. *Tristia* III. x. 71-78. *Epistulae ex Ponto* I. iii. 49-52; III. i. 13; III. vii. 13-16. Milton refers directly to this complaint of Ovid's in his "Elegia Sexta," 19-20.

13. *Epistulae ex Ponto* II. vii. 74; IV. x. 61-62.

14. Perhaps, as J. Mitchell Morse suggests *(N&Q* 203, 1958, p. 211) the reference in "Lycidas" to "Camus, footing slow" is a pun on "footing" and "pedantic."

15. For a somewhat different opinion of the structure of the poem, see my "Ovid's Exile and Milton's Rustication," *PQ* 37 (1958): 501-2. Obviously I think my present position is better.

16. I must use the term "epicedion" for "poem lamenting the death of a friend" because the usual English term "elegy" will not do. Of Milton's seven Latin poems which he called "elegiae," only two are laments for the dead. Milton decisively follows the Latin practice of using "elegia" to indicate a verse-form, the elegiac distich, and not to indicate any particular subject. I therefore follow the practice of Don Cameron Allen in *The Harmonious Vision* (Baltimore: The Johns Hopkins Press, 1954), pp. 43-45, in using the term "epicedion."

17. For example, MacKellar, *The Latin Poems*, pp. 44-45.

18. Leigh Hunt, *Leigh Hunt's Literary Criticism,* ed. Lawrence H. Houtchens and Carolyn W. Houtchens (New York: Columbia University Press, 1956), p. 181.

19. Douglas Bush in "An Allusion in Milton's *Elegia Tertia*," *Harvard Library Bulletin,* 9 (1955): 392-96, proposes that the two dead men were not Count Ernest and Duke Christian, but King James I and Maurice, Prince of Orange.

20. The last line of "Elegia Tertia," "Talia contingant somnia saepe mihi" ("May dreams like these often befall me") is a most un-Miltonic howler. It echoes Ovid's "Proveniant medii sic mihi saepe dies" ("May my lot bring many a midday like to this")—*Amores* I. v. 26. But while Milton's vision is of the saintly Bishop of Winchester in Heaven, Ovid's was of Corinna in the nude:

> Ut stetit ante oculos posito velamine nostros
> In toto nusquam corpore menda fuit.
>
> (17-18)

As she stood before my eyes with drapery all laid aside, nowhere on all her body was sign of fault.

(Grant Showerman's translation in the Loeb edition). Ovid's unsaintly poem concludes with mock reticence:

> Cetera quis nescit? lassi requievimus ambo.
> proveniant medii sic mihi saepe dies!

Who does not know the rest? Outwearied, we both lay quiet in repose. May my lot bring many a midday like to this!

21. For a discussion of the problem see H.J. Rose, *The Eclogues of Vergil* (Berkeley: University of California Press, 1942). C.J. Putnam in *Virgil's Pastoral Art* (Princeton: Princeton University Press, 1970), pp. 188-89, doubts the equation between Daphnis and Julius Caesar.

22. Throughout this work I use Fairclough's translation of *Eclogues, Georgics, Aeneid, Minor Poems* in the Loeb edition.

23. *Silvae* V. iii. 19-27. See also Propertius's vision of the beatification of Marcellus, *Elegiae* III. xviii. 31-34.

24. See Allen, *The Harmonious Vision*, pp. 43-45, for a discussion of Greek epicedia and the English tradition.

25. In *Milton's "Lycidas,"* ed. Scott Elledge (New York: Harper and Row, 1966), pp. 119-20; see also, for example, Cyril Tourneur, "A Griefe on the Death of Prince Henrie," ibid., pp. 121-25.

26. See T.P. Harrison, Jr., "The Latin Pastorals of Milton and Castiglione," *PMLA* 50 (1935): 480-93.

27. Castiglione, "Alcon," *Delitiae CC Italorum Poetarum*, ed. R. Gherus ([Frankfurt]: Iona Rosa, 1608), 1: 720. Trans. Robert M. Durling in Elledge, *Milton's "Lycidas,"* p. 72.

28. " 'To Shepherd's Ear': the Form of Milton's *Lycidas*," *Silent Poetry*, ed. Alastair Fowler (London: Longman, 1970), p. 171.

29. Richard P. Adams, "The Archetypal Pattern of Death and Rebirth in *Lycidas*," *Milton's Lycidas: the Tradition and the Poem*, ed. C.A. Patrides (New York: Holt, Rinehart, and Winston, Inc., 1961), p. 122.

30. For a more complete account of the relation of the rhyme scheme to the structure of "Lycidas," see Ants Oras, "Milton's Early Rhyme Schemes and the Structure of *Lycidas*," *MP* 52 (1954): 12-22.

31. Fowler, "Form of Milton's *Lycidas*," p. 172.

32. Ibid., p. 175.

33. See, for example, James Holly Hanford, "The Pastoral Elegy and Milton's *Lycidas*," *PMLA* 25 (1910): 403-47; and A.S.P. Woodhouse, "Milton's Pastoral Monodies," *Studies in Honour of Gilbert Norwood*, ed. Mary E. White (Toronto: University of Toronto Press, 1952), pp. 261-78.

Notes to Chapter IV

1. Hugh Maclean, "Milton's *Fair Infant*," *ELH* 24 (1957): 296-305.

2. Milton says he was seventeen when he wrote the poem, but William Riley Parker shows, in *TLS*, 17 December 1938, p. 802, that Milton must have been nineteen.

3. Woodhouse, "Milton's Pastoral Monodies," p. 262.

4. Rosemond Tuve, *Images and Themes in Five Poems by Milton* (Cambridge, Mass.: Harvard University Press, 1957), p. 37.

5. John Milton, *The Complete Poems and Major Prose*, ed. Merritt Y. Hughes (New York: Odyssey Press, 1957), p. 42.

6. Lowry Nelson, *Baroque Lyric Poetry* (New Haven: Yale University Press, 1961), p. 48.

7. Ibid., p. 51.

8. John Milton, *The Poems of Mr. John Milton. The 1645 Edition,* ed. Cleanth Brooks and John Edward Hardy (New York: Harcourt, Brace, 1951), p. 104.

9. Arthur Barker, "The Pattern of Milton's Nativity Ode," *UTQ* 10 (1940-41): 173.

10. Ibid., p. 173.

Notes to Chapter V

1. E.M.W. Tillyard in *The Miltonic Setting* (Cambridge: Cambridge University Press, 1938), pp. 1-28, dates the poems in 1631. But see Frederick W. Bateson, *English Poetry: A Critical Introduction* (New York: Barnes and Noble, 1966), pp. 108-9, and Fletcher, *The Intellectual Development of John Milton,* vol. 2, pp. 480-83, 495-96, for arguments that the Companion Pieces were written in 1629, at the same time as the Nativity Ode.

2. A.S.P. Woodhouse, *Milton the Poet.* Sedgewick Memorial Lecture (Toronto: J.M. Dent, 1955), p. 5.

3. Louis Martz, "The Rising Poet," *The Lyric and Dramatic Milton.* Selected Papers from the English Institute, ed. Joseph H. Summers (New York: Columbia University Press, 1965): 17. See also Allen, *The Harmonious Vision,* pp. 3-23.

4. Nan Carpenter, "The Place of Music in *L'Allegro* and *Il Penseroso,*" *UTQ* 22 (1953-54): 358-59.

5. David M. Miller, "From Delusion to Illumination: A Larger Structure for *L'Allegro-Il Penseroso,*" *PMLA* 86 (1971): 32, 37.

6. Douglas Bush, "The Date of Milton's *Ad Patrem,*" *MP* 61 (1963-64): 204-8; Woodhouse, "Notes on Milton's Early Development," pp. 89-91; John T. Shawcross, *N&Q* 204 (1959): 358-59; Harris Fletcher, "Grierson's Suggested Date for Milton's 'Ad Patrem,' " *The Fred Newton Scott Anniversary Papers* (Chicago: University of Chicago Press, 1929): 199-205.

7. Throughout his Latin poetry Milton tends to follow the common but not invariable Roman practice of using "donum" for gifts to or from gods or superior people, and "munus" for less honored rewards. See *A Concordance to the Latin, Greek, and Italian Poems of John Milton,* comp. Lane Cooper (Halle: Niemeyer, 1923), pp. 44-45, 104.

Notes to Chapter VI

1. Parker, *Biography,* 2: 789, n. 28.

2. Stephen Orgel, *The Jonsonian Masque* (Cambridge, Mass.: Harvard University Press, 1965), p. 152.

3. G.W. Whiting, *Milton and This Pendant World* (Austin: University of Texas Press, 1958), p. 8.

4. Enid Welsford, *The Court Masque* (Cambridge: Cambridge University Press, 1927), p. 318. See also Allen, *The Harmonious Vision*, pp. 29-30, "The poem is not a masque at all."

5. Marjorie Nicolson, *John Milton: A Reader's Guide to his Poetry* (New York: Noonday Press, 1963), p. 85.

6. Parker, *Biography*, 1: 132.

7. Jacopo Mazzoni, "On the Defense of the *Comedy*" in *Literary Criticism: Plato to Dryden*, ed. Allan H. Gilbert (New York: American Book Company, 1940), pp. 371-72.

8. E.M.W. Tillyard, "The Action of *Comus*," *Studies in Milton* (London: Chatto and Windus, 1951), p. 82.

9. Ben Jonson, *The Masque of Blackness, Ben Jonson*, ed. C.H. Herford and P. Simpson (Oxford: Clarendon Press, 1941), 7: 176-77.

10. David Wilkinson, "The Escape from Pollution," *Essays in Criticism*, 10 (1960): 32.

11. Sears Jayne, "The Subject of Milton's Ludlow *Mask*," *A Maske at Ludlow: Essays on Milton's Comus*, ed. John S. Diekhoff (Cleveland: Case Western Reserve University Press, 1968): 172-73.

12. Ibid., p. 173.

13. Quoted in Jayne, p. 185.

14. Nicolson, *John Milton*, p. 86.

15. Aurelian Townshend, *Tempe Restor'd*, in *Aurelian Townshend's Poems and Masks*, ed. E.K. Chambers (Oxford: Clarendon Press, 1912), p. 79.

16. Ibid., pp. 96-98.

17. Ibid., p. 99.

Notes to Chapter VII

1. G. Wilson Knight, *The Burning Oracle: Studies in the Poetry of Action* (Oxford: Oxford University Press, 1939), p. 70.

2. Harrison, "The Latin Pastorals of Milton and Castiglione," pp. 480-93.

3. E.M.W. Tillyard, *Milton* (London: Chatto and Windus, 1946), pp. 90-91.

4. Walter Savage Landor, "Southey and Landor," *The Complete Works of Walter Savage Landor*, ed. T. Earle Welby (London: Chapman and Hall, 1927), 5:330.

5. Andre Vitorelli in *Poesie Nomiche* (Venice: Baba, 1635), p. 310. See also Scipione Sambiasi, "Glorioso colla Spada, e colla penna," p. 280. I am grateful to Dr. Alfred Triolo for his help here and elsewhere with these Italian poems addressed to Manso.

6. Publius Papinius Statius, "Epistula ad Vitorium Marcellum," in *Silvae*, trans. J.H. Mozley, Loeb Classical Library (New York: Putnam, 1928): IV. iv. 64-65.

7. "Panegyricus Messallae," 39 (trans. J.P. Postgate in the Loeb edition).

8. "Laus Pisonis," *Minor Latin Poets* (trans. J.W. Duff and A.M. Duff in the Loeb edition).

9. Milton, *Of Education, Works,* 4: 280.

10. George Buchanan, "Ad Carolum V. Imper. Burdegalae hospitio publico susceptum, nomine Scholae Burdegalensis anno M D xxxix," *Poemata* (Amsterdam: Waesberger, 1665), p. 368; lines 7-18.

11. Patrick Hannay, "The Second Elegy," *Minor Poets of the Caroline Period,* ed. George Saintsbury (Oxford: Oxford University Press, 1905), 1: 706; lines 227-34, hereafter cited as *The Caroline Poets.*

12. Vincenzo Carrafa, "Sue lodi dispari alla fama del Marchese," *Poesie Nomiche,* p. 284.

13. *Ad C. Herennium Libri IV De Ratione Dicendi,* trans. Harry Caplan, Loeb Classical Library (Cambridge, Mass.: Harvard University Press, 1954), III. vi. 11. See also Doxopater, *Rhetores Graeci,* ed. Christian Walz (Stuttgart: Cottae, 1832), 449: 33, as quoted by Theodore Burgess in "Epedeictic Literature," *University of Chicago Studies in Classical Philology,* 3 (1902): 122; "It is the law of encomiasts to agree always that the subject is greater than words can match."

14. See Thomas Whitfield Baldwin, *William Shakspere's Small Latine & Lesse Greeke* (Urbana: University of Illinois Press, 1944), 1: 417, and Donald Lemen Clark, *John Milton at St. Paul's School* (New York: Columbia University Press, 1948), p. 193.

15. See, for example, "Ad Messallam," lines 1-17 and 177-78; "Laus Pisonis," lines 68-80; "In Robertum Sanseverinatem," f. liii^r, (lines 168-69), and f. lv^r, (lines 325-26); Henry King, "Upon the Death of ... Doctor Donne," *The Caroline Poets,* 3: 218-19, lines 1-28, 43-50; Carlo Noci, "Stile dispari al desiderio," *Poesie Nomiche,* p. 263.

16. "Praefatio Panegyrici Dicti Anthemio Augusto bis Consuli," lines 15-20.

17. "Panegyricus de Tertio Consulatu Honorii Augusti," lines 60-62.

18. Buchanan, "Ad Carolum," pp. 368-69; lines 24-28.

19. For example, "Laus Pisonis," lines 68-80.

20. Marcus Fabius Quintilianus, *Institutio Oratoria,* trans. H. Butler, Loeb Classical Library (London: Heinemann, 1933), III. vii. 11.

21. Tillyard, *Milton,* pp. 90-91.

22. Landor, *Imaginary Conversations, The Complete Works,* 5: 330.

23. Statius, "Laudes Crispini," *Silvae,* V. ii.

24. Fracastorius, "Ad Danielem Rainerium Veronae Prefectum," *Deliliae CC Italorum Poetarum,* ([Frankfurt]: I. Rosa, 1608), 1: 1096-98. See also, for example, Lazarus Bonamicus, "Ad Diegum Hurtadum Mendozam," Ibid., pp. 469-72.

25. Charles Diodati was buried on 27 August 1638 while Milton was in Italy. It is not certain when Milton learned of his death or when he wrote the "Epitaphium Damonis." John T. Shawcross, *"Epitaphium Damonis:* Lines 9-13 and the Date of Composition," *MLN* 71 (1956): 322-34, and William Riley Parker, "Milton and the News of Charles Diodati's Death," *MLN* 72 (1957): 486-88, argue that the poem was written in October or November of 1639. Meanwhile Milton met Manso in November or December of 1638, and probably wrote "Mansus" soon after. See William Riley Parker, "Notes on the Chronology of Milton's Latin Poems" in *A Tribute to George Coffin Taylor,* ed. Arnold Williams (Chapel Hill: University of North Carolina Press, 1952), pp. 130-31.

26. See, for example, Katherine Philips, "In Memory of Mrs. E.H.," *The Caroline Poets,* 1: 566; line 50.

27. The absence of explicit Christianity from "Mansus" is of course in marked contrast to "Lycidas" and "Epitaphium Damonis," especially in view of the similarity of the three poems in having a concluding vision of life after death. Perhaps two forces are at work: (1) the atmosphere of harmony throughout "Mansus," so different from the initial discord which must be resolved in the other two poems, may have seemed to Milton to create a structural situation in which a justification of God's ways to men through Christianity was poetically unnecessary; (2) Milton's fervent Protestantism and Manso's equally fervent Roman Catholicism may have led Milton to feel that Christianity was a subject better avoided in the poem. Milton himself writes of his visit to Naples: "By him [Manso] I was treated, while I stayed there, with all the warmth of friendship: for he conducted me himself over the city and the viceregent's court, and more than once came to visit me at my own lodgings. On my leaving Naples, he gravely apologized for showing me no more attention, alleging that although it was what he wished above all things, it was not in his power in that city, because I had not thought proper to be more guarded on the point of religion." *Defensio Secunda, Works,* 8: 125.

Notes to Chapter VIII

1. MacKellar, *The Latin Poems,* pp. 332-53, records 116 passages in Vergil, Horace, Ovid, et al., a staggering list for a poem of 219 lines, but G.B.A. Fletcher, "Milton's Latin Poems," *MP* 37 (1940): 343-50, attacks MacKellar for superficiality and adds eighteen more.

2. See Walter A. Montgomery, "The *Epitaphium Damonis* in the Stream of Classical Lament," *Studies for William A. Read,* ed. Nathaniel M. Caffee and Thomas A. Kirby (Baton Rouge: Louisiana State University Press, 1940), p. 215.

3. John Milton, *The Poems of Milton,* ed. Thomas Keightley (London: Chapman and Hall, 1859), 2: 456.

4. *Georgics,* IV. 168.

5. One is reminded of course of "Lycidas," 76-84.

6. Theocritus's first idyll bewailed his death and Vergil's fifth eclogue tells of the deification of Daphnis.

7. *Carmina,* II, 11, lines 17-18.

8. *Epodi,* XIII. 17-18.

9. Mark Pattison, *John Milton,* English Men of Letters, ed. John Morley (London: Macmillan, 1887), p. 41.

10. Vergil in turn is imitating Theocritus's fifth idyll, line 33.

11. See Statius, "Statius Marcello suo Salutem," praefatio to *Silvae IV;* also Quintilianus, *Institutio Oratoria,* X. iii. 7; and Aulus Gellius, *praefatio* to *Atticae Noctes,* trans. John C. Rolfe, Loeb Classical Library (Cambridge, Mass.: Harvard University Press, 1960-61), para. 6.

12. *The Reason of Church Government, Works,* 3, 1: 236

13. Woodhouse, "Milton's Pastoral Monodies," p. 268.

14. Keightley in *The Poems of Milton* (p. 463) reads "fistula" as "Latin composition"; E.K. Rand, "Milton in Rustication," *SP* 19 (1922): 124-25, n. 26, as "pastoral poetry."

15. Julius Caesar Scaliger, *Poetices Libri Septem* ([Heidelberg]: Vincentius, 1561), p. 6.

16. George Puttenham, *Of Poets and Poesy, Elizabethan Critical Essays,* ed. G. Gregory Smith (Oxford: Clarendon Press, 1904), 2:27.

17. Sir Philip Sidney, *Defence of Poesie,* ed. Albert Feuillerat (Cambridge: Cambridge University Press, 1923), p. 22.

18. Keightley, *The Poems of Milton,* pp. 463-64.

19. David Masson, *Life of John Milton* (Gloucester, Mass.: Peter Smith, 1881, reprint 1965), 1: 819; C.S. Jerram, *The Lycidas and Epitaphium Damonis of Milton* (London: Longman, 1874), p. 122; MacKellar, *The Latin Poems,* p. 349.

20. John Black, *Life of Torquato Tasso* (London: Murray, 1810), 2: 467.

21. Michele De Filippis, "Milton and Manso: Cups or Books?" *PMLA* 51 (1936): 745-56. Donald C. Dorian in "Milton's *Epitaphium Damonis,* lines 181-97," *PMLA* 54 (1939): 612-13, agrees with De Filippis, citing Pindar's comparison of an ode to a cup in the seventh Olympian ode.

22. Milton's probable source, Tasso's *La Fenice,* stresses the Phoenix as a symbol of resurrection. See Rudolf Gotfried, "Milton, Lactantius, Claudian, and Tasso," *SP* 30 (1933): 497-503.

23. See Irene Samuel, *Plato and Milton,* Cornell Studies in English 35 (Ithaca: Cornell University Press, 1947), especially "The Doctrine of Love," pp. 149-71.

24. Marsilio Ficino, *Opera Omnia* (Basileae, 1561), p. 324, quoted in Paul O. Kristeller, *The Philosophy of Marsilio Ficino,* trans. Virginia Conant (New York: Columbia University Press, 1943), p. 264.

25. Ficino, *Opera Omnia,* p. 306; Kristeller, *Philosophy of Marsilio Ficino,* p. 267.

26. Kristeller, *Philosophy of Marsilio Ficino,* p. 268.

27. Milton, *Works,* 7: 27.

28. Marsilio Ficino, *Commentary on Plato's Symposium,* trans. Sears Jayne, *University of Missouri Studies,* 19, No. 1 (Columbia: University of Missouri Press, 1944), p. 184.

29. Milton, *The Complete Poems and Major Prose,* p. 138.

Notes to Chapter IX

1. Allan H. Gilbert, "Is *Samson Agonistes* Finished?" *PQ* 28 (1949): 98-106.

2. William Riley Parker, "The Date of *Samson Agonistes,*" *PQ* 28 (1949): 145-66; Parker, *Biography* 2: 903-17; Parker, "The Date of *Samson Agonistes* Again," *Calm of Mind. Tercentenary Essays on Paradise Regained and Samson Agonistes in Honor of John S. Diekhoff,* ed. J.A. Wittreich (Cleveland: Case Western Reserve University Press, 1971), pp. 163-74.

3. A.S.P. Woodhouse, *"Samson Agonistes* and Milton's Experience," *Transactions of the Royal Society of Canada,* 3rd Series, 43 (1949): 157-75.

4. Masson, *The Life of John Milton,* 6: 662; James Holly Hanford, *John Milton, Englishman* (New York: Crown Publishers, Inc., 1949), p. 200; Ernest Sirluck, "Milton's Idle Right Hand. Appendix: Some Recent Changes in the Chronology of Milton's Poems," *JEGP* 60 (1961): 773-78; Barbara K. Lewalski, *"Samson Agonistes* and the 'Tragedy' of the Apocalypse," *PMLA* 85 (1970): 1050-62.

5. H.J. Todd, in his edition of Milton's *Poetical Works* (London: J. Johnson, 1801), 1: 124, suggests that *Samson Agonistes* "furnishes some internal proofs of its having been composed at different periods."

6. William Riley Parker, *Milton's Debt to Greek Tragedy in Samson Agonistes* (Baltimore: The Johns Hopkins Press, 1937).

7. Ibid., p. 169.

8. John Milton, *Defensio Secunda,* 8: 66-68, 63. I use the translation of Hughes in *The Complete Poems and Major Prose,* pp. 826, 824.

9. See, for example, Eleanor G. Brown, *Milton's Blindness* (New York: Columbia University Press, 1934), p. 52; Tillyard, *Milton,* p. 190; Earl Daniels, *The Art of Reading Poetry* (New York: Rinehart, 1941), pp. 35-36.

10. Johnson, *The Rambler,* No. 139.

11. Parker, *Milton's Debt,* p. 46.

12. Una Ellis-Fermor, *"Samson Agonistes* and Religious Drama," *The Frontiers of Drama* (London: Methuen, 1945), p. 32.

13. Parker, *Milton's Debt,* p. 70.

14. A.S.P. Woodhouse, "Tragic Effect in *Samson Agonistes," UTQ* 28 (1958-59): pp. 204-22.

15. I.A. Richards, *Principles of Literary Criticism* (London: Kegan Paul, 1944), p. 246.

16. *Poetics,* XIII. 1453a. Trans. S.H. Butcher.

17. Alfred Gudeman, in *Aristoteles,* Περὶ Ποιητικῆς (Berlin: de Gruyter, 1934, p. 247, proposes that, of Sophocles's plays, including those not extant, forty-three have unhappy endings (" ἐις δυστυχίαν ") and sixteen have happy endings (" ἐις εὐτυχίαν "); for Euripides, forty have happy endings and twenty-four unhappy.

18. Julius Caesar Scaliger, III. xcvii, p. 145.

19. Giambattista Giraldi Cinthio, "On the Composition of Comedies and Tragedies," *Literary Criticism: Plato to Dryden,* ed. Allan Gilbert (New York: American Book Co., 1940), p. 255.

20. George Buchanan, *Tyrannical-Government Anatomized: or a Discourse concerning evil-councellors. Being the life and death of John the Baptist. And presented to the Kings most Excellent Majesty by the author* (London: John Field, 1642).

21. Ibid., p. 27.

22. Gregorius Nazianzenus, *Operum Tomi Tres,* ed. Lewenklaius (Basileae, 1571).

23. I quote the Latin translation by Cl. Roilletus in Lewenklaius's edition of "Gregory's" Greek. The English translation is mine.

24. Ibid., p. 296.

25. Alfred Stern, *Milton und seine Zeit* (Leipzig: Von Duncker and Humblot, 1879), 2: 120.

26. Irene Samuel, *"Samson Agonistes* as Tragedy," *Calm of Mind,* p. 250.

27. Ibid.

28. Ibid., p. 252.

29. Ibid., p. 253.

30. Similarly in *Comus,* as Gilbert Highet points out in *The Classical Tradition* (New York: Oxford University Press, 1949), p. 139, the scene in which Comus is put to flight (813 f.) parallels the conquest of Circe, Comus's mother, by Odysseus in *Odyssey* X. 274 f. But in *Comus,* as in *Samson Agonistes,* this parallelism is inert.

31. Milton cites this passage of the *Aeneid* in his *Artis Logicae* in the discussion of efficient causes (1. iv), *Works* 11: 34-35. Milton's fragment "Ignavum satrapam ..." (1625?) refers to "audax Eurialus Nisus et impiger" and seems about to describe the episode when it breaks off *(Works,* 1, 1: 326-28).

32. The Nisus-Euryalus episode in the *Aeneid* parallels in many ways the foray of Odysseus and Diomedes into the Trojan camp in the tenth book of the *Iliad.* But *Paradise Lost* uses aspects of the Vergilian incident which are not Homeric, and the relation of the *Aeneid* to the *Iliad* is at this point irrelevant.

Notes to Chapter X

1. Hughes, *Complete Poems and Major Prose,* p. 1036.

2. Pattison, *John Milton,* p. 188.

3. For example, Allen, *The Harmonious Vision,* pp. 110-21.

4. Milton Miller, *"Paradise Lost:* the Double Standard," *UTQ* 20 (1950-51): p. 193.

5. Steadman, *Milton and the Renaissance Hero,* p. xx.

6. R.W. Condee, "The Formalized Openings of Milton's Epic Poems," *JEGP* 50 (1951): 502-8.

7. Gilbert Murray, *Euripides and His Age* (London: Oxford University Press, 1965), pp. 4-5.

8. See *P. Vergili Maronis Aeneidos Liber Primus,* with a Commentary by R.G.Austin (Oxford: Clarendon Press, 1971), pp. 25-27.

9. For a different view of the relation of these lines to those of the *Aeneid,* see Louis L. Martz, *The Paradise Within* (New Haven: Yale University Press, 1964), pp. 172-76.

10. Sidney, *Defence of Poesie,* p. 25.

11. David Daiches, *Milton* (London: Hutchinson's Universal Library, 1957), pp. 223-24.

Notes to Chapter XI

1. "At a Vacation Exercise," 22-23, 33-36, *Works,* 11: 20-21.
2. *The Reason of Church Government, Works,* 3, 1: 235.
3. Ibid., p. 236.
4. Woodhouse, *Milton the Poet,* p. 7; also "Notes on Milton's Early Development," pp. 95-97.

Works Cited

Abbreviations

MP   *Modern Philology.*

N&Q   *Notes and Queries.*

PQ   *Philological Quarterly.*

SP   *Studies in Philology.*

UTQ *University of Toronto Quarterly.*

JEGP *Journal of English and Germanic Philology.*

Abercrombie, Lascelles. *The Idea of Great Poetry.* London: Secker, 1925.
Adams, Richard P. "The Archetypal Pattern of Death and Rebirth in *Lycidas,"* in *Milton's Lycidas: The Tradition and the Poem.* Ed. C.A. Patrides. New York: Holt, Rinehart, and Winston, 1961.
Ad C. Herennium Libri IV De Ratione Dicendi. Trans. Harry Caplan. Loeb Classical Library. Cambridge, Mass.: Harvard University Press, 1954.
Allen, Don Cameron. *The Harmonious Vision.* Baltimore: The Johns Hopkins Press, 1954.
Aristotle. *Aristotle's Theory of Poetry and Fine Art.* Trans. S.H. Butcher. London: Macmillan, 1907.
————. Περὶ Ποιητικῆς . Ed. A. Gudeman. Berlin: de Gruyter, 1934.
————. *Poetics.* Ed. D.W. Lucas. Oxford: Clarendon Press, 1968.
Baldwin, Thomas Whitfield. *William Shakspere's Smalle Latine & Lesse Greeke.* Urbana: University of Illinois Press, 1944.
Barclay, John. *Poematum Libri Duo.* Oxford: G. Turner, 1636.
Barker, Arthur. "The Pattern of Milton's Nativity Ode," *UTQ* 10 (1940-41): 167-81.
————. "Structural Pattern in *Paradise Lost,"* *PQ* 28 (1949): 17-30.
Bateson, Frederick W. *English Poetry: A Critical Introduction.* New York: Barnes and Noble, 1966.
Black, John. *Life of Torquato Tasso.* 2 vols. London: Murray, 1810.
Brown, Eleanor. *Milton's Blindness.* New York: Columbia University Press, 1934.
Buchanan, George. *Poemata.* Amsterdam: Waesberger, 1665.
————. *Tyrannicall-Government Anatomized: or, a Discourse concerning evil-councellors. Being the life and death of John the Baptist. And presented to the Kings most Excellent Majesty by the author.* London: John Field, 1642.
Burgess, Theodore. "Epideictic Literature," *University of Chicago Studies in Classical Philology* 3 (1902): 89-254.

Works Cited

Bush, Douglas. "An Allusion in Milton's *Elegia Tertia*," *Harvard Library Bulletin*, 9 (1955): 392-96.

——. "The Date of Milton's *Ad Patrem*," *MP* 61 (1963-64): 204-8.

Carpenter, Nan. "The Place of Music in *L'Allegro* and *Il Penseroso*," *UTQ* 22 (1953-54): 354-67.

Clark, Donald Lemen. *John Milton at St. Paul's School*. New York: Columbia University Press, 1948.

Claudianus, Claudius. *Claudian*. Trans. M. Platnauer. Loeb Classical Library. London: Heinemann, 1963.

Condee, Ralph Waterbury, "Ovid's Exile and Milton's Rustication," *PQ* 37 (1958): 498-502.

——. "The Formalized Openings of Milton's Epic Poems," *JEGP* 50 (1951): 502-8.

Daiches, David. *Milton*. London: Hutchinson's Universal Library, 1957.

Daniels, Earl. *The Art of Reading Poetry*. New York: Rinehart, 1941.

De Filippis, Michele. "Milton and Manso: Cups or Books?" *PMLA* 51 (1936): 745-56.

Delitiae CC Italorum Poetarum. [Frankfurt]: I. Rosa, 1608.

Dorian, Donald, "Milton's 'Epitaphium Damonis, lines 181-97," *PMLA* 54 (1939): 612-13.

——. *The English Diodatis*. New Brunswick: Rutgers University Press, 1950.

Dryden, John. *Works*. Ed. Sir Walter Scott and George Saintsbury. 18 vols. Edinburgh: Patterson, 1889.

Ellis-Fermor, Una. *The Frontiers of Drama*. London: Methuen, 1945.

Ficino, Marsilio. *Commentary on Plato's Symposium*. Trans. Sears Jayne. University of Missouri Studies 19, No. 1. Columbia, Mo.: University of Missouri Press, 1944.

——. *Opera Omnia*. Basileae, 1561.

Fletcher, G.B.A. "Milton's Latin Poems," *MP* 37 (1940): 343-50.

Fletcher, Harris Francis. "Grierson's Suggested Date for Milton's 'Ad Patrem,' " *The Fred Newton Scott Anniversary Papers*. Ed. T.E. Rankin et al. Chicago: University of Chicago Press, 1929.

——. *The Intellectual Development of John Milton*. 2 vols. Urbana: University of Illinois Press, 1961.

Fowler, Alastair. *Silent Poetry*. London: Longman, 1970.

Gellius, Aulus. *The Attic Nights*. Trans. John C. Rolfe. Loeb Classical Library. Cambridge, Mass.: Harvard University Press, 1960-61.

Gilbert, Allan H. "Is *Samson Agonistes* Finished?" *PQ* 28 (1949): 98-106.

Giraldi Cinthio, Giambattista, "On the Composition of Comedies and Tragedies," *Literary Criticism: Plato to Dryden*. Ed. Allen Gilbert. New York: American Book Co., 1940.

Gotfried, Rudolf. "Milton, Lactantius, Claudian, and Tasso," *SP* 30 (1933): 497-503.

Hanford, James Holly. *John Milton, Englishman*. New York: Crown Publishers, Inc., 1949.

——. "The Pastoral Elegy and Milton's *Lycidas*," *PMLA* 25 (1910): 403-47.

——. "The Youth of Milton: An Interpretation of His Early Literary Development," *Studies in Shakespeare, Milton, and Donne*. New York: Macmillan, 1925.

Works Cited

Harding, Davis P. *Milton and the Renaissance Ovid.* University of Illinois Studies in Language and Literature 30, No. 4. Urbana: University of Illinois Press, 1946.

Harrison, T.P., Jr. "The Latin Pastorals of Milton and Castiglione," *PMLA* 50 (1935): 480-93.

Hartman, Geoffrey. "Milton's Counterplot," *ELH* 25 (1958): 1-12.

Highet, Gilbert. *The Classical Tradition.* New York: Oxford University Press, 1949.

Homer. *Odyssey.* Trans. W.H.D. Rouse. New York: New American Library, 1937, reprint 1952.

Horatius Flaccus, Quintus. *Opera Omnia.* Ed. Edward C. Wickham. Oxford: Clarendon Press, 1891-96.

Hunt, Leigh. *Leigh Hunt's Literary Criticism,* Ed. Lawrence H. Houtchens and Carolyn W. Houtchens. New York: Columbia University Press, 1956.

Jayne, Sears. "The Subject of Milton's Ludlow *Mask,"* *A Maske at Ludlow: Essays on Milton's Comus.* Ed. John S. Diekhoff. Cleveland: Case Western Reserve University Press, 1968.

Jerram, C.S. *The Lycidas and Epitaphium Damonis of Milton.* London: Longman, 1874.

Johnson, Samuel. *The Rambler.* Ed. W.J. Bate and Albrecht Strauss. 3 vols. New Haven: Yale University Press, 1969.

Jonson, Ben. *The Masque of Blackness. Ben Jonson.* Ed. C.H. Herford and Percy Simpson. 11 vols. Oxford: Clarendon Press, 1941.

Knight, G. Wilson. *The Burning Oracle: Studies in the Poetry of Action.* Oxford: Oxford University Press, 1939.

Kristeller, Paul O. *The Philosophy of Marsilio Ficino.* Trans. Virginia Conant. New York: Columbia University Press, 1943.

Landor, Walter Savage. "Southey and Landor," *The Complete Works of Walter Savage Landor.* Ed. T. Earle Welby. 16 vols. London: Chapman and Hall, 1927.

"Laus Pisonis," *Minor Latin Poets.* Trans. J.W. Duff and A.M. Duff. Loeb Classical Library. Cambridge, Mass.: Harvard University Press, 1934, reprint 1961.

Lewalski, Barbara K. *"Samson Agonistes* and the 'Tragedy' of the Apocalypse," *PMLA* 85 (1970): 1050-62.

Maclean, Hugh. "Milton's Fair Infant," *ELH* 24 (1957): 296-305.

Manso, Giovanni Battista, et al. *Poesie Nomiche.* Venice: Baba, 1635.

Mantuanus, Johannes Baptista Spagnola. *Opera Omnia.* Bologna: Benedictus, 1502.

Martz, Louis. *The Paradise Within.* New Haven: Yale University Press, 1964.

———. "The Rising Poet," *The Lyric and Dramatic Milton.* Selected Papers from the English Institute. Ed. Joseph H. Summers. New York: Columbia University Press, 1965.

Masson, David. *The Life of John Milton.* 7 vols. Gloucester, Mass.: Peter Smith, 1881, reprint 1965.

Mazzoni, Jacopo. "On the Defence of the *Comedy," Literary Criticism: Plato to Dryden.* Ed. Allan H. Gilbert. New York: American Book Co., 1940.

Miller, David M. "From Delusion to Illumination: A Larger Structure for *L'Allegro-Il Penseroso," PMLA* 86 (1971): 32-39.

Works Cited

Miller, Milton. *"Paradise Lost:* The Double Standard," *UTQ* 20 (1950-51): 183-99.

Milton, John. *A Concordance to the Latin, Greek, and Italian Poems of John Milton.* Comp. Lane Cooper. Halle: Niemeyer, 1923.

————. *A Variorum Commentary on the Poems of John Milton.* Ed. Merritt Y. Hughes. Vol. I, *The Latin and Greek Poems.* Ed. Douglas Bush. New York: Columbia University Press, 1970.

————. *Milton's Lycidas.* Ed. Scott Elledge. New York: Harper and Row, 1966.

————. *Poetical Works.* Ed. H.J. Todd. London: Johnson, 1801.   hes.

————. *The Complete Poems and Major Prose.* Ed. Merritt Y. Hughes. New York: Odyssey Press, 1957.

————. *The Latin Poems of John Milton.* Ed. Walter MacKellar. Cornell Studies in English 15. New Haven: Yale University Press, 1930.

————. *The Poems of John Milton. Ed. James Holly Hanford. New York: Ronald Press, 1953.*

————. *The Poems of Milton.* Ed. Thomas Keightley. 2 vols. London: Chapman and Hall, 1859.

————. *The Poems of Mr. John Milton. The 1645 Edition.* Ed. Cleanth Brooks and John Edward Hardy. New York: Harcourt, Brace, 1951.

————. *The Works of John Milton.* Ed. Frank A. Patterson. 18 vols. in 21. New York: Columbia University Press, 1931.

Minor Poets of the Caroline Period. Ed. George Saintsbury. 3 vols. Oxford: Clarendon Press, 1905.

Montgomery, Walter A. "The *Epitaphium Damonis* in the Stream of Classical Lament," *Studies for William A. Read.* Ed. Nathaniel M. Caffee and Thomas A. Kirby. Baton Rouge: Louisiana State University Press, 1940.

Morse, J. Mitchell. *N&Q* 203 (1958): 211.

Murray, Gilbert. *Euripides and His Age.* London: Oxford University Press, 1965.

Nazianzenus, Gregorius. *Operum Tomi Tres.* Ed. Lewenklaius. Basileae, 1571.

Nelson, Lowry. *Baroque Lyric Poetry.* New Haven: Yale University Press, 1961.

Nicolson, Marjorie Hope. *John Milton: A Reader's Guide to His Poetry.* New York: Noonday Press, 1963.

Ogden, H.V.S. "The Crisis of *Paradise Lost* Reconsidered," *PQ* 36 (1957): 1-19.

Oras, Ants. "Milton's Early Rhyme Schemes and the Structure of *Lycidas*," *MP* 52 (1954): 12-22.

Orgel, Stephen. *The Jonsonian Masque.* Cambridge, Mass.: Harvard University Press, 1965.

Ovidius Naso, Publius. *Heroides and Amores.* Trans. Grant Showerman. Loeb Classical Library. New York: Macmillan, 1914.

————. *The Art of Love.* Trans. J.H. Mozley. Loeb Classical Library. Cambridge, Mass.: Harvard University Press, 1962.

————. *Tristia. Ex Ponto.* Trans. Arthur Leslie Wheeler. Loeb Classical Library. Cambridge, Mass.: Harvard University Press, 1959.

Parker, William Riley. *Milton: A Biography.* 2 vols. Oxford: Clarendon Press, 1968.

Works Cited

———. "Milton and the News of Charles Diodati's Death," *MLN* 72 (1957): 486-88.

———. *Milton's Debt to Greek Tragedy in Samson Agonistes*. Baltimore: The Johns Hopkins Press, 1937.

———. "Notes on the Chronology of Milton's Latin Poems," *A Tribute to George Coffin Taylor*. Ed. Arnold Williams. Chapel Hill: University of North Carolina Press, 1952.

——— "The Date of *Samson Agonistes*," *PQ* 28 (1949): 145-66.

———. "The Date of *Samson Agonistes* Again," *Calm of Mind. Tercentenary Essays on Paradise Regained and Samson Agonistes in Honor of John S. Diekhoff*. Ed. J.A. Wittreich. Cleveland: Case Western Reserve University Press, 1971.

———. *TLS*, 17 December 1938, p. 802.

Pattison, Mark. *John Milton*. English Men of Letters. London: Macmillan, 1887.

Propertius, Sextus Aurelius. *Propertius*. Trans. H.E. Butler. Loeb Classical Library. London: Heinemann, 1912.

Putnam, C.J. *Virgil's Pastoral Art*. Princeton: Princeton University Press, 1970.

Puttenham, George. *Of Poets and Poesy*. In *Elizabethan Critical Essays*. Ed. G. Gregory Smith. Oxford: Clarendon Press, 1904.

Quintilianus, Marcus Fabius. *Institutio Oratoria*. Trans. H.E. Butler. Loeb Classical Library. London: Heinemann, 1933.

Rand, E.K. "Milton in Rustication," *SP* 19 (1922): 109-35.

Richards, I.A. *Principles of Literary Criticism*. London: Kegan Paul, 1944.

Rose, H.J. *The Eclogues of Vergil*. Berkeley: University of California Press, 1942.

Samuel, Irene. *Plato and Milton*. Cornell Studies in English, 35. Ithaca: Cornell University Press, 1947.

———. "*Samson Agonistes* as Tragedy," *Calm of Mind. Tercentenary Essays on Paradise Regained and Samson Agonistes in Honor of John S. Diekhoff*. Ed. J.A. Wittreich. Cleveland: Case Western Reserve University Press, 1971.

Sasek, Lawrence D. "The Drama of *Paradise Lost*, Books XI and XII," *Studies in English Renaissance Literature*. Ed. W.F. McNeir. Louisiana State University Studies: Humanities Series, No. 12. Baton Rouge: Louisiana State University Press, 1942.

Scaliger, Julius Caesar. *Poetices Libri Septem*. [Heidelberg]: Vincentius, 1561.

Shawcross, John T. "*Epitaphium Damonis:* Lines 9-13 and the Date of Composition," *MLN* 71 (1956): 322-24.

———. *N&Q* 204 (1959): 358-59.

———. "The Balanced Structure of *Paradise Lost*," *SP* 62 (1965): 679-718.

Shelley, Percy B. *The Defence of Poetry. Shelley's Prose: The Trumpet of a Prophecy*. Ed. David Lee Clark. Albuquerque: University of New Mexico Press, 1954.

Sidney, Sir Philip. *Defence of Poesie*. Ed. Albert Feuillerat. Cambridge: Cambridge University Press, 1923.

Works Cited

Sidonius, C. Sollius Modestus Apollinaris. *Poems and Letters.* Trans. W.B. Anderson. Loeb Classical Library. 2 vols. Cambridge, Mass.: Harvard University Press, 1963.

Sirluck, Ernest. "Milton's Idle Right Hand. Appendix: Some Recent Changes in the Chronology of Milton's Poems," *JEGP* 60 (1961): 773-78.

Statius, Publius Papinius. *Silvae, Thebaid.* Trans. J.H. Mozley. Loeb Classical Library. New York: Putnam, 1928.

Steadman, John. *Milton and the Renaissance Hero.* Oxford: Clarendon Press, 1967.

Stern, Alfred. *Milton and seine Zeit.* 2 vols. Leipzig: Von Duncker and Humblot, 1879.

Summers, Joseph H. *The Muse's Method: An Introduction to Paradise Lost.* Cambridge, Mass.: Harvard University Press, 1962.

Tibullus, Albius. "Panegyricus Messalae." Trans. J.P. Postgate. *Catullus, Tibullus, Pervigilium Veneris.* Loeb Classical Library. New York: Putnam, 1931.

Tillyard, E.M.W. *Milton.* London: Chatto and Windus, 1946.

———. *The Miltonic Setting.* Cambridge: Cambridge University Press, 1938.

———. *Studies in Milton.* London: Chatto and Windus, 1951.

Townshend, Aurelian. *Tempe Restor'd.* In *Aurelian Townshend's Poems and Masks.* Ed. E.K. Chambers. Oxford: Clarendon Press, 1912.

Treip, Mindele. *N&Q* 203 (1958): 209-10.

Tuve, Rosemond. *Images and Themes in Five Poems by Milton.* Cambridge, Mass.: Harvard University Press, 1957.

Vergilius Maro, Publius. *Eclogues, Georgics, Aeneid, Minor Poems.* Trans. H. Rushton Fairclough. Loeb Classical Library. Cambridge, Mass.: Harvard University Press, 1946.

———. *Aeneidos Liber Primus,* with a Commentary by R.G. Austin. Oxford: Clarendon Press, 1971.

Welsford, Enid. *The Court Masque.* Cambridge: Cambridge University Press, 1927.

Whiting, G.W. *Milton and This Pendant World.* Austin: University of Texas Press, 1958.

Wilkinson, David. "The Escape from Pollution," *Essays in Criticism* 10 (1960): 32-43.

Williams, R.D. "The Purpose of the *Aeneid,*" *Antichthon* 1 (1967): 29-41.

Woodhouse, A.S.P. *Milton the Poet.* Sedgewick Memorial Lecture. Toronto: J.M. Dent, 1955.

———. "Milton's Pastoral Monodies," *Studies in Honour of Gilbert Norwood.* Toronto: University of Toronto Press, 1952.

———. "Notes on Milton's Early Development," *UTQ* 13 (1943-44): 66-101.

———. "Pattern in *Paradise Lost,*" *UTQ* 22 (1952-53): 109-27.

———. "*Samson Agonistes* and Milton's Experience," *Transactions of the Royal Society of Canada,* 3rd Series, 43 (1949): 157-75.

———. "Tragic Effect in *Samson Agonistes,*" *UTQ* 28 (1958-59): 204-22.

Index